ASHES to ASHES ...
Families to Dust

False Accusations of Child Abuse:
A Roadmap for Survivors

Dean Tong

FamRights Press
Tampa, Florida

For information write:

FamRights Press
6102 Webb Rd.
No. 811
Tampa, Fl. 33615

or phone/fax: 1-813-885-6173

If this book is unavailable from your local bookseller it may be obtained directly from another source. Call **toll-free 1-800-987-7771 (orders only).**

ISBN: 0-9654833-8-X

Library of Congress Catalog Card Number: 96-86549

Additional Suggested Headings: 1. Divorce 2. Custody 3. Child Development 4. Law 5. Psychology 6. Repressed Memory

Published in the United States of America

10 9 8 7 6 5 4 3 2 1

For those within the throws of our
child protection system. May this book
be their inspiration to seek right, wrong,
truth and justice.

Contents

Acknowledgments   vi
Preface   vii
The Case Studies:
One: Massachusetts 1980-Florida 1991   1
Two: England 1977-Ohio 1991   21
Three: Colorado 1984-1991   36
Four: Texas 1986-1991   54
Five: A Summary of the Case Studies   64
Six: The Accused   68
Seven: The Accuser   73
Eight: The **SAID** Syndrome   78
Nine: The Child Victim   88
Ten: The Dolls   102
Eleven: The Agencies   114
Twelve: The Courts   129
Thirteen: A Critical Review   143
Fourteen: Fighting Back   163
Fifteen: A Summary of Problems and Solutions   177
Sixteen: An Attorneys View-Charles Jamieson, Esq.   188
Seventeen: What You Need To Know-Ken Pangborn, Trial
Consultant, The A-TEAM   199
Eighteen: Self-Help Guide   212
Appendix A: A Questionnaire   221
Appendix B: Fake or Factual? Speedy Identification of Child
Sexual Abuse Allegations   224
Appendix C: Family Rights Organizations   226
Appendix D: Attorney Referral List   231
Appendix E: Caselaw and False Accusations   237
Appendix F: Internet On-Line Resources   243
Appendix G: Investigative Intake Process Flow Chart   252
Epilogue   254
Bibliography   257

Acknowledgments

Words cannot express my appreciation, for the steadfast support and guidance of Lily, my wife to be.

To my parents Kenneth and Claire Tong, for their emotional, psychological, and financial aid during my times of trials and tribulations..

To my grandfather Cyrus Gardner, who, although deceased, taught me early on to stand up and fight for what is right.

To my grandmother, Emma Gardner, who recently passed away; thank you, Gram!

To Rick Thoma, Herm Ohme and Terry Dawson, for their internet support.

To Mayford Davis of Illinois VOCAL for his cover contribution.

To Ken Pangborn and Charlie Jamieson, Esq, **The A-TEAM**, for their carefully crafted contributions.

To Reid Kimbrough, friend and colleague, and to the False Memory Syndrome Foundation, for their last minute contributions.

And, finally to all of the organizations and individuals who I have not mentioned here, but who have been huge contributors to this work, directly or indirectly!

Preface

Sexual allegations in divorce, involving the minor children of estranged parents, have become the weapon of choice in bitter divorce and custody battles across the nation. This phenomenon has become common enough that there is now a name attached to the action. Blush and Ross called it the SAID Syndrome (Sexual Allegations In Divorce).

ASHES to ASHES ... Families to Dust is the result of my rise from dormancy, an attempt to awaken the American public and legal profession to the trendy national hysteria of false sexual child abuse allegations.

The four case studies presented in this book all represent examples of how devastating the use of child sexual abuse charges as a weapon is, not only for the accused but, equally important, for the children who are the alleged victims. Child victims of unfounded accusations are treated for conditions that do not exist, frequently. They are non-abused children treated as abuse victims. The empirical data extracted from scientific studies of non-abused children, who were rendered unnecessary therapies, clearly demonstrates the ramifications are neither benign nor innocuous.

The alleged perpetrator of this crime is usually the father, who has requested or sued for joint or full custody, although the allegations may be made against others involved in the family unit, as in the case of William Smith, whose story is one of those featured. These stories, painstakingly true, depict the trials and tribulations of several **innocent** individuals-people who became entangled in a system which operates on the premise of 'guilty until proven innocent.'

There are myriad individuals, agencies, attorneys, therapists, counselors and other professionals who inevitably become involved when allegations of sexual child abuse surface. Theoretically, all are acting in the best interest of the child.

Whether that is, in fact, true is one of the questions raised in the later analyses of these cases and the ways in which they were handled. The book exposes the real world of the various social service agencies and so-called child 'protection' teams, illustrates the inadequacies of our current court system and its procedures, and cries out to our legislature for help!

Given the effects of such allegations on the <u>alleged</u> perpetrator, the <u>alleged</u> victim, and the associated family members, it is critical the treatment for <u>alleged</u> abuse be carefully considered and its effects be analyzed and, if necessary, adjusted to truly serve the best interest of the child. There is more than a little doubt that the children in the cases we studied were well served by the system charged to protect them, the accusing parent, or those involved in their treatment.

Sexual child abuse is a taboo, and for a good reason. It goes without saying that real abuse is intolerable and must be stopped. And that the guilty must be prosecuted with vehemence to the fullest extent allowed by law. Make no mistake about it...child abuse is a problem in America today. But, the cure has compounded the problem itself!

With federal and state laws that mandate 'uneducated and untrained' professionals to report abuse, invite and entertain anonymous hotline callers who are protected by 11th amendment immunity, define child abuse vaguely and make no provisions to punish false accusers, it is no wonder why false allegations of child abuse have mushroomed to numbers of unimaginable proportions.

There were 3,200,000 **reports** of alleged child abuse and neglect in America last year. Of those, only 16% incorporated sex abuse complaints. Of those, 75% were deemed unfounded, without foundation. Ironically, 1995 depicted 6,500,000 children had access to only one (1) parent, largely due to false child abuse charges.

I, for one, am grateful President Clinton signed Megans Law...requiring convicted child molesters to report their whereabouts to the local authorities. In Florida, I endorsed the Sexual Predator Law in 1993, a similar measure.

But, as of this writing and on the flip side of the coin, we must balance the child protection playing field for innocent parents and professionals alike. We must, in part, repeal the Mondale Act (Child Abuse Prevention and Treatment Act of 1974), to ensure equity for non-abused children and innocent adults.

ASHES to ASHES...Families to Dust represents to America the destruction that is incurred by families due to **false** allegations of child abuse. This same destruction is responsible for the disintegration, death and future extinction of families, internationally. Since women's rights, children's rights, biased judges, timid legislators and political correctness are responsible for fueling and accentuating the 'child abuse industry,' it is necessary to arm innocent parents and legal practitioners with a tool to aid them in their defense. That tool is the self-help roadmap **ASHES to ASHES ... Families to Dust.**

Chapter One

Massachusetts, 1980 – Florida, 1991

She was a beautiful young woman, small to the point of being petite. Her shoulder-length, dark hair fell in natural waves, serving as a frame for the sparkling eyes and flashing smile that she shared with most of us at the Medical Center. That smile brightened the day for employees in the lab where I worked, and in the veteran benefits section of the Center where she was a volunteer helper. It was July of 1980. I was twenty-four years old and Carla was twenty-two.

We initially met through my work as a lab technician in the outpatient laboratory. Carla had been diagnosed with epilepsy, which was controlled by medication. Once a week, I ran the tests that monitored her drug levels to assure her continued health. During those weekly visits, I learned that Carla had been honorably discharged and retired from the Army as a result of the epilepsy. I also learned she was going through a divorce from her first husband and was naturally upset and depressed by the domestic situation.

Our laboratory friendship quickly progressed to courtship. Gradually we began sharing more and more of our previous experiences, current hopes, and future dreams. As I began falling deeply in love, I envisioned our life together: sharing all the good times and bad times, building a family, growing old in the glow of the love we felt for each other. I recognized the serious nature of Carla's illness and was concerned with the frequency of the seizures, but Carla never let it get her down. She often viewed the seizures as a joke and, when people commented sympathetically on her condition, she made it clear that she didn't feel sorry for herself and neither should they.

Unfortunately, during the late summer and early fall of 1980, Carla's seizures began coming more frequently and were of longer duration. After talking with her doctors in Boston, we made the decision to relocate to Fort Pierce, Florida, in the hope that the warm Florida climate would decrease the seizure activity.

In fact, her convulsions and their frequency worsened, often requiring that she be rushed by ambulance to the local hospital. An increasingly bad temperament was directly proportional to the prevalence of her seizures, both getting worse as time passed. This was a result not only of the natural progression of the disease, but, more importantly, because Carla was often careless about taking her medication, often neglecting it totally.

We had our up days and our down days, as does any new couple. They sometimes seemed more extreme, because of the added stress of dealing with Carla's illness and her intense mood swings. I blamed her periodic withdrawals and days of shrewish behavior on the illness, the drugs, anything I could stretch to use as an excuse for her behavior. There was no way I could accept the fact that the woman I had fallen in love with had been a temporary personality, now replaced by the "real" person behind the mask.

In January of 1981, Carla announced we were to become parents. This placed our relationship in an entirely new light. Up to this point, Carla and I hadn't worried about the legalities of living with and loving each other; it hadn't seemed important. Now, however, we agreed that we wanted a family, we wanted our children to have a mother and father who were legally bound in the eyes of God and the state. We flew back to Massachusetts on Memorial Day weekend and were married in a private ceremony attended only by my family and close friends.

Carla's pregnancy was a difficult time for her, although the frequency of her seizures was reduced. Initially, during the first few months, she was not only lethargic but, like many pregnant women felt miserable. For a period, I felt I was running in circles, changing hats from lover to nurse to orderly, then playing house-husband and breadwinner. The first few months, Carla required being waited on hand and foot.

To my dismay, we grew further apart during the course of the pregnancy and our relationship became one of not only disharmony, but distrust. When she began feeling better, Carla returned to her job as a cocktail waitress at Franky & Johnny's Lounge and I would periodically slip into the bar to watch her. Her actions did nothing to alleviate my concerns about her feelings for me, the future of our new marriage, and the prospects for a happy family. It was not unusual to watch her use her skimpy uniform to gain the notice and attention of the male customers. I tried to justify her actions by telling myself she was trying to make me jealous, afraid that as she gained weight with her pregnancy I would no longer find her attractive. Her actions over time progressed from flirtatious to promiscuous.

Our daughter, Diane, was born on November 3, 1981, almost exactly a year after we had relocated to Florida to start our new life. I had hoped the birth of our daughter would mark the beginning of a resurgence of love and togetherness in our marriage, the beginning of the happily-ever-after envisioned when I first asked Carla to come to Florida with me.

Our marriage, however, continued to be a series of ups and downs. We had delightful days at the beach, watching Diane daring the tide to touch her toes, pleasant evenings out to dinner or the movies, shopping expeditions to the mall and fishing trips in our boat on the Indian River. Interspersed with the good times was Carla's ever-present jealousy, which included my success in my career, any contact I might have with other women professionally, and my close relationship to Diane. Added to the jealousy were anger and the ever-present seizures. Nonetheless, we both worked hard to develop a good marriage. Carla wanted another child, a son. She saw Diane as "Daddy's girl" and commented on the close father/daughter relationship, saying she wanted to enjoy the same natural mother/son closeness. Carla had hoped that Diane would be a boy; we decided to have another child and this time Carla got her wish.

With the realities of two children, rapid inflation and the diluting of opportunities in the lab technician field, I decided to attend medical school at the University of St. Lucia, even though it meant a temporary separation from my wife and children. Of primary consideration was the fact that St. Lucia did not require taking the Medical Collegiate Aptitude Test, thus the qualifying time was greatly reduced and I was able to gain quick acceptance into their medical school, an important fact given our family and financial requirements. In addition, their acceptance criteria was easier to meet and they taught all courses in English, even though they were located in the West Indies. The decision, when made, seemed a resolution to the many problems we were facing as a result of an increasing family and decreasing cash flow and an answer to my yearning to help others.

Robert was born in July, just before I was to leave for school. Carla was elated with the new baby, but distraught over my departure for school. We had moved to Boston so Carla and the children could live with my parents while I was away. This arrangement assured the grandparents the opportunity of knowing their grandchildren and, more importantly, assured that Carla would have assistance in caring for two babies and someone always available should she have any medical problems.

Carla continued to waver in her attitudes and emotions, and in November I was called home because of her persistent irrational behavior and pseudo-seizures. While I was at school, she sent a continual stream of depressing correspondence, noting her increased seizure activity, how much she and the children missed me and how unhappy they all were. In addition, she and my mother were constantly bickering, until they finally reached the point of fisticuffs. When Carla was admitted to the Medical Center the first of November, it marked the end of my medical studies.

We returned to Florida, this time settling in St. Augustine, where I could work as a medical technician and Carla still had the advantage of warmer weather throughout the year. My return to the states seemed to have no positive effect on Carla's personality, our marriage, or her irrational mood swings. Her behavior became more and more negative. She persistently ignored medical advice, often, in fact, going against the advice of her physicians. Her care for the children became erratic. It wasn't unusual for me to arrive home and find Diane in soiled diapers, left lying in urine-soaked sheets. When I changed the sheets and diapers, an argument over the necessity of such actions and my trying to "take her place" would inevitably ensue. The marriage was rapidly deteriorating and Carla was not subtle about seeking solace elsewhere. In September of 1984 she moved in with a male friend from one of the local bars, and I learned what being "Mr. Mom" was all about.

Two months later, Carla returned to the house and we once again attempted a reconciliation. Within days, things were back to normal, with Carla unhappy and unpleasant, myself unhappy, confused and frustrated, and the children confused and frightened by the frequent screaming and shouting. Feeling it unfair to expose them to our continuous fighting and wanting to subject them to as little change as possible, I moved out of the house and found an apartment near my job, in a town about fifty miles away. Little did I realize that this error would have long-reaching effects. Unbeknownst to me, Carla moved her boyfriend into our home almost as soon as I moved out, a fact of which I was unaware for over two weeks.

My wife now had full control of the children, their environment, their well-being and their emotions. In the state of Florida, it is the public policy to assure that each minor child has frequent and continuing contact with *both* parents, after the parents separate or the marriage is dissolved. Both parents are encouraged to share the rights and responsibilities of child-rearing and, theoretically, the father is given the same consideration as the mother in determining the primary residence of a child, irrespective of the age of the child.

Carla sued for divorce and temporary custody in mid-December. With the "live-in" environment that existed at the house, my wife's irrational and inconsistent behavior over the past few years, and potential future medical problems, I felt it appropriate for me to counter-sue, requesting full custody of the children.

I sought the legal assistance of a local attorney, being unaware at the time that, in cases of custody disputes, one is best served by locating and retaining an individual with extensive knowledge and experience in the ways of divorce courts, public agencies, and ex-wives. Had I initially retained such an individual, there is the possibility that he would have forewarned me of the potential for not only a long up-hill fight, but the real possibility that not all fighting would be clean and straightforward. Unfortunately, I knew none of this at the time.

At this point in the process, I made a major mistake in reacting to my concern for my children. After an evening visit in the children's home, Carla and I had one of our frequent verbal disagreements just prior to my leaving. A short distance from the house, I realized I had left my jacket. Returning to the house, I found the front door ajar, the master bedroom door closed and the children left unsupervised in their respective bedrooms. Taking advantage of what I thought to be the perfect opportunity to remove the children from a negative environment, I hid in my son's bedroom.

At 3:00 a.m. that following morning, I packed up the children and drove north to my parents' home. Arriving in Massachusetts, I immediately contacted an attorney to try and get custody of the children. His efforts were a waste of his time and my money. . .a superior court judge ruled that Florida had jurisdiction over the children.

The following day we returned to St. Augustine. Within twenty-four hours of our return, I was not only served with divorce papers, but advised that my wife had motioned for a restraining order. Under the Shared Parental Responsibility Act, Carla had moved the court for temporary custody. The end of that month I counter-petitioned for full custody under the Uniform Child Custody Jurisdiction Act of 1977. Because of innuendos Carla had included in her motion, intimating that I had done such things as physically abused her, had kicked the front door ajar and had threatened to wreck her car, for example, I filed a motion for contempt. Because of my response to her innuendos, she motioned for contempt. The actions, first by my wife and then by myself, began a game of back-and-forth accusations and innuendoes that built a mountain of evidence that could be used to the detriment of either party.

A hearing was set for February 27, 1985 in St. Augustine. During the two months prior to that time, Carla's behavior continued to fluctuate. Early in February she brought the children to my laboratory office, despite repeated orders from her doctors that she was not to drive. Her visit resulted in a heated argument, witnessed by my co-workers who expressed concern about her irrational and belligerent behavior. While her erratic behavior could, in a minor way perhaps, be attributed to organic or seizure-related causes, the behavior was primarily inorganic in origin. Carla's actions were the result of personality factors that would be identified in later psychological tests.

A few days later, Carla apologized and we conversed on a mature adult level. Prior to the court hearing, Carla allowed me to visit the children, creating no problems and initiating no arguments. The children appeared well cared for, Carla's attitude seemed stable and I began to feel the game of tug-of-war was not in the best interest of the children. I still loved my wife and felt guilty in the extreme for the situation the children were in.

The hearing, held the end of February, proved to be non-adversarial. Carla and I appeared with our respective attorneys and I reluctantly gave Carla temporary custody of the children, toddlers ages three and one. This error in judgement on my part would complicate future problems tremendously. Carla was to receive three hundred dollars a month in child support and I was granted reasonable rights of visitation.

The judge did not grant dissolution of the marriage that day. He instead ordered the Department of Health and Rehabilitative Services (HRS) to conduct a home study, witnessing the interaction each of us had with the children. The findings of that study would be instrumental in the final decree of custody. Although such studies are not routine during a divorce proceeding, they are typically ordered if there is disagreement between parents regarding custody rights. Such a study supposedly allows HRS to recommend to the judge which of the individuals is the most fit, most mature and best all-around parent for the children.

Under the visitation order granted at the February hearing, I saw my children twice a month. During this period of time, I

began to suspect physical abuse was occurring in their home—
bruises on Diane's legs and on Robert's arms raised my concern
about their well-being. I took photographs of the children, showing the bruises and documenting my concerns. Additionally, the
general overall health and appearance of the children deteriorated
and I began regretting my decision to afford Carla temporary
custody.

In early April, I made another of many mistakes that would
have long-term and negative ramifications. Concerned about the
children and unable to discuss the situation rationally with Carla,
I called the local hot line number and reported questionable
physical child abuse and potential neglect, naming Carla as the
perpetrator of the abuse. The call incited an investigation of the
report by the Department of Health and Rehabilitative Services,
which was handled by an unmarried male in the local office. The
result of the investigation was that neither physical nor emotional
abuse could be substantiated and nothing more was done by HRS
concerning the matter. At the time, I questioned the agency's
handling of the report and ensuing investigation, but was unfamiliar with standard procedures and policies.

I know now that there was a much better way to handle my
concerns. Given that I already had the pictures, my best course
of action would have been to take the children to a doctor for a
physical examination and then contact my attorney, requesting
he motion for an immediate court appearance. My experience has
proven that the one constant, when involved in a divorce and
custody battle, is to avoid the HRS at all times.

Unfortunately, my allegations set the stage for Carla's
revenge. Unknowingly, I had taken a number of steps that would
place me in the classic setting for a SAID Syndrome case, Sexual
Allegations In Divorce.

I was at work at the lab, running routine tests and making plans
for the weekend visit with Diane and Robert. It was April 18,
1985, and the divorce was not yet final, nor was the question of
custody resolved. Responding to a paged message, I cradled the
telephone receiver against my shoulder as I examined the
specimen in my hand. It was my attorney.

"Dean, it's Ron. I've just been advised that you've been accused of sexually molesting Diane."

Dropping the serum specimen, I stared at the shattered pieces of glass on the floor as I stated, "Ridiculous hogwash, Ron. She's only three-and-a-half and I'm her father!" There was silence on the line.

"Is Diane OK? Why would Carla do this, Ron? It was Carla, wasn't it?"

Ron confirmed that Carla had made the accusation. Supposedly, Diane had complained to her mother that "she hurt down there," after returning home from the last weekend visit with me. Ron advised me that a court hearing had been set for determination of probable cause on April 21, 1985.

At the onset of the hearing I was, of course, nervous, but felt I had no reason to be intimidated, as I had done nothing wrong. The judge informed both parties of the proffered medical evidence. . ."vaginal lacerations." I began to wonder why my attorney didn't question this evidence. Where was the M.D. who reported the findings? How could we cross-examine a report, hearsay evidence?

The judge ruled the accusation was unfounded or unsubstantiated, based on the fact that Diane would not talk. In other words, there was a lack of evidence. I had mixed emotions. I felt relieved that the court sought justice and I was not going to be charged. However, how could they rule "lack of evidence?" There was no evidence at all! Suddenly I had more questions than anyone had answers for: Why had DHRS gone through such steps to try and have me charged? Why was my young and innocent daughter brought into this courtroom? Why didn't Carla testify? What was I doing here?

I had several concerns, in addition to protecting myself from Carla's actions. The major concern, of course, was the evidence of vaginal lacerations. Since I hadn't seen or talked with the doctor issuing the report, I had no idea exactly what he meant by the statement nor how he determined the existence of such. If there were lacerations, how had they really happened? Could

Carla be extreme enough, in her search for vengeance, to hurt Diane in order to get at me?

Was it possible that her current live-in boyfriend was responsible for the lacerations? I had learned that in two-thirds of the cases of child abuse in a divorce setting, the abuse occurs at the hands of the live-in boyfriend or step-father.

Was there a chance that Diane had hurt herself while masturbating? She was going through a rough time, adjusting to her father being gone and a new man in her house, her mother's care and attention being given sporadically. It is not unusual for young children to masturbate when under emotional stress of some kind and Diane's fingernails were unkempt most of the time.

I wondered about the possibility of Diane's soiled underwear causing irritation and discomfort, the lacerations occurring when she rubbed or scratched herself in response to the itchiness.

Finally, of course, there was the possibility that Diane had fantasized the entire ordeal and Carla had taken advantage of it. Although I continued to probe and prod at these questions and possibilities, there were no conclusions.

Carla motioned the court twice, attempting to suspend my visitation rights, based on the first allegation of child sexual abuse. Her efforts were unsuccessful. Our divorce was finalized on May 6, 1985. The HRS home study recommendations called for Carla to be awarded primary residential custody with myself having liberal visitation.

On September 24, 1985, I was in Orlando, Florida at a sales demonstration meeting. It was my third week as an employee of Professional Medical Sales, a distributor of clinical laboratory products, and I was optimistic about my new position, if nothing else in my life at that time.

During the meeting, I received a message to call Ron at 9:15 a.m. Knowing Ron would only call me at this meeting if there was something important happening, I obeyed the summons. My attorney advised me tersely that I had, for a second time, been accused of sexually molesting Diane. I dropped the phone, left the meeting and drove home to Baldwin, pondering this second allegation and reviewing every detail of my last visit with the children.

As soon as I arrived home, I was on the phone with Ron, a conversation that lasted an hour and a half. We went through the events of the most recent visit with the children the previous weekend, and I assured him it had been without incident, as always. "Did you have anyone with you and the children? Anyone who could attest to the activities of the weekend, state that no abuse occurred?" With a deep sigh, I responded, No. It simply hadn't occurred to me that it would be necessary to have someone always at my side, to testify as to my behavior with my own kids. The attorney asked what I wanted him to do. I didn't know.

Two days later, a juvenile detention hearing to determine probable cause commenced at the county courthouse. DHRS had filed a petition for dependency against me to get the hearing— Ron and I were totally unprepared for the hearing, let alone its outcome.

Entering the courtroom, I saw several faces there I had never seen before. Although my attorney urged me to remain calm, I was nervous and I was beginning to get angry, feeling the victim of a conspiracy, an ambush. Carla was flanked by her new attorney, a DHRS intake counselor, and an assistant state attorney. In spite of my innocence—or because of it—I was beginning to feel a strong sense of paranoia building.

My fate was sealed by hearsay evidence presented by the intake worker. The "evidence" that led to losing my children consisted of a social worker repeating a statement she claimed Diane made, a social worker repeating the statement of an unnamed doctor who stated there were vaginal abrasions present, and a social worker stating that Diane had acted out the sexual actions with dolls while a video tape was made.

It is interesting to note that the first hospital physician to examine Diane found no evidence of abuse. However, two hours later, at another hospital, a Child Protection Team physician found positive evidence of trauma. I had not seen my daughter in the two-hour period between the two examinations. The second physician's report was accepted as evidence of abuse.

My next shock was at the amount of authority and judicial latitude assumed by the presiding family court judge, the same judge who had presided over the hearing when the initial allegation had been made. Based on the hearsay testimony of the intake worker, he found probable cause that I had sexually abused my daughter and terminated my visitation rights with *both* children, pending further investigation by the DHRS.

My mind went blank and my body was numb as I walked out of the courtroom. I was devastated from the experience of a living nightmare. I couldn't even express my feelings and the pain I felt. I didn't want to talk to anybody, especially my attorney. I thought I might still see the children for a last weekend visit. That of course, did not happen. I didn't know when, or if, I would *ever* see my children again.

The first weekend after the hearing was tearful and depressing. I stared at the toys laying motionless in my living room while my home seemed to cry out for the children's presence.

I became easily agitated, not wanting to associate with anybody. Nothing held any interest for me—the television, radio, working on my car. I couldn't sleep, my mind constantly racing with thoughts that circled to no conclusion. I was finding it difficult to simply function as a person.

Throughout this entire ordeal, my parents were, fortunately, a very positive support for me. During that first weekend, I talked with them several times on the phone. They encouraged me to persist in my efforts, to fight for what I knew was right. I agreed, but thought they were seeing things too simply, not understanding the complexity of all I was facing. Nonetheless, throughout, they prodded and encouraged me to be strong for myself and for the children, to always remember this wasn't Diane's fault.

On Monday, September 30th, I received yet another call at the office from Ron.

"There's a warrant out for your arrest, Dean. . .criminal charges of sexual battery. You need to turn yourself in. I'll meet you at the Jacksonville Sex Crimes Unit at nine o'clock Wednesday morning."

I hung up the phone, nauseous and shaky. After a trip to the men's room to splash my face with cold water and try to get a grip on my nerves, I went to see my supervisor. Putting into words the fact that I had been accused of such a horrible action toward my daughter made it no more real, but a great deal more painful. We talked briefly and I tried to explain the sequence of events, my beliefs as to what might be behind the accusation, as I assured him of my innocence. He accepted my verbal resignation.

My reaction to the criminal accusation was predictable—a mixture of chills, sweat, and tears.

I arrived at the Sex Crimes office as scheduled and found my attorney waiting for me there. We were greeted by a detective, who informed me I was under arrest for probable cause of committing sexual battery, handcuffed me and sent me off to jail. I'd had no time to confer with my attorney.

Following instructions, I emptied all my belongings onto a counter as another officer read my arrest report. He looked at me in total disgust and yelled, "That's sick, man! That's sick!" While I had not seen the report, I knew the charge and could only agree to how sickening the entire fiasco was, as I stared at the ground, listening to his abuse. My short stay in the booking room convinced me that, until I could prove my innocence, I was guilty. . .in everyone's eyes, it appeared.

I used my one phone call to contact my mother, calling collect to bring her up to date on my current ordeal.

When I entered my cell, the eyes and odors of twenty other inmates greeted me. My intuition told me that they knew what I was in for. I hadn't even made it to my bunk, when a black man growled in my face, "Baby Raper." As the sweat poured down my brow and between my shoulder blades, I reminded myself that I had to maintain control of my thoughts, emotions, and actions.

With lightning speed, the bond hearing the following morning came and went. Although my attorney was dependable and likable, he was not experienced in the area of criminal law and, as a result, the judge denied me bail. Back in my cell, I tried to remain calm, despite my spinning head and shaking hands. It seemed that the state must feel they had a solid case against me, if bail had been denied, and I realized their goal was to send me to prison. The fact that the majority of my cell mates were hardened, repeat offenders, familiar with various prisons throughout Florida, did nothing for my morale or feeling of well-being.

The first week in jail passed slowly. There were constant questions, chasing each other through my mind. Why did it take so long to get another bond hearing? What will this do to my reputation? Could I get another job? Should I—could I—sue for false arrest. Was this really America, where the arrested are suddenly guilty until proven innocent? The more questions I asked, the more depressed I became.

Once out of jail, my parents having managed to raise the twenty-five thousand dollars in bail money, fighting the false allegations was time-consuming and costly. In December of 1985, HRS closed the arrest case as "indicated," and I was placed on the Child Abuse Registry for seven years. An "indicated" case is one in which the HRS feels some type of abuse did occur, but leaves the perpetrator unnamed. Ron was replaced by two attorneys experienced in criminal law. First there was the psychosexual testing. Then my attorneys viewed the videotape of Diane with the dolls, a tape taken by the Child Protection Team, which is a branch of Child Protective Services affiliated with the HRS, and obtained Carla's deposition. I knew the two attorneys and psychologist fees had to be expensive. I knew I couldn't afford it. How could my parents pay for such expenses?

I was referred to Dr. David More of Jacksonville by Frank's request. I had no idea what to expect or what he expected. Did he think he was meeting and evaluating a sexual deviant? Was that what he was supposed to look for and verify? I spent an entire day with Dr. More, exposed to a battery of psychological tests. Unfortunately, the results were cloaked in secrecy and it was months before I had any indication of what those tests had revealed.

We received no notification of anything that was happening or had happened and I had to obtain all of my files personally. This further accentuated the stigma of being an accused abuser of children.

So far, there had been no criminal charges formally filed, for which I was thankful. Frank said the state's case against me was growing weaker every day. However, the assistant state attorney, who was prosecuting the case, wanted me to see a "psychologist for the state." He wasn't satisfied with Dr. More's conclusions, which I still had not seen. I wasn't looking forward to another session with another psychologist, but it appeared I had little choice. I didn't want to face a future arraignment and criminal indictment.

The first part of 1986 I met the "psychologist for the state" in Orange Park, Florida. It was clear this was not going to be an objective relationship and things were tense from the beginning. The doctor's direction was clear. He was to interview me and conduct a variety of tests, then recommend whether or not the state should prosecute. His analysis and conclusions as to whether or not I was a pedophile would be persuasive, directly affecting the actions of the state attorney's office.

The results and conclusions reached by the state's psychologist were contradictory in a number of areas and only increased my frustration, confusion and growing anger at a system that more and more appeared *not* to have the best interests of my daughter or justice as a priority.

Initially, his statements were encouraging: "Mr. Tong's Minnesota Multiphasic Personality Index (MMPI) is one which necessarily raises doubts about his capability for responding to therapeutic intervention." With this statement, I was in total agreement. Since I had not compromised my daughter, why would I want to respond to "therapeutic intervention?"

"His responses to the group of psychosexual disorder questionnaires fall within normal limits, i.e., there are no findings from these self-reported instruments that this father endorses aberrant or deviant values or beliefs about any form of engagement in sexual behavior and, in particular, there is no reflection of overt pedophilic tendencies."

I thought that made things pretty clear. However, the report continued. "In this psychologist's consultations with professionals who interviewed Diane, it was their strong belief that the child's reports of having been molested by her father were credible. My review of the videotape of Diane, taken by the Child Protection Team, also points to the same conclusion." Suddenly, I couldn't believe what I was reading.

The psychologists final conclusions were damning as far as I was concerned. "This clinician would be reluctant to render any conclusive and unequivocal opinion regarding the actuality of the allegation that Mr. Tong has molested his child." Well, that meant he wasn't recommending prosecution, at least.

"However, there does appear to be a strong likelihood that Mr. Tong has engaged in some form of inappropriate, erotic behavior with his young child. Accordingly, it is my recommendation that Mr. Tong be referred for therapeutic participation in an outpatient sex offender program to further explore his responsibility for misdirected affectual behavior with his young child. While the charge that Mr. Tong has molested his daughter is certainly a serious one, I do not see a compelling cause to prosecute this individual, provided he shows a willingness to cooperate in correcting his psychological and sexual deficiencies. This psychologist would support the present exclusion of parental and other visitation rights of Mr. Tong."

I was devastated. First the man states that I am "normal" in the areas of sexual behavior and have none of the characteristics of a pedophile. He further stated his doubts that I would respond to therapeutic intervention, based on the results of the MMPI. He then turned around and recommended that I continue to be denied access to my children and, while he wouldn't recommend prosecution, that recommendation is qualified by the requirement to attend therapy for an action he indicates I don't appear to have committed. By this point, I was convinced I was the victim of a conspiracy by the state agencies and my ex-wife.

Not only was the report of the state psychologist contradictory, he and his findings never were presented in court, nor was the doctor ever cross-examined. As seemed to be the case throughout the long ordeal, a doctor or agency seemed to know all about me, while I knew nothing about them.

Frank's job was to keep me out of jail and he was delighted that I wasn't recommended for prosecution. I was happy to stay out of jail, but I wanted more than that. I wanted my innocence proven and I wanted to see my children.

I went to a session of outpatient therapy, at Frank's advice. There I sat, in a room filled with twelve "guilty" sexual deviants, individuals who blatantly stated they committed inappropriate sexual acts. When my turn came to speak, I said nothing. I knew I shouldn't be there in the first place. I wasn't guilty, as they proclaimed to be. My personal story was none of their business.

I called Frank the next day, told him of my actions and reactions at the therapy session and said I wasn't going back. Frank informed me that, if I didn't complete the ninety-day program, my case would linger in the state attorney's office. I was willing to let that happen. Perhaps forcing the state to either prove my guilt or admit my innocence was the only option left.

In November of 1986 I moved the court for supervised visitation with my children. The family court granted my motion, after learning that the state was going to drop the felony charge. In December of 1986 the sexual battery charge was dropped. I was never indicted and this was not a case that was "nolle prossed." That term is the state's way of saying that, even though you've been formally charged, they decline to prosecute at that time. In my case, I was not formally charged, only arrested and detained for probable cause.

It had taken fourteen months and thirteen days for the capital felony charge of sexual battery to be finally dropped by the State Attorney's office. During this time, I had been under a court order not to see or contact my children. I had no visitation rights at all, even though I had been arrested for probable cause only. Although formal charges were never filed against me, I still had to prove my innocence to the juvenile and family courts and the world. I had to prove that it was safe for the children to be with me.

In October of 1986 I moved to Georgia, hoping the change of residence would aid my emotional state. I began seeing Dr. David Fox, for assistance in dealing with my depression, isolation, and other negative emotions. He attempted to work with the Florida Department of Health and Rehabilitative Services, but wasn't even afforded the courtesy of responses to his letters, let alone any increase in my visitation with my children. That spring I went through another series of tests with a psychologist in North Carolina and these tests and interviews again stated that I was not pedophilic. In June I hired Hoffman and Associates, known as the "A Team" for their extensive knowledge of and work with false allegations of child sexual abuse. Mr. Hoffman filed the appropriate motions for visitation. A month later I went to Athens, Georgia where I underwent a series of psychosexual tests, including the penile plethysmography test, which indicates an individual's natural and involuntary reactions to a variety of audio and visual sexual stimulations. As in earlier cases, my test results clearly indicated that I was not an individual with any pedophilic characteristics. This information was added to the results of my polygraph, which proved that I was not lying when I denied any inappropriate behavior with my daughter.

In April of 1988 there was a hearing at the St. John's County Courthouse which included expert testimony from the Georgia doctors, David Fox and Henry Adams, all supportive of my case.

In June of 1988 there was another hearing at St. John's County Courthouse following our motion for normal visitation and/or a change in custody, a restraining order against Carla, a requirement for her to have a psychological examination, a finding of contempt or removal of the children to a foster home.

The following day we received an order giving us one full day at a final hearing to be held the end of September.

In July my attorneys lodged a vigorous objection to the admissability of using the videotape of Diane with the anatomically correct dolls as evidence in court, stating that the tape was unduly prejudicial and contrary to due process, and that we would need to question the Child Protection Team (CPT) personnel who were involved with it.

Carla had a psychological examination on September 13th, ten days before the final hearing, which really wasn't final at all.

On October 21st, Carla's recommendations were submitted to the court. A week later, on the 27th, we submitted our final arguments. In spite of the results of the psychological evaluations and testimony submitted to the court, in spite of the fact that Carla was proved an unfit mother, in spite of the fact that Carla had threatened a day care center with an accusation of child sexual abuse to avoid payment of her bills, on December 5, 1988 the court awarded Carla full custody of Diane and Robert and allowed me only supervised visitation with my children. We filed an additional memo, but were denied a motion for rehearing.

On January 5, 1989, I filed my first Notice of Appeal against Health and Rehabilitative Services. On the 27th of the month we filed a rebuttal memorandum and an amended motion for rehearing. As a result of this action, the judge set aside the order of December 5th. However, five days later, when he issued his second order, there was little difference from the first. Carla retained custody and I still had only supervised visitation. However, this order did contain the stipulation that HRS was to investigate Carla as a result of some question about her being an abusive parent. This investigation was never performed.

On March 8, 1989 I filed my second Notice of Appeal, this time against Carla. On the 17th of the month, the Fifth District Court in Daytona Beach granted my Notice of Voluntary Dismissal and the HRS Appeal was dismissed. Three months later, in June, the HRS case was dismissed in full.

In August I submitted my initial brief to the Fifth District Court. The end of August my supervisor for visitation was changed again—for the fifth time—and my visitation increased to provide for nine hours on alternate Sundays, four hours the other Sundays.

In November of 1989 I filed a Motion for Oral Argument and to Expedite Appeal. On December 7th my motion to expedite the appeal was denied. We never did receive a ruling on the Motion for Oral Argument.

In early March of 1990 I lost my Appeal, as the Fifth District Court deemed the case Per Curiam Affirmed (PCA), not even rendering an opinion. This meant the Appellate court reaffirmed the lower court's decision. On the 20th, we filed motions for Rehearing on Clarification and also attempted to go to the State Supreme Court and request the entire Fifth District Court of Appeals to review my case. On the 22nd the PCA became a mandate because of untimely filing of these motions by my attorney.

On April 3rd we filed motions to recall the mandate and to reconsider my motions. On the 20th, all motions were denied and ruled as "moot."

In July of 1990 I had a one-hour hearing before the trial judge to modify visitation. For the first time in five years I was allowed unsupervised visitation with both children, four hours on one Sunday, nine hours the following Sunday, progress indeed.

During the course of the five years following these allegations, I spent over eighty thousand dollars, hired six attorneys, saw five psychologists, took a polygraph test, a penile plethysmography test and was subjected to countless other psychosexual tests. Although I proved a prima facie case of my innocence and my ex-wife was declared an unfit mother in court, she retains custody of the children. It wasn't until late summer of 1990 that I was allowed to see my children without the supervision of an appointed chaperon. Regardless of my innocence, I was still considered guilty by the system that regulated my relationship with my children.

As of this writing, I find it necessary for me to always have at least one other adult in attendance whenever I am with Diane and Robert, as insurance against further potential allegations by my ex-wife.

I am currently pursuing joint custody of my children. In addition, I have filed a federal lawsuit against my ex-wife and the HRS for monetary and equitable relief of the fiscal and emotional costs of the false allegations.

Chapter Two

England, 1977 – Ohio, 1991

William Smith was an unhappily married man. His wife of seventeen years had gone back to college in the early seventies. The children were almost grown and she wanted her own career, her own life. William was in the process of starting his own business in an effort to raise their standard of living. The return of his wife to college, and her constant and consistent exposure to the new men of the seventies and the new attitudes, created a number of situations with which William was uncomfortable, but which neither of them chose to face or discuss. William quietly decided to wait until the two children left home and obtain a divorce.

Into this set of circumstances walked Patti, twenty years younger, entrancing, vivacious and beautiful, with a mind that was active and bright. William tried to ignore Patti, knowing she was provocative in the extreme to him, knowing he was not yet a free man and his master plan said he would get a divorce and then take his time finding a woman with whom to begin anew. Love doesn't necessarily follow one's management plans for life.

Patti began her studies at music college and William vowed to put her out of his life and out of his mind. For a few months, he honored that vow. Until he got a call that Patti wanted to meet him. Events moved rapidly, their love being the stuff that romances are made of. William left his wife, and he and Patti lived together. William had met with Patti's father, to explain his intentions, and was happy to find that her father wished them well. However, he had cautioned William that she often had emotional and personality swings, but both men considered these would be resolved as she gained maturity. Following the finalization of William's divorce, they were married on August 27, 1977.

Life with Patti was an emotional roller coaster. She'd run for days in high spirits and then crash down into the 'blues.' Much of this appeared to be the result of her relationships with her family. Her mother seemed to have an unusual effect on and control over Patti. One day her mother approved of the couple, the next she withdrew that approval. One day Patti loved her mother, the next minute she hated her.

In 1978 Patti was pregnant with their first child. Her relationship with her mother worsened during this period. They were happy, however, finalizing plans to move to the United States from England, so William could help start a business there. Patti looked forward to putting some distance between her and her mother and regaining full control of her life. All was going well and planning took much of their time.

One morning, after leaving home with the usual happy farewell, Patti waving goodbye from the front door, a movement in the rearview mirror caught William's eye as he started down the quiet main road—a parked car pulled out from the side of the road and turned down their lane. He slowed and swung the car around, back to the village. As he circled the one-way street, William saw the car parked outside the cottage and a man entering the front door, greeted by his very pregnant wife. Caught in the system of one-way streets, he was unable to get to the house before the man, warned by Patti, had returned to his car and left. She claimed the man was someone from her past and it was all unexpected, that he had called to see her on impulse. William had strong suspicions this was not true, particularly as the man had appeared to be purposefully waiting for his morning departure, but, loving Patti and considering her condition, he didn't feel he should pursue the matter.

That fall, the Smiths moved to the United States, visiting the East Coast sights before settling in Ohio. They had a lovely home and he worked out of the house, developing new ideas for machinery and supporting a new license for his original technology. Janice had been born the winter of 1978 and Johnny was born in 1980. In spite of his love and the children, Patti still seemed to be haunted by her personality problems, the problems her father had tried to explain to him before he and Patti had married.

In 1981, a young man had moved in with the neighboring couple, whether a friend or relative was never clear. Much of the time he'd appeared to be out of work and would be in the house with Patti when William came back from daily business excursions. William was curious and concerned, but gave his wife the benefit of the doubt. Years later, he learned from the neighbors that they had sometimes seen the two hand in hand. During one of William's overnight trips, they had seen the young man returning to the house early in the morning, bare-footed and with no shirt. Eventually, the young man had gone off to Oregon with another male neighbor. There were other dubious situations. It seemed almost as if Patti had two personalities, in total contrast to each other. William tried to put the concern out of his mind.

In 1982, through a combination of "innovative financing" and money from his late father's estate, William moved the family to a beautiful house with woodland acreage and a small lake in a suburb of Cleveland. Life with Patti and the two children seemed close to perfection.

In 1983, William went to England for a week on business. Shortly after his return, Patti had mentioned inviting a man to tea. William tried to find out just what that meant, but with no success. It was two years later that he was advised that the man had stayed at the house for several days during his absence.

By 1984 he was getting on his feet, although they were not nearly as wealthy as they appeared to be. The future looked good, his technology was being accepted well and his company was set to receive growing royalties for years to come.

William's oldest son from his first marriage graduated from London University and, at Patti's invitation, came to live with the family the first of the year. As was true with the various members of her own family, she seemed to have a love/hate relationship with Brandon after he arrived. He got a job and moved into his own apartment in May. Patti's mother came out to visit that summer. Although Patti said she dreaded the visit, when her mother arrived, she acted as though she'd been reunited with her best friend. They had lengthy conversations, which stopped when William came near, and he began to feel uncomfortable and upset. It seemed that her mother's pub in England was failing and Patti asked if she could come live with them. He said definitely not, knowing what her mother's constant presence would do to Patti as well as to him.

William found that he needed to take a long overdue business trip to Japan and Australia that fall, if his business was to continue to prosper. He would have preferred to stay home, fearing that Patti might go to pieces again while he was gone, but felt forced to schedule the trip for October. Usually, Patti was not keen on his leaving, but this time William was surprised to find that she actually supported his going. On the day of his departure Patti was angry and jealous about his older daughter's graduation from London University. Patti dropped him at the departure area for the two-week trip and drove off.

During that two-week trip, he talked to Patti every day, with the exception of one weekend when he couldn't reach her at the house. William arrived home on November 10th, exhausted and looking forward to time with his family. Patti met him at the airport, alone, and advised him that something terrible had happened to the children. Fearing an accident or serious illness, William was stunned when Patti handed him three documents— one from a social worker, one from a psychologist, and one from a physician, all stating that the children had been sexually abused. With little expression, she informed him that Brandon was in jail, a rape charge had been filed and William's choice was between Brandon or her and the children. He got the distinct impression that his wife was enjoying herself.

Arriving home, William discovered that Patti's mother had come over from England and was staying with them. Suffering from the shock of the accusation and the jet lag that accompanies a trip such as that he had just completed, William kept quiet and simply listened. Later that evening he went down to the police station. His son's first words were, "Dad, I'm sorry about Patti." Not knowing what Brandon meant, William simply nodded his head and assured himself that Brandon was okay.

Over the next few days, he began to pick up facts and pieces of information that started to confirm a rather ugly picture. With an air of arrogance, Patti informed him, that she had slept with Brandon earlier that year. Now, Brandon's comment, made to William in the jail cell, made sense. A second visit to the police revealed that Patti had told them she had slept with Brandon, while he was residing in her home, and had done so to stop him from abusing the children. This made no sense at all to William, as he knew she had asked Brandon to baby-sit over the several months following her having slept with him. Therefore, she was either knowingly leaving the children with a child abuser or she was lying. The police officer told William that he had considered the abuse allegations a "set-up" after the first interview with Patti and he had another officer confirm that he'd stated so at the time. However, the police said they were bound to proceed because the Human Services were proceeding. William felt that they were playing a political game and was thoroughly disillusioned. He was now totally on his own.

Later, while putting his passport away in the file, he found that Patti's passport and those of the children were missing. Although he shouldn't have been surprised, he was.

Within a week, Patti began developing scenarios aimed at getting William out of the house. On one occasion, he was tickling the children's feet, as requested by Janice and Johnny, and she walked into the room, stating he was abusing the children. Walking up behind him, she struck him on the head with heel of her high-heeled shoe, as her mother watched. Instead of retaliating as she had hoped, William called the police and showed them the cut. He has since learned that actions such as these are commonly employed by the wife, who hopes the husband will retaliate and she can then have him removed from the house on the basis of domestic violence.

William insisted upon attending what appeared to be a routine follow-up interview with the children by the psychologist who had stated, in writing, that the children had been sexually abused. He perceived the report as unscientific and therefore dangerously unprofessional, since it stated that abuse had definitely taken place. He got a shock when, in front of him, the psychologist gave

Janice a "good touch-bad touch" book and proceeded to ask her if the bad touches were ever given to her by her father. At this point, it appeared that the case could take on an additional angle.

Patti's mother returned to England, but the following weeks were difficult at best. Patti continued her attempts to bait William into some type of negative action, while acting the distraught mother who hoped to see Brandon rot in jail. Throughout this period he met several social workers of one sort and another, not one of whom impressed him, but rather convinced him that they were running the investigation on some agenda other than that of truth.

On December 17th, Brandon was indicted for eight counts of rape and four counts of gross sexual imposition. Four days later, William took care of the children while Patti went to the Witness/Victim Center to sign a release. He asked her to bring him a copy, but her only response was anger. The task that was supposed to take an hour stretched into six hours, but Patti refused to discuss where she had been or what she had been doing, although she was visibly upset when she returned. The next day she attacked William with a kitchen knife, in full view of the children. When her attempts at forcing William out of the house failed, Patti left the house with the children, coming back with the police for some of her possessions and moving to a Women's Shelter in Cleveland. She then filed for divorce. The divorce request included domestic violence and the fact that Brandon, his son, had been indicted for sexual abuse of the two children.Unknown to William and unauthorized to do so, she had withdrawn all of the money in the company account, totalling eight thousand dollars, and had run up a bill for fifteen hundred dollars worth of clothes on a credit account.

The events that followed were an ongoing nightmare. Christmas Eve was a perfect picture as snow began falling over the landscape. The children's presents were grouped at the foot of the Christmas tree and William's faithful German Shepherd remained at his side. Somehow, William retained his sanity.

The weeks that followed blur in retrospect. William could see that Patti had become deadly, not caring about anyone, not even the children, in her attempts to crush them all. He would wake in the night, thinking it was all an impossible bad dream.

In early January, William received a letter from the Department of Health and Social Services (HSS) requesting he meet with them. During a telephone conversation regarding that request, he learned that Patti had alleged that he had also sexually abused the children; HSS never pursued those allegations. During this time, Patti advised the police that Brandon had a criminal record of child abuse in England—they found this to be untrue when they attempted verification.

William began the process of obtaining legal representation for the divorce. Since Patti had stolen the money from the company, he had to find money to cover the operating bills. Meantime, Brandon's grandparents sold their home in England to come up with the twenty-five thousand dollar down payment for a criminal defense lawyer for him. There were two cases— Brandon's criminal case and William's divorce case—and he had to be prepared to fight a potential criminal case against himself as well.

On January 24th, with no warning of any kind, Patti fled to England with Janice and Johnny, leaving via Canada. She filed and had the children made "Wards of Court" in England. Patti's affidavit made unbelievable claims, including statements that both Brandon and William had been found to be sexual abusers against Janice and Johnny. She further claimed that the family burned coal in their home, and that it was damp and cold. The documents arrived within hours of a hearing in which William would have lost all his rights as a parent. Although this appeared to have been Patti's intent and purpose, he managed to get a British attorney immediately. More debts.

Finally, in February, William was allowed to see Johnny and Janice under the supervision of a policeman. Although it seemed to him that both children were depressed, they had always had a close relationship and were almost immediately as close as they had been before Patti's flight to England. For the next several months he was allowed to see them one hour on Friday and one hour on Monday every fifth week, in England, under the supervision of a social worker.

The agreement was that if all went well after several months of supervised visits, there would be support for his contention that the children should return to their home in the U.S.A. After several months, he was told the children obviously loved him, but it would be traumatic for them to leave England. William felt that both he and the children had been tricked by the change in the terms and he told the social worker/supervisor so. He managed to ask the kids what they wanted, out of hearing of the supervisor. They said they had no regard for their mother, because of all that had happened and because she had told them they didn't have a father anymore. They hated living with her family and complained about their treatment. Fortunately, their mother had been unable to destroy the close relationship William had with the children. Even at such an early age, Janice and Johnny were able to see themselves as part of a team and to exercise patience, knowing they were working together to be together.

Finally, in June of 1985, William had his ammunition. The rape case had been dismissed as "Nolle Prosequi" in April. The Ohio police had written to Patti in March about leaving unlawfully with the children and about her availability for the local case against Brandon. Also in March, the Guardian ad Litem issued an affidavit for the return of Janice and Johnny to Ohio. The fact that there had been two full months of non-protective guardianship of the children later raised some question as to her competence. Armed with new passports for Janice and Johnny, William flew to England, not knowing when or if he would be returning to the states. It seemed so bizarre to him. He was then still a British subject, about to put himself in jeopardy with the British authorities in order to get two American citizens back to their own country. None of this should have been necessary in the first place. (There is now a Hague convention in place between Great Britain, the United States, and other countries to ensure the return of children to "their place of habitual residence.")

William had to consider more than the next few hours or days. He questioned Patti's mental condition and what she might do to the children in the short and long term. What she had done thus far had been grossly abusive to all of them in different ways. . .she had obviously intended to put Brandon in prison for the rest of his days and then follow up with the same fate for William. In doing so, it appeared she was willing to destroy the children's family and their lives.

As on his other visits, William stayed with Patti's father, Fred, and his second wife, Annie. They could see what was going on and shared his concern for Janice and Johnny. When he announced that, somehow or other, he was going to get Janice and Johnny back home to the states, Fred jumped right in and announced his help. This meant risking his livelihood as a dental surgeon and his friendship with local members of the royal family. Nonetheless, he was with William one hundred percent.

William had several outlined plans for the escape, intending to settle on the best option by midweek. There were several major obstacles to be gotten over: how to get the children away from under the nose of the supervisor and out of the building; how to travel several hours to an airport or seaport, past police; how to get past security and immigration checks. It was inevitable that there would be a national security system alert within minutes of their leaving the building and he was well aware of the efficiency of that system. Once and for all, he had to make sure the children knew exactly what they were doing, and had no doubts about their actions or leaving their mother.

On Friday, the children secretly reaffirmed their wish to go back to the States, fully aware that their mother might not follow them home. In fact, their enthusiasm to get going and their lack of interest in Patti's plans was somewhat overwhelming to both Fred and William, a subject that they often discussed afterwards. By nine o'clock that evening, William, Janice and Johnny were in France, ready to fly to Cleveland. The next day they were back in the United States.

William had complete responsibility for the children for nine months. They had a grand time together and the children gradually opened up about what had occurred when Patti started the rape allegations two years earlier. According to their matching stories, they had been taken to a motel about a mile from the house over the weekend while William was in Japan. This was not a total surprise, as he had found the receipt for the stay at the motel.

Janice told him that she and Johnny were told, over and over again, what to say about Brandon having sexually abused them. Patti had even drawn pictures of what had happened. They had no toys and Janice remembered playing with tissues and having to sleep on the floor. Johnny remembered Patti calling the police to come talk to them at the motel, but the police didn't come. Both children covered other details, such as when they were finally interviewed by the police and Patti sat behind Johnny, pinching and flicking him with her fingers. It appeared that the pressure may have caused both children to lie as instructed, although Johnny remembered saying "No, No, No" to a social worker. Having listened to the tape made by the HSS agency, it had been apparent to William that the children were pushed by the social worker over and over again until she received the right answer. However, the real crux was that both children denied ever being touched wrongly or abused in any way by Brandon, or anyone else for that matter. It was apparent they were thoroughly disgusted with the whole subject.

During the time William had the children, they were in counseling, which confirmed the above reports they had given him and identified their negative attitude towards their mother for having put them through the trauma of the sexual abuse allegations, their removal from their home, their father, their country and their loss of Brandon, whom they considered a great friend. Brandon had moved out of the area, away from the family, and was attempting to build a new life of his own. Patti had returned about three months after William returned the children to the United States. Throughout this time, she failed to comply with any of the court-ordered, twice-weekly visitations with the children, although she was living nearby in Cleveland. Nonetheless, she continued to make her presence felt through various legal motions and William was ordered to pay her support money. He started to do so, but stopped due to a lack of money and the fact that he was close to going under financially. In January of 1986, Patti entered an affidavit, accusing William of violence towards the children. In what William considered to be a move to stop her father from being a witness against her in the pending divorce and custody case, Patti accused her own father of having sexually abused her as a child. Through her mother, pressure was brought to bear on the English court to bring about two allegations of child abduction, citing the children's return to the Untied States. William won against both charges.

Shortly after Patti's return to the states, both parties were to complete a Minnesota Multiphasic Personality Index (MMPI) test. Upon completion, the results of Williams's testing was available but, mysteriously, Patti's results never came to light. Patti changed attorneys and her new attorney and he and the Guardian ad Litem for the children quickly requested that new tests be done for both parties, but by another psychologist. Amazingly, both MMPI tests were allowed to be taken at home and without supervision. A report was later submitted to the court, based on the interpretations of these latest MMPIs and interviews with the family.

William had questioned the psychologist as to the validity of the MMPIs, since under the testing circumstances, they could have been completed by anyone and could well have been done by an outside party. His concern was ignored. For reasons best known to himself, the psychologist had Patti take yet another test some months later. That in itself was not scientific, because William was not asked to repeat the test. The question was (and is) why? That and more became the subject of a lawsuit.

In March of 1986, a hearing was scheduled regarding the children's current and future custody. After waiting for hours, the judge said she had made up her mind—the children were to be returned to Patti. This decision was made without benefit of hearing William's witnesses or reading the psychological reports from the children's counselor. His attorney was astounded and attempted to have a full hearing scheduled. At five-thirty that afternoon, they were advised that the hearing would be held that evening and that it must be completed within an hour and a half. At that point, their witnesses were long gone, but Patti's attorney had two on standby. One of these was the psychologist and the other a social worker who testified that, among other things, William had a face like a martian's sex organs. From this, you may imagine the quality of the hearing. The end result was that

William had to instruct Johnny and Janice to gather their belongings and go to their mother. They didn't cry, they screamed.

Dr. Hill, the children's counselor, immediately protested to the Ohio court authorities that the hearing had been improperly held and that significant information had not been available regarding the children and actions in their best interest. There was no response from the courts or the Guardian ad Litem and custody was established as twelve days with Patti, two days with William. Those involved with the children were stunned. Throughout the preceding months the children had constantly and consistently repeated that they had been made to lie about the sexual abuse, and had evinced a great deal of anger toward their mother for making them lie and for taking them to England and away from their father.

Next began years of pain, frustration and expense, as William set out to prove not only that the allegations of sexual abuse were false, but that it was in the best interest of the children for him to have at least joint, if not full custody of the children. On the advice of his attorney at the time, William took the children to Dr. Carl at the University of Arizona, in the event there might be further allegations of child abuse against himself. Dr. Carl stated that, in her opinion, the children had not been molested by their father and that she considered him a good candidate for custodial parent.

In November of 1986, Janice described a clash with her mother, regarding her being made to lie in the original allegations against her stepbrother. According to Janice's report, Patti had tried to smother Janice by putting one hand over her mouth and holding the girl's hands and knees with the other. She said the act was interrupted by an inquiring neighbor.

After hearing this, William took both Janice and Johnny out of state for an in-depth evaluation at Loyola University. The evaluation was recorded on video and was the subject of a comprehensive report, which was later blocked from use as evidence on a technicality raised by the Guardian.

William's concerns about Patti's emotional state increased as it became clear that the children were being subjected to physical, verbal, and emotional abuse, this fact being confirmed by psychologists considered experts in the field of child psychology.

There were what seemed to be continuous motions, appeals, and counter appeals to the legal system and the state HSS agencies. Each time there was a chance for a change in custody, the children became hopeful. Each time custody remained with Patti, the children resisted that custody, more than once having to be forcibly taken to their mother's home. No one, it seemed, thought it necessary or advisable to listen to the children.

William had filed a police report due to his concern for the safety of the children if Patti became desperate about the discovery of her perjury and brainwashing of the children. In November, Janice wrote a letter to the police, asking that it be given to the judge in charge of their case so they could return to their father.

In January of 1987, prior to the divorce and custody hearing which had finally been set for May of 1987, William learned from the children that they had been taken for drug tests at the local General Hospital and that they had been questioned about his giving them drugs. William received the bill for the tests.

He couldn't afford an attorney by the time of the divorce hearing and represented himself. The case ran for most of a month and, although the outcome was predictable from the start, William was determined to bring out evidence and put it on record for future use. Of the thirteen witnesses he'd brought in, perhaps the most interesting was the teacher who testified to being approached by Patti and asked to lie, to say that she, the teacher, had started the abuse accusation. William had always suspected that Patti would do her best to cover her tracks.

For three years, William continued to battle for custody. For three years HSS and the courts refused to listen to the pleas of the children or to consider the reports from the University of Arizona, from Loyola Medical School, and from Ross Counseling, where the children had been under consistent therapy at the order of HSS.

During the course of 1989 and 1990, Janice and Johnny suffered further physical and emotional abuse from their mother. On one occasion they called the police to their mother's home. On another occasion, they ran away from their mother outside the Juvenile Court and defied six police cars in the local garage.

Johnny, at the age of ten, fought two sheriff's men so as not to be returned to his mother, who was watching the struggle. Although at one point a judge declared there was "clear and convincing evidence of abuse," the case was dismissed without a hearing days later. HHS told William to keep the children and then denied doing so to a judge who subsequently stopped William's visitation. Never once were the children allowed to testify, to act as witnesses.

In June of 1990, Janice, then twelve years old, filed an affidavit with the court, documenting the events of the past six years. In that affidavit, she pointed out that filing the affidavit was especially important as she and her brother had never had the chance to speak or to be heard in a court.

Janice first stated that while her dad was away, their mother took them to a motel and kept them there for two days, telling them that their stepbrother had done bad things to them and drawing pictures for them to look at. She told of being taken to England by her mother, who told them they didn't have a dad anymore, and then of returning to Ohio with their father. She stated that they were very happy living with their dad and that they didn't want to see their mother, but were taken away from William and forced to go live with her.

Janice documented the fact that her mother had physically abused both her and her brother and that she was afraid of her mother. After a particularly frightening display of abuse, Janice had confided in her father during their weekend with him. She said William made some calls and they were allowed to stay with their father until they could go to court and tell the judge everything. However, when they arrived at the courthouse, they were not allowed to see the judge and were sent home with their mother.

One of the saddest parts of this particular case study was this affidavit and the statements made by Janice regarding the dilemma of the children:

"I told a social worker about that (physical abuse) when she came to visit us. Mrs. M said she was my friend and that I need not tell anyone because my mother and father were going to get together again. I asked my dad and he said it wasn't true."

"I told a teacher at our school, Mrs. K, and she said she would help us. I also told Mrs. R. They didn't."

"This year my mother began to punch Johnny and I tried to stop it. I climbed out a window to get help. The police came and they said they would help us. The police did not help us."

"I talked to a man on the phone and he told me that Johnny and I could stay (with William) until they came to see us. They never did come to see us."

"I tried to see the judge, but they wouldn't let me. It was the worst day of our lives and Johnny and I tried to run away but the police caught us and made us get in the car with our mother."

"A lady called Cheri talked with us and said she would help us speak to a judge the next day, but it never happened."

"It is another summer and the court has stopped my father from seeing us. It is so difficult living with our mother because we never know what she is going to do. We have asked our dad to never give up fighting for us."

As of this writing, William continues to be denied any visitation with his children. He continues to pay child support and lives abroad much of the time. Each month the children are growing stronger and closer to freedom from a strange oppression. Like the Berlin Wall, William believes it is inevitable that time will tell and the barrier of lies separating him from his children will crumble.

Chapter Three

Colorado, 1984 – 1991

Marsha and Rick were married in 1977 and had three children, Andrew John, born in 1979, Cecil Wayne in 1980 and Sheila Marsha in 1982. Like most couples, they had their fights, but Rick loved her dearly and thought she loved him. He was concerned about the fact that she was a "screamer," instructing and disciplining the children in a strident voice that made Rick as nervous as it did the children. During the course of their marriage, Rick was often concerned about the many times she stayed out late with girlfriends, later learning that she had been lying to him about where she was and with whom.

The couple separated for three months in 1979. In July of 1984, they again separated. Marsha filed for divorce in November of 1984, but stopped the proceedings based on the belief she and Rick could work out their difficulties. She returned to him in April of 1985 and they made a second attempt at a working marriage. Rick had purchased a large cabin for the family and was doing finishing work on their new home while Marsha and the children lived in a trailer in town. Marsha had termed the cabin unlivable and Rick was trying to bring it up to her standards. She left him again in June of 1985 and they lived separately thereafter. Rick had continued working on the cabin, ever hopeful that once all the comforts had been installed and the finishing touches completed, Marsha and the children would move back there to live. He and Marsha had been seeing a marriage counselor and, although Marsha felt they could not reconcile their differences, Rick continued to hope.

Throughout the spring and summer, Rick continued to see his three children, although not as often as he would have liked. Marsha contended that his attempts to see her and the children constituted harassment. On one occasion when Rick came in to see the children while she was visiting her mother, Marsha had him arrested for causing a major disturbance, threatening to take the children and damaging her car. A few weeks later Marsha had called the Sheriff's office, contending that he was harassing her at work.

Unknown to Rick, Marsha had contacted a therapist in June and taken the children to see her. When he learned of the therapy and asked Marsha what was going on in the sessions, she told him she couldn't say exactly. In August, Rick advised Marsha that, because of her behavior in seeing other men and her inability to support the children, he was going to sue for custody.

On a sunny day in September, Rick heard the crunch of gravel and looked up to see Marsha's car coming down the drive. Since she rarely came to the cabin, he started toward her car, hoping she was coming to see how work was progressing. It was then he saw the second car. The officer in the squad car had come to arrest Rick for sexually molesting his three-year-old daughter.

From the cabin, Rick was taken directly to jail and refused any contact with friends or relatives, told the phone was out of order and generally ignored. The next day he was taken to court for formal charges and returned to jail. Three days later, he was taken to a second court for filing of criminal charges. Fortunately for Rick, the criminal court judge was so agitated about the manner of arrest and confinement, he ordered Rick released on his own recognizance. It was only during the court appearance that Rick found out the charges had been made by a policeman. Later investigation revealed the charges had been made based on Marsha's allegations. The policeman was Marsha's boyfriend, who had frequently been seen at the trailer by neighbors.

Marsha had filed a hand-written affidavit, in which she had made the allegations of child sexual abuse, stating it had occurred when the children had one of their rare overnight visits with Rick. The visit had originally been scheduled to take place at his parent's home. Following an argument with him, Marsha decreed that the children would, instead, spend the night with her mother and Rick was so advised. He went to his mother-in-law's house, picked up the kids and returned to his parents' home, as had been originally planned.

Marsha's allegation stated that Rick had taken the children for visitation the 26th of August, spending the weekend at his parents home. When the children returned, Marsha learned that the boys had slept upstairs and Sheila had slept downstairs with Rick. When Sheila went to the bathroom she said "my pee-pee hurts." Checking her daughter, Marsha noticed the entire vaginal area was red. She asked her daughter what happened and Sheila replied, "Daddy kissed my booby and pee-pee." Then Sheila said no, her daddy didn't do this, her grandfather did. Then Sheila said no, her grandfather didn't do it, it was because she had slept on the carpet. Marsha contacted Social Services the next morning.

As is common in cases such as this, Rick had no idea of the steps Marsha had taken that resulted in his arrest. Marsha was a good friend of a therapist at Department of Social Services (DSS), and with her assistance had set up an entire scenario to establish charges of child sexual abuse. As a result, the County DSS, Juvenile Division had filed a petition stating that Sheila had been sexually abused and both boys had been physically abused. The dependency petition, dated September 26, 1985, stated that the boys said their father had hit them with his belt and left bruises. It further stated that due to Sheila's age (she was three at the time), she could not talk about the abuse and referred the child to an agency therapist (ironically, the same close friend of Marsha's) for purposes of obtaining more information on the sexual abuse to substantiate the allegation. The agency therapist's letter to the DSS stated that she had received a call on August 30, 1985 from Sheila's mother stating she had reported further information supporting the allegation to Social Worker Jane Storey. In a letter to the social worker, the agency therapist said that in her sessions with Sheila, the child had remained consistent about her father having laid on top of her with his clothes on and that he goes "potty" on her.

In the meantime, a report had been filed by a District Attorney Investigator, following an interview with Marsha. During the course of that interview, Marsha made clear allegations of sexual abuse. She began by discussing the fact that from the time Sheila was three weeks old, she had noticed a thick white discharge with a strong offensive odor coming from the child's vaginal area and contended that during the periods when she was separated from her husband, the discharge and odor seemed to be reduced. Marsha also stated that Rick walked around their home often with no clothes on and expected to engage in intercourse when the children were in the bedroom. She specifically discussed an incident when Rick was in a chair with no clothes on and Sheila, crawling into his lap, grabbed his penis and said "Daddy, you got a big peter." Marsha said Rick laughed about the incident.

According to Marsha's report, when she left Rick the second time in June of 1985, she made an appointment with the agency therapist at the County Mental Health for therapy for the children. She also took Sheila to see a doctor, who said it would be hard to determine sexual abuse unless Marsha brought Sheila in immediately upon noticing anything out of the ordinary.

When he was released from jail, Marsha and Rick met at the marriage counselor's house. She had gone to him earlier to try to undo what she had done that week. She showed Rick a list of the written charges she had made against him and a list of the recantations, telling him she had not meant for him to be arrested, but things had gotten out of hand. He was absolutely shocked at what she had done and the charges she had made and immediately asked for a divorce.

In the short period of time that had elapsed, a week that had seemed like a month to Rick, the District Attorney had gotten involved as well as Social Services. The recantations meant nothing to them. . .they contended Rick had threatened Marsha into making them. In addition, there was a charge of physical abuse, based on an incident when he had lifted Sheila over a porch railing. In the process, she hurt her elbow and they had taken her to a doctor to have it checked. There had been no report of abuse by the doctor, as it had been a simple accident. Social Services viewed it as another weapon in their arsenal and used it against Rick in future hearings and considerations.

Suddenly Rick had only very limited access to his three children—supervised visits were required. More often than not, these were either scheduled when he was working or Marsha canceled them arbitrarily. Because he refused to confirm the charges and maintained his innocence, he eventually lost all rights to visit the children at all.

On September 26, 1985, based on a letter from the social worker stating it was her opinion that sexual abuse had occurred, an edict was issued by the Department of Social Services, stating that Rick would not visit with the children unless supervised by the County DSS or an assigned agency; that the Sheriff's department and DSS would be notified of when Rick would be visiting with the children (time, place and date) and that, should the agreement be broken, visitations by Rick would immediately cease and the children might be removed from their home.

The formal statement from the social worker asserted, "Based on information Sheila and her mother provided me, it is my opinion sexual contact has occurred between Sheila Doe and her father, Rick." Rick's access to his children was based primarily on statements made by his ex-wife and Marsha's interpretation of Sheila's statements, which she repeated to the social worker.

No one seemed to be listening to anything he had to say. All actions were based on what Marsha said or what the Social Services workers said.

The following weeks were an ongoing nightmare. Rick saw his children only under supervised conditions, the supervisor being the Department of Social Services or an assigned agency. Because of agency policy, most visits continued to be scheduled during Rick's work hours and Marsha continued to cancel the visits arbitrarily, usually at the last minute. Meantime, the children—his two sons as well as his daughter—were in on-going therapy under the direction of DSS, who treated all three children as if they had, in fact, been abused and issued consistently damaging reports and summaries regarding Rick's actions with the children and their feelings about their father.

On May 12, 1986, the agency therapist sent a letter to the County DSS, stating her concern about the visitations of Rick with his children. Criminal and juvenile petitions were still pending, alleging physical and sexual abuse of the children and Rick was to meet the conditions set out in the September edict. The agency therapist contended that Rick was not following the rules, that he had frequently been in the presence of the children and had been emotionally abusive to them, telling them he didn't love them, he didn't want them. She further stated that the children reported being frightened of their father and of his following them and Marsha around. The therapist recommended that visitation be disallowed until the disposition of the criminal and juvenile matters. She based her recommendation on her analysis of the children's reports, Rick's hostility towards DSS and her feeling that his attitude was disrupting their therapy progress.

On May 16th, the therapist sent a letter to DSS stating that Rick's son Cecil had shown her, with anatomically correct dolls, "bad touches." He indicated that Rick had touched his penis, fondling him when he was in bed, and also showed her how his father had fondled Sheila's vagina.

A comprehensive report was submitted by the agency therapist on July 1, 1986 to DSS. This report indicated that both Marsha and Rick had previously been married, that Rick had two daughters who lived with his ex-wife. Marsha said the ex-wife had told her that Rick had been physically abusive to her during their marriage and Marsha contended he had continued that pattern during his marriage to her. Over the ten years of their marriage, Marsha and Rick had separated several times.

The agency therapist contended that all three children demonstrated behavior characteristics of physical, emotional, and sexual abuse victims. According to the therapist, Andrew exhibited an extremely low self-concept and had difficulty expressing any positive item about himself, frequently stating he was "unlovable." He perceived the world as an unsafe environment, showed antisocial behavior, and acknowledged little personal responsibility. Both Cecil and Sheila were said to demonstrate a mistrust of adults. Cecil demonstrated difficulty in concentrating and a basic "don't care" attitude. Sheila exhibited angry, defiant, oppositional behavior to any monitoring or restructuring of her activities. In summarizing the benefits of the therapy the children had been undergoing, the agency therapist stated that Cecil's increased feeling of being protected allowed him to discuss the incestuous behavior of his father. She further stated that Sheila's progress included improved identification of her feelings concerning the sexual abuse and improved expression of feelings concerning family roles, boundaries, and relationships. (I find this to be an impressive accomplishment for a three-year-old, as did Sheila's father.) In conclusion, she recommended that legal custody of the children be returned to Marsha and, due to the fact that criminal and juvenile court petitions were still pending, a strong case management system be implemented.

At the end of July, the court gave legal and physical custody of the children to Marsha Doe with DSS retaining protective supervision, requiring that the children and Marsha remain in therapy and stating that Rick was to have no visitation and no contact with the children unless he agreed to enter therapy, at which time the restrictions would be reviewed.

On August 1, 1986 the courts issued the divorce decree, recognizing the orders in effect from the juvenile court, denying Rick any contact with his children and stating that Rick was not to visit Marsha unless a time had been previously arranged and a third person of Marsha's choosing was present.

On August 27, a motion was filed requiring that the victim (Sheila) be made available for a psychiatric examination prior to Rick's trial on child sexual abuse.

While Rick's attorney was successful in getting the criminal charges of sexual abuse dropped, due to lack of any substantial evidence, he was not helpful in his suggestion that Rick plead nolo contendere to the charges of physical abuse. Following his attorney's advice, in an effort to simply end the nightmare, Rick made a fatal mistake in this pleading, a mistake that resulted in the possibility of the juvenile court using that plea to prevent Rick from ever seeing his children again.

Unknown to Rick, a videotaped interview of his daughter was ordered by the Deputy District Attorney, based on the therapist's opinion that it would be emotionally traumatic for Sheila to testify in court. The tape was made, but Rick was not present, never saw the tape and, when he learned of it and asked to view it, his request was denied. Unfortunately, this is not unusual in cases of this nature.

It is interesting to note the list of questions asked during the interview, a list provided by the Deputy DA. In any analysis of interviews, the types of questions often dictate the types of answers received and it is quite possible to lead the witness through the proper questions. Included in this listing were a number of closed and leading questions which placed the interviewer in a much more active role than the child. Questions such as:

Has Rick Doe ever touched her where she didn't want to be touched?

Where did he touch her?

With what did he touch her?

Did he touch her more than once?

Did the touching hurt?

Has Rick Doe ever laid on top of her?

Has she ever laid on top of him?

Did they have their clothes off?

Has Rick ever made her touch him?

Where?

Did Rick ever tell her not to tell anybody?

Although the sexual abuse charges were dropped by the criminal prosecutor, due to a lack of any substantial evidence, Social Services held to the sexual abuse as well as the physical abuse charges.

The public defender, who represented Rick, advised him to plead nolo-contendere to the physical abuse. . .after all, the incident in which it was alleged his daughter's arm had been hurt did happen. So there he was, charged with child abuse, sentenced to four years probation and denied any access to his three children. Rick found himself in the typical position of one who has been falsely accused of sexual abuse. The agencies and courts were determined to treat a condition that didn't exist and solve a problem that wasn't there. Meantime, his children were deprived of any contact with their father.

In final court orders, Rick's ex-wife received full custody of the three children, Rick was put on probation for four years, ordered to pay four hundred and twenty dollars a month in child support, as well as full restitution to the court, and advised by the court that he would never see his children again. Any attempts to visit or contact the children would result in his arrest. It was a no-win situation. He couldn't admit to sexual child abuse that had never occurred, he couldn't see his children and he couldn't find anyone to help.

On October 8, 1986, the agency therapist drafted a clinical summary update in which she recommended that the County Social Services discontinue their involvement with Marsha and the children. She indicated that all three children were afraid of their father. She stated that the agency continued to work with Cecil and Sheila as incest victims and that Marsha had joined a weekly adult incest group.

On November 11, 1986, a memo from Rick's probation officer stated that he had a letter from their family counselor, stating that Marsha had told him she had trumped up the charges against Rick because she believed she had been caught by him in an incriminating relationship with another man. Marsha had initialed the report from the counselor. The memo further included statements from Dr. R, indicating that he did not believe Rick suffered from mental illness, was not an alcoholic, and did not appear to him to be a child abuser. The probation officer recommended Rick participate in mental health counseling.

The court-ordered evaluation done by Dr. R was, for all practical intents and purposes, ignored by the court. Overall, the evaluation pointed out that Rick was a candid, straightforward man, one incapable of perpetrating child sexual abuse. It is interesting to note that Dr. R questioned the use of the anatomically correct dolls, pointing out that an inappropriate setting and the use of leading questions can provoke desired responses, rather than accurate or true responses. He indicated that the Public Defender felt Rick was the victim of a legal sequence of events derived from what he felt was incorrect procedure, poorly carried out, in Aspen by the mental health worker. In closing, Dr. R cited the fact that Marsha had admitted to the marriage counselor that she had made false allegations of both physical and sexual abuse in an effort to protect her custody of the children in the face of her extra-marital relationships. He then stated: "Accordingly, then, the whole issue of counselling may be moot, since there is, in my opinion, no significant issue to be dealt with."

Two months later, January, 1987, in spite of the above positive report, DSS issued a six-month treatment plan for Rick that required the following: Therapy with a professional whose background experience was in working with perpetrators who have sexually abused; a psychological evaluation; no visitation or telephone contact with his children, unless specifically recommended by Rick's therapist and agreed to by the agency therapist; entry into a perpetrator's group, preferably with DSS's recommended Mental Health Center. The stated goal of the treatment was "to have Mr. Doe in therapy so that he is able to resolve past issues that led him to abuse his children."

Rick was referred to a female therapist. She insisted he admit to sexual abuse prior to any therapy. Because he was innocent of those charges, he refused. DSS then referred him to a second therapist, the agency therapist who was convinced he was an abuser, who had filed allegations based on her work with his ex-wife and three children, and who continued to counsel the children as sexual and child-abuse victims.

As a result of maintaining his innocence and refusing to enter a perpetrator's group and admit to being an abuser, the court, based on recommendations of DSS in August of 1987, dismissed the juvenile case with the following orders: Legal and physical custody of the children would be with Marsha; Rick would have no custody and no visitation or contact, direct or indirect, with his children; Rick would enter therapy and be evaluated; Rick should be in individual therapy for one year to work on issues related to sexual abuse of children. If Rick progressed through this therapy, he would then have to attend parenting classes for a minimum of eight weeks and, following that, enter counseling with Marsha to allow them to establish a dialogue in which the two could work toward the children visiting their father. Meantime, Marsha remarried, providing a substitute father figure for the children who were denied their own father by the system.

In December, the agency therapist left the Mental Health Center and was replaced by a second therapist. Unknown to Rick, the second therapist provided the District Court with a Clinical Summary Update on April 6, 1987. Many of her statements and recommendations were in marked contrast to those of the original therapist, i.e. "recognizing and working through personal concerns such as ambivalent feelings toward their father and mother, age-appropriate issues around trust and abandonment which may be exacerbated by their family problems."

The new therapist further stated that she thought it important to the children's emotional well-being for them to re-establish a healthy relationship with their father. Toward this end, she recommended Rick consistently attend a minimum of twelve consecutive weeks of therapy in individual or group format and attend eight weeks of parenting classes, following which he should be allowed supervised weekly or bi-weekly visits with his children. She also recommended that Rick and Marsha attend joint therapy for purposes of helping them function together in the children's best interests.

At the same time this occurred, the Social Services agency in their county was under fire from a number of families who had been treated much as Rick had been and whose rights had been badly abused. There was a great deal of media attention, resulting in a state investigation which culminated with resignation of the director and a general shake-up in the employees.

During this time Rick continued to look for a good lawyer. Most didn't want the case, as they felt they could be of little help due to his pleading guilty to the child abuse. Others didn't want to fight the Department of Social Services. Finally, he located an attorney who said he could approach it from the standpoint of restoring Rick's visitation rights. At least, he might get to see his children again after three and a half years.

In April of 1989, Rick went back to court for reinstatement of visitation rights, represented by a new attorney. It had now been more than three years since he had seen his children. One of the items pointed out by the attorney was that Rick found himself in a lose/lose situation. The psychological report indicated no basis for the charge of sexual abuse and no issue for which to seek resolution through therapy. His ex-wife admitted she had concocted the charges. The criminal courts had dropped the charges. Yet, as a condition of seeing his children, he was required to admit he had perpetrated sexual abuse and enter a year's therapy. Rick's attorney sought supervised visitation, supervision to be supplied by a clinical psychologist who agreed with Dr. R's findings regarding Rick and who had offered his services to assist in establishing contact between father and children.

On October 17th, an order was issued regarding visitation. Initial visitation was scheduled in the DSS office, with the agency therapist supervising. It was ordered that, prior to Christmas, reports would be filed by the therapist and the Guardian ad Litem describing the course of the visitations and addressing the issue of holiday visitation.

Marsha's response to this request was to file a motion asking that visitation reinstatement not be considered until after a Guardian ad Litem was appointed for the children and said guardian had the opportunity to review the case and make some judgement regarding the merit of reinstating visitation. The motion requested that the Guardian ad Litem who had been appointed for the juvenile case be reinstated.

A Guardian ad Litem was appointed and in December she entered a report to the court in which she recommended that visitation continue, but that there be no unsupervised visitation allowed at that time. She requested that she be allowed to determine when unsupervised visitation became appropriate.

Attached to the Guardian ad Litem's report was a report from the therapist, indicating that the visitation was occurring on a weekly basis with both Rick and Marsha attending the visits. She stated that the children exhibited increasing comfort in Rick's presence and some lessening of prior levels of fear, although they continued to express strong reluctance to be alone with their father. It was recommended that the children spend an extended Christmas Eve visit with Mr. Doe at his parent's home, with his parents supervising. She further recommended that visitation times be increased and be supervised by a non-related person, gradually moving into an unsupervised visit in a public place, then at Rick's home.

Rick's girlfriend encouraged him to continue to fight for his innocence, but the attorney told them this would cost a lot of money. If they wanted to put his kids through college, he didn't mind, but he was very discouraging regarding the cost. At that time, the end of January, they felt they had their hands full just dealing with the visitation issue. The Guardian was prejudiced against Rick from the court records she had read and her interviews with Marsha and the therapist during the supervised visits had once worked with DSS, and the only thing keeping the couple going was their visits with the kids. The children remembered Rick, in spite of the years of separation, the father and children began getting acquainted again and their hope was that time would resolve the problem.

Eventually the Guardian and Rick began communicating, her attitude seeming less one-sided. She was bothered by some things she'd heard from his ex-wife, some things that didn't click. Over the course of several visits, Rick gained ground with the Guardian. His girlfriend sent the Guardian a copy of an article she had seen in an issue of the *Florida Bar-Commentary* and suddenly, the visits were extended and unsupervised. When the Guardian ad Litem advised Rick of her approval of unsupervised visits, she cautioned him that his girlfriend should always be present. It seemed that his ex-wife would cooperate under those circumstances. Rick now got to see the kids for two hours one day a week and every other Saturday from 9:00 a.m. to 7:00 p.m.

In April of 1990, Rick and Marsha were asked to draw up a visitation agreement with the Guardian ad Litem for purposes of establishing visitation. Both Rick and Marsha were dissatisfied with the supervision and therapy of the second therapist and asked for her dismissal. Rick signed the agreement drawn up by Marsha, unaware that both agreements were to have been reviewed by the Guardian ad Litem. As always, his major concern was avoiding delays in spending time with the children.

Rick's agreement had requested unsupervised visits of eight hours in length, beginning in April, every other Saturday. He had then requested overnight visitations beginning in June and including either Friday or Saturday night stays every other weekend, increasing in July to visits every other weekend starting on Friday evening and ending on Sunday evening. Provision was made that if visits were missed because of their mother's plans, those visits would be made up.

Marsha's agreement, which he signed, provided for visits every Tuesday night for two hours and every other Saturday from nine in the morning to five in the evening, such visits to be unsupervised *if* the children were comfortable, Dr. T. recommended such and the judge approved. She requested freedom to change the visits if unforeseen plans occurred.

The spring of 1990, Rick again filed for joint custody of the children and liberal visitation. In May, Marsha produced two letters, one from Cecil's teacher and one from Andrew's teacher. The letter from Cecil's teacher was particularly upsetting to Rick, as she stated that his visits with Rick were having very negative results on the child. She also said that she was familiar with children who had suffered from physical and sexual abuse, clearly indicating that she felt Cecil's problems were directly related to his being abused and forced to visit with his father. No one seemed to consider that the issue here might not be visiting with Rick, but the fact that the time with Rick was restricted. Perhaps, if they had been allowed more time with their father, these problems would have gone away.

During 1990, psychological evaluations were ordered on all three children, partially as a result of the above letters. Andrew's evaluation was done first, consisting of testing and interviewing Andrew, then interviewing both Marsha and Rick. The evaluations were done by a psychologist requested by Rick's ex-wife (not an independent Ph.D.), one who appeared to accept the allegations of abuse as fact and whose findings on all three children indicated behavior "consistent with abuse."

Her summary of emotional considerations included statements that Andrew had a distorted image of an aggressive father figure, that he wished a less powerful figure in that role. During the Children's Apperception Test, she stated that after producing a plot, Andrew could not resolve the hostile conflicts between parents and children unless the father figure was killed or left. The Sentence Completion Test, in conjunction with an interview, suggested to the psychologist a cry for help in improving his relationship with his stepfather and resolving his ambivalent feelings of wish/fear towards his father. In addition, she stated that he seemed to have great difficulty relating to the mother figure during the Rorschach testing and that he was angry and unfulfilled by parent figures. Scattered throughout the evaluation were comments such as, "The physical and emotional abuse has clearly had a significant deleterious effect upon him"; and, "He suffers significant emotional problems consistent with a physically and sexually abused child."

Included in Andrew's evaluation were recommendations for family therapy and focus points. She felt it was important that Andrew work through his aggression and his fear of Rick in order to re-develop a more positive relationship and, at the same time, work to develop a stronger attachment with his stepfather and stronger bond between him and his mother.

The evaluation report on Sheila, now eight years old, was submitted in July. In the summary of emotional considerations, the psychologist stated that Sheila described the family environment as a hostile, dangerous place in which the father was angry at the child and physically attacked the mother. In her stories, she and her siblings routinely rescued and protected the mother from the powerful father. The psychologist then stated that Sheila believed that her natural father had sexually molested her, which resulted in Sheila's significant anxiety and ambivalent feelings toward him. The constant thread throughout the evaluation and recommendations was recognition of the fact that Sheila often felt sad, lonely, and insecure and that she needed a much closer, more trusting relationship with both parents and her stepfather, but particularly her mother.

Cecil's evaluation also was done in June of 1990. He was ten. The summary of emotional considerations indicated that Cecil was seeking adult help in solving, among other things, the continued strife between his parents. The psychologist stated that Cecil seemed angry at both parents and court officials for not hearing or understanding what he was saying. Emotionally, Cecil appeared very attached to his mother. The psychologist stated that, because of his fear and unsafe feeling with his father, Cecil said he could not ask his father to stop the bitterness between the two families. She felt Cecil had a strong attachment to his stepfather, but felt confused and tense when Rick did not support Cecil's affiliation with his stepfather. One of the key issues of this evaluation was the negative impact being caused by the bitterness between Cecil's parents, his desire for everyone to be happy. It appeared that Cecil was sensitive to the anger and tensions between his mother and father and sought to solve the conflict by severing contact with Rick. During his interview, Cecil indicated that he wanted to get along with his family and that meant he didn't want to see Rick. At one point, he reported to the psychologist that when he was two or three he sat on Rick's lap, and Cecil thought Rick had touched him. This conflicted with the original report of abuse filed by DSS years earlier.

In a letter to the psychologist, Rick's attorney raised several points. Among these was the fear that some of the allegations made against him were a result of the separation and divorce and had nothing to with abuse, that the child-abuse charge to which he pleaded no contest had been an excuse for those allegations.

After reviewing the psychological evaluations, the attorney sent another letter to the psychologist. In this letter, he raised a number of questions. First, the parties involved in the upcoming August hearing had agreed to the necessity of not bringing up old rumors and allegations concerning child abuse, yet the reports from the psychologist seemed to dwell on the past to a large degree. Secondly, he questioned the assumption that the aggressive father figure was Rick, not the stepfather. Andrew had referred to the aggressive and abusive figure as "dad." The attorney pointed out that the children were not allowed to call Rick "father" or "dad," but were to refer to him by his given name, while instructed to refer to their stepfather as "dad." He went on to question the fact that in Sheila's evaluation and Andrew's evaluation the exact same opening to a statement was made: "I would do anything to forget the time that I had bad bruises from Rick." "I would do anything to forget the time that I was hurt by Rick, his bad touches." He pointed out that the fact the same wording was used is a potential indication they were told what to say.

A hearing was scheduled for July of 1990 to address Rick's requests. Marsha asked for a continuance of that hearing and again requested that the court appoint a Guardian ad Litem to represent the best interests of the children. An order was issued, granting her requests.

Court hearings were canceled three times. The therapist was out of town and the Guardian ad Litem was tied up with a different case, and Marsha's lawyer requested a continuance. Finally, a November hearing was scheduled. Rick's girlfriend called the attorney weekly, ascertaining there would be no more changes, no more delays. Waiting for the hearing was a long, difficult exercise. Always, the situation was on their minds; always, they faced the possibility that Marsha would come up with new and different schemes, more attempts to alienate the children.

It was hoped that by forcing the issue of therapy/mediation between Rick and Marsha prior to the court date, some truth might be revealed which would counteract the negative effects of Marsha's manipulation. However, the Guardian denied their request for Dr. S. to serve as therapist. Rick was already behind on his debts to lawyers and therapists as well as his support payments and it was contended he didn't need additional debt. In addition, Marsha wouldn't agree to the therapy.

When they finally had their day in court, it all seemed very strange. The two opposing attorneys chatted amicably and it was agreed that Rick should have the normal visitation he had requested. Effective immediately, he would see his children one day every week and every other weekend, as well as having them for a week during Christmas break and two weeks during the summer. Nothing was mentioned about the alleged abuse.

The judge stated that she remembered the case from years ago and was impressed that the parents now seemed to be cooperating, on behalf of the children. A therapy session for Rick and Marsha was instated, both of them seeing Marsha's therapist, whose involvement was left to her discretion. Although nothing was resolved as far as Rick's innocence, there was satisfaction in knowing his visits with the children had been successfully negotiated and court-ordered.

Currently, Rick has what appears to be normal visitation and the ability to return to a somewhat normal life. But the fear and uncertainty are always there. Will his ex-wife continue to cooperate or will she do something to disrupt the visits yet again? Will the children, who are still in therapy, be treated for what is really wrong or will the focus of the therapy continue to be abuse that never occurred? For how long must Rick and his girlfriend walk a tight rope, before they can really relax and be natural and open around the children?

And finally, will Rick's name ever be cleared? Will he be removed from the Central Abuse Registry? And what of the emotional trauma and financial ramifications resulting from the false allegations? Will life ever return to what most people perceive as normal?

Chapter Four

Texas, 1986 – 1991

The Mark Doe case is making headlines in Texas and throughout the nation. As a result of the many negative ramifications caused by false allegations of child sexual abuse filed against him, Mark has filed a multi-million dollar lawsuit against his ex-wife, her attorneys, Texas Child Protection Services and mental health institutions and professionals who were involved in the case, alleging malicious prosecution and conspiracy, citing the violation of his constitutional rights and extortion and racketeering attempts used by his ex-wife and her attorney to gain divorce and custody settlements. Among other charges he states that the individuals involved knowingly provided false information to the County District Attorney, false information that led to his indictment on child sexual abuse charges. Mr. Doe has also engaged the RICO Act (Racketeer Influenced and Corrupt Organizations). Although the charges against him were dismissed in August of 1988, as of late fall, 1990, Mr. Doe still has severely restricted visitation rights with his children and it remains to be seen what effect or feelings of alienation may result from the events of the last four years. Currently, Mark Doe is fighting for a two-fold purpose—to gain normal, unsupervised visitation with his children, or better yet, custody, and to set a national precedent as the hallmark case in false child sexual abuse charges.

Mark and Judy Doe were married in 1978. A year later their son, Norman was born. In 1984 they had a second son, Bill, and in March of 1986 became the proud parents of a daughter, Paula.

Mark owned two successful businesses, a cafeteria and a medical equipment supply firm. Unfortunately, their marriage was not building as successfully as their family and businesses, as Judy had been seeing other men. The couple separated in September of 1986 and, in October, Mark filed for divorce and custody of the three children, on grounds of adultery and abandonment. He had been both mother and father to the children for some time prior to the separation. The court awarded Mark temporary custody of the three children. Mark consented to joint custody, pending the arbitration property settlement proceedings, hoping that Judy would want to become a parent for the children's benefit.

In January of 1987, Judy's attorney, Mr. L., filed an application for a family study to be conducted by the County Child Protection Service (CPS). This request is highly unusual as, by law, the CPS is not involved unless there is suspicion of, or allegations of, child abuse, as occurred in my case. At that point, there had been no indication of abuse of any sort. Mark's counsel was not advised of the request. It was later learned that the order for the home study was never signed, nor entered by the family court. The motion, as filed, was in violation of the court's orders for non-interference by attorneys during the arbitration process.

As is often the case in custody disputes, the Does were instructed to undergo psychological evaluations to determine the best interests of the children. The evaluations were done by a professional recommended by Judy's attorney.

By the time the psychologist saw Mark Doe, she had already seen Judy and Bill several times, and had concluded that Mark had sexually and physically abused his son. She had stated this opinion to the authorities. With her conclusion already made, she reviewed Mark's tests as pathologically as possible, concluding he had "obsessive-compulsive tendencies, high defensiveness and an intense need to control," that "his rigidly defensive posture does not adequately bind the underlying anxiety and trepidation of doing poorly." Later review by forensic psychological experts indicated that nowhere was this conclusion supported by empirical data, nowhere did the psychologist indicate that not all tests were performed under supervision, and nowhere did she give any allowance for the acrimonious situation in which Mark currently found himself.

The psychologist's interpretations of the Rorschach, stating she saw "an undercurrent of anxiety, unrequited love, and cloaked sexuality. . .difficulty with relating appropriately to others. . .polymorphous perverse orientation to the environment. . .fantasies (that may include) homosexual, bisexual, and exhibitionist feelings. . .hostility toward woman. . ." were termed by the forensic experts later reviewing the case to be arbitrary, personal, subjective, and idiosyncratic interpretations.

Citing serious omissions in her educational requirements, the experts reviewing the case raised questions as to the psychologist's competency and training for providing the type of services she did for the Doe family, and questioned her competency in representing herself up as an expert and making the far reaching recommendations regarding the entire family.

Throughout the evaluation process, the psychologist had numerous contacts with Judy's attorneys, a highly irregular occurrence. As an objective arm of the family law court, her mission should have been to form an impartial evaluation of the family members, based on contacts with those family members, not on contact and information supplied by the wife's attorney. Throughout this period, there was no contact with Mark or with his attorney.

Arbitration broke down on April 28, 1987, with no agreement on property settlements or custody arrangements. On April 29, 1987, Judy began seeing a therapist and taking Bill, their three-year-old son, with her. The therapist agreed to prepare a statement that she suspected Bill was the victim of physical or sexual abuse. Although she stated in notes, documenting her meetings with Judy and Bill, that she suspected abuse, Ms T. did not report the suspected abuse to CPS, as she is required to do, in writing, by law. As a matter of fact, although Ms T. saw both Judy and Bill numerous times and concluded there had been child abuse, there were no case notes available to be surrendered to the criminal court regarding any of these therapy sessions. However, such information was made available to the court and counsel when she was *personally* sued by Mark Doe. In this instance, the therapist had perjured herself in criminal court by denying the existence of notes and records.

In June of 1987, CPS received a call from Bill's day-care school. The school had been requested by Mark's ex-wife to report that they suspected sexual abuse because of his behavior. The suspicion was ruled unfounded on July 2nd, after CPS initiated an investigation. Bill denied having been abused by anyone when he was questioned by the CPS case worker. In spite of these findings, Judy and her attorney persisted in making the allegation an issue in family court proceedings, attempting to force Mark to settle the divorce and custody issues on their terms.

On July 9th, less than a week before the family court hearing, Judy called CPS from the psychologist's office to report Bill's declaration that he had been abused by his father. This allegation made no sense, as Judy stated that Bill had told her about the abuse on July 6th and again on the 7th. Yet, Judy had allowed Bill and his older brother to stay overnight with their father on July 7th and 9th—after Bill had allegedly told her about the abuse. The report to CPS wasn't made until the 9th. That report alleged that Bill had told his mother that Mark had tied his legs with a chain and played with his penis. Based on Judy's allegation, CPS reopened the investigation into allegations of child sexual abuse involving Mark and Bill.

On July 10th, unknown to Mark or his attorney, Judy took Bill to the CPS offices, bringing with her a blue bicycle chain. Bill was interrogated by CPS and later interviewed on videotape. During the videotaped interview, Bill repeatedly denied having been touched in his private area. Finally, the caseworker led Bill to mumble, "Daddy touched me there." Terminating the interview, the caseworker asked Bill if he was telling the truth or a lie. Bill responded, "It's a lie." The same question, eliciting the same response, was repeated three times.

As too often happens, the interview was conducted using a number of repetitive and leading questions and employed the use of anatomically correct dolls, which are highly suggestive by their very design. A review of the tape showed clearly that this was not Bill's first introduction to the dolls or to the questions being asked of him. In the video, he identified the dolls as the ones he had seen at his mother's house and it appeared that he had been coached by his mother in using the dolls and responding to questions and comments. Nonetheless, his answers were confusing and not credible. Throughout the interview, the caseworker routinely touched or pointed to the "private parts" of the doll when asking where Daddy had touched Bill. In addition, Bill was not yet toilet-trained at the age of three and, naturally, his father would have touched what the caseworker referred to as "private parts" when cleaning him after an accident or when bathing the child in preparation for bed.

However, where Judy and her attorney were concerned, the only important part of the tape was that Bill said, "Daddy touched me there." In spite of the fact that CPS knew the Does were involved in a bitter divorce and custody battle, generally the type of situation that fosters the possibility of false allegations, no further investigation was done.

As too often happens, the social worker made an immediate initial decision that Bill exhibited the behaviors and attitudes of an abused child, based on the assertions of the child's mother. The therapist's subsequent opinions, conclusions, and recommendations were derived solely from information and opinions provided her by Judy Doe. Ms T. became Judy's support person and, due to her prejudice, was unable to act in the best interest of her supposed-to-be client, Mark's youngest son.

On July 13th, at five in the afternoon, Judy and her attorney filed allegations of child sexual abuse and the next morning the psychologist submitted her report to the family court, stating she suspected Bill had been physically and sexually abused by his father. A review of the evaluations done on Norman and Bill showed that, while the psychologist recognized that the stress of the acrimonious divorce was causing problems for Judy and Norman, she concluded that Bill's problems were due to his having been physically and sexually abused, "most likely by his father."

Mark wasn't advised of the allegations against him until immediately prior to the family court hearing. Judy's attorney and the trial court judge expelled Mark Doe from the courtroom during the proceedings. *Why?* The psychologist and the therapist had prepared highly biased and inaccurate reports, in which they represented themselves as experts and concluded Bill was *probably* the victim of sexual abuse and the abuse was *most likely* from his father. She recommended that Judy be given sole custody of the children and that Mark be allowed only very limited and closely supervised visitation. She further recommended that Bill be hospitalized for further evaluation and psychiatric treatment, based on her statement that Bill exhibited the demeanor of an abused child.

Mark's visitation rights were immediately terminated. On the 17th, during the courtroom negotiations finalizing the divorce, negotiations between Mr. L and Mark's attorney, the psychologist issued her threat, telling Mark's attorney that unless Mark agreed to Mr L's property settlement, the custody arrangements, placing Bill in a hospital for psychiatric evaluation and treatment and submitting himself to therapy, she would use her efforts to have all three children removed to foster homes. Consumed with fear and concern for the three children, Mark, on his attorney's recommendation, agreed to the terms, having been told he had no real choice. He certainly didn't view foster care as being in the best interest of the children.

On July 20th, the divorce papers were signed by the court. Mark paid one hundred thousand dollars to Judy's attorney, as "agreed" under the terms of the settlement he had been forced into accepting. Mr. L again reminded Mark that if he didn't go along with the terms and the system, he would never see his children again. Mark took the threat very seriously.

Bill was hospitalized at Duchein Children's Center on July 21st, based on the psychologist's recommendation and with CPS approval. While the medical staff at Duchein was aware there was no evidence of abuse, they provided treatment as if such abuse had occurred. In addition, the psychologist diagnosed the three-year-old as enuretic and encopretic when, in fact, the child was simply not yet toilet-trained, and neither diagnosis is valid at such a young age. Nevertheless, Duchein treated these conditions as well. Mark was refused permission to see his son for forty-five days. A week later, the CPS caseworker was instructed to follow up on criminal charges against Mark.

It became apparent to Mark that CPS was not going to conduct any further investigation of the alleged abuse and it was equally clear that the staff at Duchein had decided there had been abuse and that Mark was the abuser. He contacted CPS, the psychologist, and the doctor at Duchein, informing them that he intended to find out if Bill had actually been abused and, if so, by whom.

Mark took a polygraph test and submitted the results to the Duchein staff and all professionals involved. The lie detector test indicated he had not abused his son. In addition, he obtained affidavits relating to his ex-wife's live-in boyfriend and the sexual molestation of the boyfriend's three daughters. Judy subsequently married the boyfriend, a convicted child sexual abuser. The information was submitted to everyone involved: the trial court, attorneys, professionals, and hospital staff. As Mark continued his battle, he obtained evaluations by forensic psychologists.

After a great deal of thought, Mark decided to go back to domestic court and attempt to regain custody of his children, trusting that the psychologist would be reluctant to force his children into foster homes, with the evidence he had gathered showing the falsification of the allegations, and hoping that Judy wouldn't allow such a thing to happen, out of vindictiveness towards Mark.

On September 4th, Mark went to CPS to inquire about child visitation rights and rulings. He found that all records of the investigation were missing. When Mark spoke with a CPS supervisor and explained the situation, the supervisor's reaction was, "Oh no, not again!" When Mark questioned the man's reaction, he explained that there were other cases he was aware of, in which Mr. L., Mark's ex-wife's attorney, had injected charges of child abuse or child sexual abuse in custody battles. Further investigation into Mr. L's records has already revealed there are at least five other parents and their children who have suffered as a result of this attorney's tactics.

Mark was becoming more and more concerned about his children, particularly since he had learned that Judy's live-in boyfriend had a documented history of child sexual abuse. He was equally concerned about the psychological and emotional effects that staying in Duchein might have on his youngest son, particularly given the fact that the staff continued to treat him as a victim of child sexual abuse. Bill was the youngest child there. Duchein had been designed to treat disturbed adolescent or prepubescent children and there were no programs available for Bill, who was only three years old. The therapies used by the staff were too advanced for Bill. The staff had decided that Bill had been abused by his father. The observations, interpretations, and diagnoses were made with the goal of supporting those allegations, rather than investigating the possibility of abuse.

One incident particularly bothered Mark. It occurred the first time he was allowed to see Bill within the supervised confines of the hospital. Bill had greeted him with a hug and they had played a variety of games. When Bill was hit on the nose with a nerf ball, he ran to Mark, who kissed it to make it better. Bill, hearing noises, appeared frightened and said someone was coming to get him, that a lady would take him back to the unit and instead he wanted to go to his daddy's house. The observer's interpretation of this was that Bill was frightened by his father's close physical reaction, stating she felt the physical closeness triggered a reaction in Bill.

On October 27, 1987, Mark was indicted by the County Grand Jury for allegedly having sexually molested his son Bill, in spite of psychological evaluations clearly stating that there was nothing in his background, nothing in the interview, and nothing in the evaluation results to suggest any reasonable concern. It was further stated that he did not exhibit the personality characteristics, behaviors, background, or attitudes typically associated with individuals who do admit to such inappropriate acts. The evaluation psychologist pointed out that the level of involvement he has with his child is unusual for the typical sex offender. Mark persisted in denying the allegations and began the long, frustrating, and expensive process of seeking to prove his innocence.

Evidence introduced against him was all hearsay—the allegations of his ex-wife and statements from biased therapists who persisted in treating Bill as an abused child. On July 15, 1988, the criminal trial court judge ruled that Bill was not a competent witness and therefore could not provide credible testimony. . .once again, an incompetent witness, whose statements are only given credibility when repeated by an adult.

Throughout this period, Mark went through the emotions and turmoil typical to one who has been falsely accused. He was unable to focus attention on anything but the false accusations and their ramifications. He suffered the frustration of not being able to see his children, and experienced deep concern about Bill and the potential effects of his experiences at Duchein. Mark was humiliated, frightened, and lived in self-imposed isolation. He experienced a constant state of severe depression. He still cries out in his sleep at night.

In addition, investigation that included examinations by a forensic document examiner revealed that records at CPS and the mental health clinic had been altered in order to bolster the case against Mark. Ultimately, the Assistant District Attorney became convinced that the state wouldn't be able to prove its case and the indictment was dismissed on August 1, 1988.

As of this writing, Mark Doe continues to seek custody of his children and the media-riddled suit is pending in federal court. As a result of conditions contained in the divorce settlement, Mark religiously attended the parenting therapy required by Dr. G, seeing the director of the Fairmont College of Medicine Sex Abuse Clinic. During the first three months of therapy, the discussions related primarily to Bill. During the following four months, discussions centered on the situation of the false allegations. It was Mark's belief that following this action would lead to discovery of the truth and restoration of his children.

In February of 1988, Mark was released by his therapist when the therapist found that Mark had hired one of the foremost defense attorneys in Texas (a federal court specialist) to represent him, an attorney with a reputation for "catching liars." The state's district attorney, apparently fearful, avoided Mark's attorney, neglecting to show up in court for scheduled hearings until so ordered by the trial court judge.

The institution where Bill was sent was sued by the State of Texas for Medicaid fraud and, in a plea bargain settlement, paid back the money identified as defrauded from Medicaid.

In spite of the fact of his innocence, Mark will live the remainder of his life under the dark cloud of a serious social stigma, the result of false allegations brought by a malicious attorney and his ex-wife. He will never be able to be a Boy or Girl Scout Leader, an activity he had hoped to share with his children. He will never be able to work with and teach blind children, something he had done in the past. And, to this date, there are many people who will never forget the accusation and indictment reported in the local papers for all his friends and customers to see.

Chapter Five

A Summary of the Case Studies

Unfortunately, these four cases are not isolated or unique situations. False allegations of child sexual abuse are occurring daily across the country, being made against teachers, day-care providers, coaches, volunteer program directors and psychologists. However, the most frequently accused perpetrator is the ex-husband or divorcing husband who is involved in a visitation dispute and/or custody battle where young children are involved.

The similarities in these case studies and other cases reviewed should sound a warning to individuals, professionals, and agencies.

First, all cases studied involved divorcing parents. Second, all cases studied involved a current or potential custody suit. Third, these cases all involved an ex-wife who perceived that there might be good reason for her to be denied full, residential custody, thereby losing the benefits of child support and control of the children, as well as social standing as the best parent.

In all but one case, the fathers had moved out of the house, thereby giving the wife control of the children and an open opportunity for coaching and convincing the children. In the William Smith case, the allegations surrounded an incident alleged to have occurred while he was out of the country. When he refused to be coerced into leaving his home, his wife removed herself and the children, first to a shelter, then out of the country.

In all cases, the allegation was made to some agency that dealt with social services and, by extension, child protective services.

The allegations were made by the ex-wife and assumed to be true by the social worker, who then set in motion interviews and therapies to support and substantiate the charge. Not once could I find evidence of an objective investigation to seek facts from *all* parties involved before therapy was begun.

In all cases, the accused, the husband, was the last to know anything was going on. When interviews, physical examinations, videotapes, doll sessions, and therapies all occur without his knowledge, culminating in an allegation that usually leads to criminal charges as well as stiff sanctioning in family court, it is no wonder that the falsely accused begins to feel he is the victim of a conspiracy.

In three of the cases studied, it is clear that the accused did not initially have benefit of adequate or competent counsel, an attorney familiar with the ramifications of a SAID Syndrome case. Even an experienced divorce attorney who has not come face to face with this issue, who has not educated himself into the machinations and ramifications of such a case, may flounder under the weight of defending false allegations of child sexual abuse. In Rick's case, the advice of the public defender that he plead no contest to physical abuse charges, in the interest of diffusing the sexual abuse charge has had far-reaching negative ramifications for Rick and his three children. In Mark's case, the fact that his own attorney suggested he had no choice but to agree to the extortionate demands of his wife's attorney has resulted in untold emotional damage for his middle son and a lengthy and expensive battle to regain any kind of access to and relationship with his three children.

In my own case, a reliable civil attorney simply did not have the background and expertise to deal with the criminal charges of child sexual abuse. And a competent and effective criminal attorney didn't have the expertise to carry the battle successfully back through the family courts.

In all cases studied, the criminal charges of child sexual abuse were dropped or the father was acquitted. However, in all cases, the allegations stood in family court and, based on testimony of social workers and agency-selected therapists, the father was either denied access to his children, or provided extremely limited and supervised visitation.

In all cases, the children were ordered by the court to continue in therapy and the father was ordered to enter therapy as an alleged abuser, in spite of never having been found guilty in criminal court, in spite of the fact that they repeatedly and steadfastly maintained their innocence of the charges.

In all cases, the evaluations of video tapes by child psychologists have routinely identified the leading and coercive questions used to gain a child's testimony.

In all cases, positive psychological and psychosexual evaluations and summaries regarding the alleged perpetrator have either been summarily ignored or have led to requests for further evaluation by state-selected psychologists, who could be counted on to provide an evaluation to support the allegations of child sexual abuse.

In all cases, there is serious doubt that the events of the last several years have, in fact, been in the best interest of the children.

There are a number of things to be aware of if you are to protect yourself from false allegations of child sexual abuse and a potential abuser, a number of questions you can ask that may indicate what is coming.

1. Has the marriage been stormy?

2. What are the benefits derived by your ex-wife if she can win sole custody?

3. Is there another man in the picture?

4. Does your ex-wife have any reason to believe she might have difficulty proving herself the best parent?

5. If there has been a history of animosity and lack of cooperation throughout the divorce and/or custody battle, are you suddenly being treated in a more cooperative manner?

6. Has she ever brought an accusation or threatened to bring an accusation against anyone else?

The next section explores the many facets and complexities of the individuals, professionals, agencies, and systems involved when an allegation of child sexual abuse is levied, as well as outlining the characteristics of the SAID Syndrome.

Chapter Six

The Accused

How do you describe the feeling, the reaction, to being accused of sexually abusing your own child? There are a myriad of emotions, all negative.

One of the first realizations you have is that, in spite of the premise upon which our justice is supposed to be based, when it comes to this allegation, you are assumed guilty. *Immediately. Period.* The abhorrence with which sexual offenses against children are viewed fills the majority of the population with righteous indignation toward the accused, even before any evidence has been presented.

In cases of child sexual abuse, hearsay evidence from doctors and nurses, whom you will probably never see, from social workers and the accusing parent is commonly used to circumvent the unreliability and short memories of children. Because no one is in favor of child abuse and everyone wants to do their part for the children, there has been a steady erosion of the accused's rights to confront his accuser and a corresponding rise in the use of hearsay evidence. Since there is rarely actual evidence of child sexual abuse, the accused finds himself fighting a phantom. Given the current trend of believing that "children don't lie," any allegation, even based on hearsay, is assumed to be valid.

All of these facts don't change the way you, the accused, feel. In reality, being labeled an abuser may produce many of the personality characteristics later cited as the causes of child abuse—anger, bitterness, defensiveness.

The waiting is the worst. And the waiting breeds questions which never seem to have answers. One individual, accused of abusing his two-year-old daughter, even began questioning himself. Could he have scratched her the last time he bathed her? Did she have an irritation he should have noticed, something that caused her to scratch herself?

The emotions engendered by false accusations of child sexual abuse are endless and devastating. Sleep is forever elusive, night-terror becomes common-place and depression is a constant companion. Rarely is there any support to be found within the community and rarely is there any sympathy for the falsely-accused. The frustration and anger increase with every day that goes by and each incident that occurs, affecting you and your children. The realization that winning in one court doesn't mean winning in another makes the ordeal seem to go on forever. Throughout it all, you must bear the title "abuser," until you prove otherwise, if you can. Disorientation, denial, shock, confusion, anxiety, and disbelief are constant. Lack of concentration is a chronic problem, exceeded only by the frustration of being denied the right to see your children.

During this battle, understand that numerous negative emotions are going to become a part of your every day life. Disorientation, denial, confusion, and depression become "normal" day-to-day feelings. Often the shock felt by the accused makes concentration difficult, if not impossible, while they try to deal with the anxiety and disbelief. Some contemplate suicide.

The temptation to give up can be strong. You can't see your child, you can't get any information about the charges, the evidence, the test results, or current events. Your ex-wife seems to win on all fronts, using evidence that is patently untrue, evidence that has been fabricated and cannot be disproved. Even when evidence is disproved, it doesn't seem to matter. The state is paying her legal fees, evaluation, and therapy fees, while you are footing the bills for your attorney, court costs, child support, and seemingly never-ending psychological and psychosexual tests to prove your innocence. The paranoia begins to overtake your common sense and your ability to function in your best interest and that of the children. Everything seems so helpless that, sooner or later, every victim of a false accusation asks the same question: What have I done to deserve this?

There is a grieving process that is an on-going part of this fight against false allegations of child sexual abuse. Your children have been taken from you. If a child had died, there would be a period of grieving, a period that would end when the fact of death had been accepted. However, the child is still alive and only artificial circumstances, circumstances over which you seem to have no control, are separating you from your child, resulting in a roller coaster of grief, sadness, hope, despair, anger, frustration, and bitterness.

Accept that grief is an inherent part of the process, as are anger and resentment. You grieve for the time lost with your child, you grieve for the important milestones that you are missing, you grieve for yourself and your loneliness and you grieve for your child and his or her current circumstances. Since the battle against false allegations is an on-going process with no immediate end in sight, there is no finality, no way to put closure to the grief and no way to say, "This will be over in two weeks."

When Mark was accused of molesting his son, he found he was unable to focus on anything but the false accusation and the results of same. He was humiliated and wanted only to run away, seeking self-imposed isolation and sinking into a deep depression. As a result of his emotions, Mark experienced severe headaches, stomach disorders, high cholesterol, and a host of other stress-related disorders. He became obsessed with concern for his children, the loss of his children, and his personal future. This obsession and the attendant physical problems led to the loss of a highly-successful business he had been running for a number of years.

One individual we spoke with was fighting for custody against a wife who had a history of drinking and drug use, a promiscuous sex life, and was physically abusive of the children. He knew what she was and what her problems were. Whether he could have proved her unfit in court, whether a judge would have believed him was beside the point. She knew what she was and she knew that no judge in his right mind would give her custody, so she resorted to desperate means.

Ken Pangborn, a paralegal and well-known expert in false child-abuse cases, who works with the "A" Team in defending against false allegations of sexual abuse, states that, in his experience, many of the women who make false allegations have something pretty terrible to hide, a knowledge that they are not, in fact, fit to have custody of their children.

Gather a support system to get you through this period. Friends, relatives, lawyers, mental health specialists, and victims' support groups. The process of working through and disproving a false allegation of child sexual abuse is a long, draining, lonely process and you will need on-going support for those times of frustration, depression, and weariness. You will spend most of your time feeling (and often acting) defensive, fighting the unfair social stigma that says, "If he was accused, *something* must have happened.

You don't need someone to tell you what to do, so much as you need someone to listen, to hold your hand, to pat you on the shoulder and encourage you to keep on pushing, keep on working toward the day when your children will be yours again.

Self-imposed isolation is a natural reaction, a method of avoiding embarrassment and hiding the shame you feel about the fact that anyone could even consider accusing you of such an action. Draw strength from your support groups, get out in the world and try to function as a part of it. In addition, isolation is hard on the mental and emotional system and you need all the positives you can get at this point, to allow you to meet and deal with the myriad issues of the allegation in a mature, controlled, sustained manner.

In addition to your personal support group, find an organized support group such as VOCAL or Men International, Inc., or one of the several organizations that have begun forming over the past few years. A list of current supportive groups is included in the Reference section of this book and I urge you to locate a group that can give you not only moral support, but often provides resources of which you may be unaware.

Most important, please believe you are not alone in this situation. Others have been there and are there today. We know the questions and doubts you have, the emotions you are encountering and the frustrations that seem to mount on a daily basis. We are aware of the questions you are asking, questions like the following:

1) How did it happen?

2) How can my relationship with my child be terminated without an investigation?

3) Don't my constitutional rights protect me from indiscriminate and irresponsible government intervention?

4) How could this situation take so long to be resolved?

5) Will I succumb or will I prevail?

Be prepared to deal with a host of negative emotions, recognize that depression, grief, anger, frustration, and confusion are an inherent part of your reaction to the accusation leveled against you.

The critical issue, if you are dealing with false allegations of child sexual abuse, is to maintain your innocence, locate a competent and experienced attorney, be prepared to spend a great deal of money and find local support groups to assist you with your battle.

Chapter Seven

The Accuser

There was a common thread running through the personalities and actions of the accusing ex-wife in all four case studies examined during the preparation of this book. This same thread has also been identified by individuals studying the dynamics of SAID Syndrome cases.

In several of the cases, accusations of child sexual abuse were used by the accuser against additional individuals or organizations, other than the husband. In my case, Carla used the threat of a child sexual abuse allegation to avoid payment of tuition fees at a day-care center Diane had been attending. The tuition was refunded and charges were never formally brought by Carla. In another case, the ex-wife accused not only her husband, but her own stepfather and a cousin of abusing their daughter. Neither incident was ever substantiated or prosecuted. Patti, who accused her stepson of abuse, later accused William of abusing his daughter, but that allegation was never pursued.

In all cases, the allegations were made during the course of a custody dispute, brought by wives who had reason to believe they might need additional support for their claims as custodial parent. In all cases, the custody dispute was acrimonious. In all cases, the ex-wife was in some way involved with another man or other men. In all cases, the wife initially had custody of the child and was in the perfect position to manipulate the child's statements and encourage the child to make and sustain accusations against the father.

A review of the various evaluations done on the accusing parent shows many common personality traits. The evaluation of one accusing ex-wife included the following comments: ". . .is quite capable of antisocial behavior and her MMPI clearly demonstrates a propensity for fabrication. She is an angry woman. . .and very sensitized to sexual abuse."

Dr. Larry Spiegel, a psychologist, was falsely accused of child sexual abuse by his wife. In his book, *A Question of Innocence*, he points out that the actions of an accuser like his wife are not just extreme examples of revenge, but stem from severe psychological problems. Speigel's ex-wife perceived herself to be rejected by her husband. A psychological examination indicated that she had admitted to her hatred of her husband, and further indicated that she was quite capable of projecting her own emotional turmoil, doubt, and sexual pathology onto her daughter.

In the case of William Smith in Ohio, his ex-wife had a history of mood swings and depressions. Like Marsha, Judy, and Carla, Patti also had a history of relationships with other men during her marriage to William, in this instance, adding William's oldest son to her stable. One evaluation of Patti indicated she was an overly self-confident, energetic, and distinctly defensive individual who was rebellious, willful, and rather impulsive. It also revealed a passive-aggressive personality harboring considerable conflict and tension in the independent-dependent sphere. A psychological test done a year later noted the wife's feelings were similar to psychotic or severely neurotic patients. A third test, done yet another year later, indicated that Patti's self-confidence had plummeted, her manifest anxiety level had increased considerably and her capacity to cope with day-to-day problems had been considerably undermined. She exhibited paranoic indicators. However, the psychologist administering the test, a state-appointed doctor, qualified these findings by pointing out that she was under considerable stress as a result of the on-going custody dispute, indicating that these findings shouldn't be considered in a negative light. That factor is rarely recognized when the accused exhibits such test findings.

In my case, Carla's psychological evaluation indicated that she chose her answers so as to give a strongly favorable picture of herself. While the psychologist stated that this type of response bias is often seen under such circumstances, it is not necessarily present to such a degree. She denied any anger or hostility, but the results showed it much more likely that she is denying a significant amount of that hostility, not only to others but to herself. Carla was very defensive, very afraid of exposing her real nature and, for that reason, the psychologist felt the results of the testing had questionable validity. Although there were many positive character traits identified in the testing, there was indication that Carla would go along in a conforming sort of way while inwardly being quite rebellious. Indirect, rather than direct, anger appeared to be usually expressed, being in general over-controlled, yet violent or aggressive outbursts may occur. The evaluating psychologist requested that Carla retake the tests, having been made aware that her biased responses would certainly invalidate much of the data. Carla did not retake the tests and the psychologist qualified all the test scores and responses with the statement that there was a "need to interpret the test results with the assumption that weak points, problem areas and therefore the clinical scales of the MMPI have been suppressed." Consequently, we had an evaluation that even the professional giving the test said was inaccurate. Other evaluations indicated Carla's use of projection and her elevated K scale on the MMPI went along with her display of manipulative and dishonest traits.

In an article by Matthew Miller, published in the *Family Law Commentator*, the writer addressed the issues of child sexual abuse allegations. "Mothers are falsely accusing fathers of sexual abuse or child abuse at an alarmingly increasing rate in order to gain leverage or advantage in custody/visitation disputes. . ." He went on to point out that these women often become obsessed with punishing the ex-husband and using the allegation to gain desired advantages, often losing sight of the effect on the child.

Can a malicious accuser manipulate the system to produce conviction for a false allegation? Unfortunately, given the way the system currently operates, it is all too easy for an individual to manipulate it to their benefit, particularly in cases of custody or visitation. An embittered ex-wife, if she knows the system and is capable of any degree of manipulation, will usually find support and belief within the offices of the social workers and case investigator. Since she is working with individuals who are prone to believe anything the child says, or anything she tells them the child said, about abuse, she's off to an easy start.

The accuser recognizes that the use of a sexual abuse allegation gives her an easy and almost instant win in the custody battle against her ex-husband. The family court system encourages the accusations, since the almost universal result is to deny the accused any access to his children, and assure the ex-wife the ability to further manipulate the child. In addition, she retains receipt of child support payments, a strong incentive for some parents. Finally, the accuser will always emerge as the "fit" parent, whether she truly is or not.

Feudal law in the Middle Ages recognized the economic value of the child to its parents, either for purposes of helping in the family business, earning money to be used for support of the family or, for females, making an advantageous marriage. We consider ourselves to be an enlightened society. Yet, is there not a hint of this economic consideration when bitter custody battles revolve around the issue of child support payments and the changes in lifestyle that may result from support monies being increased, decreased, or lost altogether because of a change in residential custody?

There are certain characteristics that seem to be consistent throughout the actions and circumstances surrounding false allegations of child sexual abuse within the parameters of a custody dispute, as pointed out in a study done by The Joint Custody Association of Los Angeles, California.

The accusing parent commonly exhibits impulse control problems, excessive self-centeredness, strong dependency needs, and poor judgement. Often the individual is overzealous, dishonest, histrionic or combative. The mother has a need to tell the world about the incident, as opposed to the more common reaction of being secretive and embarrassed. An accusing parent often demands that decision makers act quickly and is unwilling to consider other possible explanations for the child's statements or behavior. She will insist on being present whenever the child is interviewed, and will shop for other professionals who will verify her suspicions and allegations. Regardless of the impact on the child, a mother making false accusations frequently demands the investigation continue or be intensified. The varied accuser profiles are identified in the next chapter.

It is important to be aware of the benefits that accrue to the accusing parent in a custody dispute. The most important is being awarded custody of the child. Even in those instances where both parents have recognized problems and neither parent is clearly better than the other, when allegations of child sexual abuse are present, custody almost always goes to the accusing mother, as occurred in all case studies reviewed for this book.

In my case, the mother was termed "unfit" by the court. However, rather than award custody to me, even where abuse hadn't been supported by the evidence, the court awarded the children to her and assigned Health and Rehabilitative Services to oversee the lives of the children and the actions of the mother, suggesting or requiring parenting classes for her.

Chapter Eight

The SAID Syndrome

While almost anyone can be the victim of false allegations of child sexual abuse, more often than not, whenever there has been a breakdown in the family resulting in divorce or separation, the accused is the child's natural father and the accuser is the mother. Frequently, the allegations have nothing to do with the best interest of the child, but are perpetrated in an effort to either satisfy the anger, frustration, or vindictiveness of the mother, to fulfill her requirement to "win" over her husband or ex-husband or to assure the mother the ongoing income provided by the child support payments.

In 1986, Dr. Gordon J. Blush and Karol L. Ross presented their study, prepared for fellow professionals in the field of child advocacy, dealing with Sexual Allegations in Divorce (SAID). In this study, Blush and Ross pointed out that sexual allegations made within the framework of a divorced or divorcing family environment need to be addressed in a discriminately different way than sexual abuse allegations made within a non-divorcing family. The study was done in a family services clinic, which served as a diagnostic agency within a circuit court. Primary in the evaluation process were cases in which custody and visitation problems existed, involving minor children.

It is common, when dealing with the two parents in a divorcing family situation, to find that each parent wants to present the other parent in the least complimentary manner possible. Each parent wishes to establish that he or she is the best choice for custodial parent and this is often done by placing the other parent in a negative light. Unfortunately, over recent years, allegations of sexual impropriety are being heard more frequently in custody disputes. This type of allegation results in the alleged perpetrator not only fighting a custody issue, but finding him/herself in a position where access to the minor child can be terminated without due process of any type. The individual is completely excluded from their children's lives and, in addition, suffers the social stigma of the allegation, and often has to contend with felony charges within the criminal court system.

The sad thing about allegations of child sexual abuse is that once accused, the alleged perpetrator finds himself in the position of being guilty until proven innocent, a state in direct conflict with the basis of our country's judicial system and beliefs. This position is strengthened by the actions and activities of the various social agencies who become involved when such an allegation occurs. In many instances, cases are systematically built on a false allegation that, through manipulation of facts and children's testimony, can create damning "evidence."

Several papers, presented by expert psychiatrists and psychologists over the last ten years, have pointed to the strong potential for false allegations of child sexual abuse within the framework of a divorcing family, particularly when there is a dispute over custody and/or visitation rights.

An article in the Denver *Post* on April 9, 1989 referred to studies done by Dr. Richard Gardner of New Jersey in regard to the SAID Syndrome, which found numerous instances in which children had been brainwashed by one parent in an acrimonious divorce to accuse the other parent of sexual abuse.

Blush and Ross caution that child sexual abuse allegations should be viewed within the context of the entire family picture to determine whether there may be more involved than concern for the child by the accusing parent. According to their study, there are six "red flags" which should form the focus of investigating the allegations. While these are not conclusive indicators of a SAID case, they are valid clues to the possibility of such a situation. The six red flags to be observed are:

1) Evidence of a family on the verge of marital breakup;

2) Divorce proceedings already in process;

3) Divorce proceedings that have been unsuccessfully in progress for some time;

4) Unresolved visitation or custody problems;

5) Unresolved money issues related to the divorce in process;

6) Involvement of either or both parents in ongoing relationships with others.

Any one of these circumstances may provide a clue that the allegations are a part of the SAID syndrome. In each of the cases studied for this book, as well as in my own case, three or more of these "flags" were in evidence, yet none of these considerations were addressed in the consideration of the allegations levied against me or the other accused fathers.

Too often, agencies involved in the investigation of allegations of child sexual abuse are, in fact, therapeutic in nature as opposed to investigative. Treatment of the involved child is begun before the cause of the child's action or alleged action is investigated. If more social agency employees were required to be aware of the SAID syndrome and its effects, there would be fewer lengthy and expensive court cases crowding our judicial system calendars, most of which have no basis. As a consequence, these agencies and the courts would be better able to pursue true child-abuse cases involving valid allegations.

In the interest of avoiding false allegations, as well as anticipating such, it is important to note that Blush and Ross identified personality types that may well bring such allegations against an ex-husband or soon-to-be ex-husband.

In the first profile, the individual may present herself as a fearful person, believing she is the victim of manipulation, coercion, physical, social, or sexual abuse in the marriage. She tends to see men as a physical threat, a means of economic retribution, or as a person who does not understand the physical safety and psychological needs of children.

In the second profile, the ex-wife manifests the characteristics of the "justified vindicator." This individual is a hostile, vindictive, and dominant female, who often becomes insistent that formal legal measures be taken immediately—not waiting for reasonable proof of the allegation. This personality often appeals to experts in both the mental health and legal communities and often has concurrent criminal action pending alongside her domestic legal action.

The third pattern is that of an accuser who is potentially psychotic. Although rare, these individuals are functioning in a borderline reality in which what they want to believe, in order to protect their current status, is more clear to them than what is actually occurring.

Regardless of the profile exhibited by the accusing female, in all cases her emotional basis of appeal can be very convincing and misleading to the inexperienced or well-intentioned professional. For those reasons, the "red flag" considerations need to be incorporated in *any* investigation of child sexual abuse occurring during the course of divorce/custody hearings.

In those infrequent cases where the accusing parent is the male, the personality is usually found to be intellectually rigid, with a significant need to be "right"; often, he has been hypercritical of his wife throughout the marriage and exhibits a number of "nit-picking" examples of her unfitness as a mother. In the instance of such a male accuser, the allegations are generally against the male(s) with whom the mother has become involved, rather than directly against the mother. The accusations against the mother generally involve her leaving the children in inappropriate or incompetent care, or generally placing them in an "at risk" situation at home.

Children involved in these situations typically occupy the key position in the adversarial struggle. Parents who cannot—or will not—communicate directly with each other, communicate through the child, thereby providing the child with a part of their adult insight, feelings, and information. Children in this position often evolve into miniature dictators at a very early age, given the ability to manipulate and control both parents because of their knowledge and insight. Younger children tend to align their requirements and their emotional allegiance with the dominant or custodial parent and frequently mirror that parent's descriptions or feelings concerning a situation. Children in these situations often reflect one or more of the following behaviors:

☐ Giving responses that appear to be rehearsed, coached or conditioned;

☐ During interviews, initiating conversation by quoting the same phrases as those used by the controlling parent who presented the complaint;

☐ Using verbal descriptions inappropriate to their age, with no demonstrated practical comprehension of the meaning;

☐ Offering spontaneous and automatic reports of the act(s) perpetrated upon them, without any direct questions being asked to solicit this information;

☐ Offering inconsistencies in various aspects of the reported incident(s), such as the specifics (who, what, where, when), frequency (once or twice, exaggerated to numerous times) and subjective perceptions of the experience (very frightened, not scared, hurt, not hurt);

☐ Lacking the appearance of a traumatized individual, from an emotional and behavioral standpoint.

It is important to note that Blush and Ross found that as children approached adolescence and developed into their teenage years, they developed a more vindictive agenda. Whereas young children tend to mimic the dominant parent, adolescents develop their own requirements and desires, often built around getting or not getting their own way.

In cases of allegations of child sexual abuse where the red flags of a potential SAID Syndrome situation are present, it is also important to consider the general personality profile of the alleged male perpetrator, as the characteristics exhibited by a victim of the SAID Syndrome are similar to those of individuals who actually do engage in sexual abuse of children.

Typically, the following characteristics may be demonstrated by the alleged perpetrator:

☐ An inadequate personality, with marked passive and dependent features;

☐ A socially naive perception of the adult world;

☐ Evidence of a caretaker role taken toward the female during courtship and early marriage;

☐ A need to "earn" love, by yielding to the wants and demands of the spouse.

Because of these characteristics, this type of male typically finds himself in a relationship with a more dominant female. Further, the male victim is puzzled and at a loss to explain what has happened to him. He may be unable to effectively or appropriately respond to the allegations of the spouse, the children or other adults drawn into this situation. The allegations, in effect, create a relatively helpless and ineffective individual, whose lack of direct or assertive response may give the appearances of guilt. Because of this—the similarities between the typical male victim of false allegations and the individual actually guilty of inappropriate sexual behavior—it is critical that the overall home and family situation be closely reviewed for indications of the red flags of the SAID Syndrome.

In the early 1980s, when Dr. Mel Guyer started the Family and Law Program at the Child and Adolescent Psychiatric Hospital in Ann Arbor, about seven percent of the two hundred-plus divorce custody cases studied each year included allegations of sexual abuse. He says that now, thirty percent of the custody cases include allegations and he believes that seventy percent of those alleged abuses never occurred.

In divorce custody disputes, child sexual abuse has become the accusation of choice. Many psychologists who evaluate such cases for the courts estimate that from a third to half of the cases they deal with include this allegation and, they believe, most of these claims are unfounded.

An allegation of child sexual abuse is so powerful and so effective, others may encourage the wife to consider it as a valid and conclusive weapon. Dr. Guyer, who is an attorney as well as a psychologist, suggests a possible scenario:

Suppose you have an attorney who knows his reputation and income depends on winning cases. He's not hired to do what's best for kids. He knows that success, for him, is getting custody for the woman. So, he sits down and takes a very careful history of the marriage, asking some very pointed questions. Does their father ever bathe the child? Have you ever noticed anything inappropriate? Does he put the child to bed and linger in the child's room?

By asking those types of questions, he can lead the client to think in a certain way. Actions that once seemed tender in a happy home, seem suspect, once a couple is separated or divorced.

The parent, in the privacy of her own home, actually does the first interview. While I don't know what occurs when the parent arrives home, I can imagine her questioning the child about what he or she does while they're at Daddy's house. Normal child care activities suddenly become distorted to possible acts of sexual inappropriateness, when placed in improper perspective by a spouse who is not objective or impartial, who most likely is under stress and possibly bitter.

It is important to note that the professionals within the social agencies can also be victims of the SAID Syndrome, if the red flags are not considered. Many times, the accusing parent immediately takes the child to a therapist or some other intervention specialist and reports the child has been sexually abused. The professional receives information that, because of legal and social implications, takes on great importance. The original introduction to the case is within a limited and biased environment and too often the professional responds immediately to the presenting parent's report.

Since most intervention professionals are trained to believe children and accept what they have to say regarding sexual abuse, these professionals become potential victims by accepting what the child or accusing parent has to say at face value. There is the additional fact that professionals who do not report suspected abuse face serious trouble for non-reporting.

As pointed out by attorney Robert Pope, most children are natural mimics. Therefore, the question of whether or not innocent children are capable of lying is somewhat rhetorical. We teach children to speak by repeating to them, over and over, a word or a phrase, until they can mimic that word. Why then, is it so difficult to accept the possibility that a vindictive accuser may coach the very small child by repeating to them an accusing phrase. The child is certainly not lying intentionally, only repeating words which have earned him or her positive rewards. Once the accusation is made, social workers further this cycle by asking questions that will lead to accusing answers because of what the child has been told. When the child provides the expected response, they are told that is "very good." When the child does *not* provide the expected response, it is assumed that he/she isn't paying attention and the question is repeated until the expected response is forthcoming, at which time the child is again praised. It is often upon this skewed manner of reporting and investigating that the guilt or innocence of an individual is determined.

Based on the child's report and the standard methods of intervention, therapy and investigation, "facts" are created which shape the entire situation. This results in social and legal agencies accepting a created reality as truth. Once a professional opinion has been formed by a therapist, that individual is generally reluctant to change his or her perception. Because of the effect of professional opinions and the credence attached to them, it is critical that every effort be made to accurately assess the overall situation in the initial stages.

Because of the legal and social ramifications, as well as the long-term effect on the entire family, it is important to investigate the possibility of divorce and family dysfunction leading to false allegations of child sexual abuse before assuming actual abuse occurred. Blush and Ross point out that one or more the following situations indicates a need to investigate the possibility of the SAID Syndrome:

☐ The allegation surfaces after separation and legal action for divorce has begun;

☐ The family has a history of dysfunction, with unresolved divorce conflict;

☐ The personality pattern of the female parent tends to be that of the hysterical personality;

☐ The personality pattern of the male parent tends to be passive-dependent;

☐ The child is a female, under the age of eight, who shows behavioral patterns of verbal exaggeration, excessive willingness to indict, inappropriate affective responses and inconsistencies;

☐ The allegation is communicated by the custodial parent, usually the mother;

☐ The mother takes the child to an "expert" for further examination, assessment or treatment.

At this point, the expert often communicates to a court or other authority a concern and/or confirmation of apparent sexual abuse, usually identifying the father as perpetrator. The court typically reacts in what it considers a responsible manner, suspending or terminating visitation, foreclosing custodial arguments or, in some way, limiting the child-parent interaction after allegations are recorded or criminal charges are filed.

More and more, the courts are relying on the behavioral and social science community for recommendations in protecting the best interest of the child. If the professionals providing these recommendations are not familiar with the SAID Syndrome, and are more interested in therapy than in investigation, rarely will the accused perpetrator receive just and equitable treatment and rarely will the courts find in favor of that individual.

Too often, social workers have not familiarized themselves with the indications and ramifications of the SAID Syndrome and are using information, methodology, and approaches that were valid when the bulk of child sexual abuse cases were of an incestuous nature, where the major concern was that the child might not admit to the abuse, that the mother wouldn't believe her husband capable of such an act, and everyone wanted to hold the family together. Today, the majority of false allegations are occurring in divorce situations where a bitter custody battle is being waged and child support and social status are important issues. The theory that a child would deny the abuse in the interest of holding the family together is no longer necessarily valid. The child may be denying the abuse because, quite simply, it never occurred.

Many agencies continue to use the methodology and percepts of the Child Abuse Accommodation Syndrome, published by Dr. Roland Summat in the early eighties. A review of the five components of this theory indicates that this methodology is based on cases where the issue is incest, far different from the SAID Syndrome cases currently reaching epidemic proportions.

Chapter Nine

The Victim

An alleged victim of child sexual abuse, whose father success-fully fought the allegations and was awarded sole custody of his children, made several telling statements in an interview she granted me for this book.

. . .They need to be aware that it hurts the kids the most. The mothers think they're hurting the other parent, but they're really not, they're hurting the kids. It hurts the parents a little bit, but that's not going to stop them from living. They're already grown-up, they know the facts of life and stuff. The kids don't really have a way to know what's going on and that basically destroys a part of their life and I think that's wrong. . .

Mary was five years old when her mother used false allega-tions of child sexual abuse, citing instances of oral sex involving Mary and her sisters, to block her father's motion for a change of custody.

Now sixteen, Mary has been living with her father for eight years and, in the interest of other children who are or may be potential victims of false allegations brought during a custody battle, she agreed to speak out about her feelings. We asked Mary, more or less as an expert witness speaking in the true best interest of the children, for her feelings, her opinions, her thoughts on the issue of false allegations of child sexual abuse and its effect on the children involved.

Mary's messages to mothers, fathers, social workers, and mental health care professionals are probably more valid and more valuable than the most learned dissertation on this subject from a degree-bearing specialist.

. . .Basically, the mothers or fathers—whoever thinks about making false allegations—tell them to think twice. It's a stupid thing to do and it hurts. It hurts more and different people than they know. . .

In Mary's case, not only did the allegations cause questions and, in fact, fear of her father, but Mary truly dislikes her mother because of the lies that involved her entire family. There is a rift between Mary and her sisters, and Mary doesn't know if it will ever be healed. She doesn't trust women in general although, fortunately, she is close to her step-mom who has, over the past eight years, proven herself to be a person deserving of trust and respect. Mary's trust in authority figures has been seriously undermined, partly by the fact that the counselors and therapists—people with authority—worked with her mother to perpetuate the lies.

As a result of the lengthy, consistent, and intense attempts to substantiate her mother's accusations, Mary knows a permanent seed of doubt has been planted. Although she sincerely loves and trusts her father, Mary admits that a doubt will always be there. She doesn't think the question of whether it happened or didn't happen will ever go away, and is learning to accept that this is something she may always have to deal with in her life.

. . .Tell the fathers to talk to their kids. Not directly about that, but about things that are related, like how not to lie and how to tell a truth from a lie. Try to have fun with the kids so they can tell the truth from a lie, don't let them be able to have ideas planted in their heads by other people. . .

. . .Fight for your kids, but don't say bad things to them about their mom. My dad didn't say bad stuff about Mom. I think, if he had, it would have made me mad and I'd have hated him as much as I hate my mom now. . .

. . .Tell the mothers it's wrong. They're teaching the kids bad values, bad thoughts. . .destroying their trust. . .

Today, Mary says she's very careful who she is friendly with, let alone who she dates. Lying is totally abhorrent to Mary, and what a person is like "inside" is critical to her. Because of her mother's allegations and the actions of primarily female social and mental health care workers, Mary readily admits that she doesn't hold women in very high regard and frequently wishes she was a man. She feels most women need to make themselves worth something and would like to have more respect for herself than most women seem to have. With a maturity unusual at the age of sixteen, Mary candidly admits that it may be wrong for her to feel that way, but right now she can't help it, it is the way she feels.

. . .Tell the caseworkers, counselors, and therapists not to take sides. They do take sides, all the time—the mother's side. Don't tell the kids what happened, what to do. Don't dwell on the accusations. Listen to the kids and help them deal with it, work with them. Don't act like another parent. You're supposed to be a friend, someone to help us. . .

In Mary's case, she says she felt like it was her against the world—against her mother who was, in fact, physically and emotionally abusive to the girls; against her father, whom she hadn't seen for four and a half years and couldn't remember; against the social workers and therapists, who kept asking the same questions, repeating the same accusations, raising the same issues, and questioning her dad's actions.

. . .Why, she asks, would people keep asking these questions? They kept repeating them over and over and finally, I thought, My God, maybe he did do that and I don't remember. What's a kid supposed to think? Even though you don't remember and you don't know that it happened, it gets planted, the doubt, the question is there. It makes me sick. . .

We asked Mary what it felt like to be in the middle, to know her parents were fighting over her.

. . .We see in our minds that our parents are in a fight, they're trying to get back at each other and you think they're fighting to get custody of you just to try to get back at one another more than they're fighting because they want you in their home. We really didn't know if they were fighting because they really wanted us with them, or fighting just to fight each other. It's stupid. . .

. . .When Dad won, we thought he'd won against our mother, not a fight for us. . .

In Mary's case, even though life was abusive with her mother, the children were truly scared of their father. They hadn't seen him for four years, as a result of his ex-wife's efforts to discourage and later prevent his custody attempts, Mary had been a year old when he left home and the girls had heard nothing good about him. They were the spoils of war, going to a victor about whom they knew nothing except what their mother had told them.

Mary's mother fought to regain custody of the children after they moved in with their dad. Mary's recollection of that period is that she and her sisters felt their parents were still fighting each other and that they, the kids, were simply the rope in an on-going tug of war.

Unfortunately, Mary's situation is no more unique or unusual than the four case studies presented at the beginning of this book.

Because of their age and vulnerability, the children find themselves being manipulated by a number of different, and often unfamiliar, adults. The accuser often brings in a host of supporting witnesses from agencies, hospitals, and schools and uses various means to substantiate the claim.

Children can be taught to say various things, which may or may not be true, as a result of either direct teaching or subtle teaching through reinforcement such as verbal responses and encouragement, body movement, and facial expressions. Discussions of the incident between the child and mother, the child and friends or other family members can serve as an effective learning process, reinforcing the child's knowledge and recital of a contrived event.

As a general rule, children seek to give the answers they think are desired, rather than deal with facts that may get negative reactions. Through the use of facial expression, body movement, or verbal responses, an interviewer can make it plain what type of answer gains approval and what gains disapproval. A strongly-biased interviewer can shape a child's response by reinforcing the child with smiles, hugs, and "good girl" statements when the answers are what the interviewer wants to hear.

Children placed in this situation become pawns in a game which they don't understand, a game they shouldn't be expected to understand, let alone be forced to play. It is not unusual, in divorce situations, to find one parent pitted against the other, often making negative remarks and accusations in front of the children. In these instances, children are torn—loving both parents, wanting to be loyal to both parents, wanting to please both parents. In the case of child sexual abuse, the accusing parent has made it clear that the other parent is bad and is to be blamed.

A false allegation of child sexual abuse places a child in an intolerable situation: They don't want to hurt Daddy; they don't want to lie; they don't want to disappoint Mommy or make her angry. Placing a child in this position is itself child abuse at its worst.

Children are easily coached and easily manipulated, especially when they are emotionally and physically dependent upon the accusing parent for all their needs. During the course of an investigation of child sexual abuse, the child is expected to go through the same questions and exercises, time after time, to satisfy everyone's requirements for testimony. By the time the child has been exposed to the same round of questions and the same round of coaching over a period of weeks, it is not difficult to convince the child that the incident actually occurred. He or she has a tape recorder going in his or her mind, giving the responses that people want to hear and receiving the praise they've come to expect for being "a good girl and helping us so much." Even though he or she may not be convinced, the question, the doubt is planted and will remain throughout his or her life, as Mary has pointed out.

In the Colorado case, all three of Rick's children were placed in therapy and "treated" for sexual and physical abuse, starting as soon as Marsha made the allegation. These children became victims of the system and victims of their mother's vengeance, not victims of child sexual abuse. They were and still are thoroughly confused. They were separated from their father, denied any contact at all, and are now having to learn to know him again. They have a stepfather whom they are required to call "Dad," while instructed to refer to Rick by his first name. They don't understand their mother's attitude and are trying to cope with what she did. Meantime, they have been treated like victims and made to feel like victims, losing much of their childhood trust and dreams and pleasures in the process.

Forcing a child to lie, or to accuse a parent whom they love, may well cause permanent and irreparable harm to the child who is, in all probability, unable to cope with the situation. We recognize that the adult who has been accused has tremendous difficulty accepting and adjusting to the accusation. Why can't we recognize what the situation is doing to the young child?

The Connecticut Bar Association's Guidelines for Courts and Counsel states, in connection with custody cases, ". . .counsel should act to move the proceedings toward conclusion as speedily as possible, since undue delay in the resolution of the custody or visitation dispute is rarely in the best interest of the child. The minor will suffer more than any of the adults as a consequence of the anxiety of uncertainty."

Unfortunately, it seems that few social service workers, prosecutors or family court judges, in Connecticut or anywhere else, appreciate the validity and importance of this directive.

In cases involving allegations of child sexual abuse, where the allegation is made by one parent against another, the case customarily deteriorates into a series of interviews of the minor child, and attempts by the accuser to introduce hearsay statements into evidence.

We are routinely asked to believe that children do not lie. Research has indicated that, in cases of divorce and custody disputes, the child is often affected by the psychological functioning of the accusing adult and adult agendas, which impose their ideas upon the children, making the children pawns and victims of the directive adult, who is using the allegations and the child as a weapon.

A. Matthew Miller, in an article in the *Family Law Commentator*, made the following comments:

> "Too often the child is the innocent victim of the failure of the marriage and becomes a mere pawn between parents competing for the love and loyalty of the child. . .Unfortunately, a custodial/residential mother with vengeful attitudes may perceive the child's relationship with the father as the only means of getting even."

A child usually reflects the emotional responses of the adult with whom the child resides. A child's ambivalent feelings for the non-custodial parent may well be the result of the influence of the custodial parent, or the child's emotional perception of that parent's feeling for the non-custodial parent. The child's need to please and be loved by and accepted by the custodial parent creates a dependency or identification with that parent. Rarely is testimony of the mother, child, or social services people carefully reviewed to determine the extent, if any, of the mother's bias, interests, or anger. As it currently operates, the system encourages manipulation of the child by the custodial parent, provides support for the accuser, and is an effective aid in assuring maternal custody.

What happens when the allegation is proven false? The child has probably still been subjected to endless interrogation and often sexual abuse therapy that is confusing and probably emotionally damaging. He or she may have been taught the role of victim. A young child has probably learned a great deal about explicit and deviant sexual behavior long before they would normally have had that type of exposure.

Too many social workers and mental health care workers approach an interview with the belief that, if the child said it or the mother said the child said it, then it must be true—the child has been molested. The child is given positive feedback when he or she provides the sought-for answers, i.e. say "yes" and Mommy is proud of you. Negative feedback and contradictions result from his/her denial of any abuse. Say "no" and the child is asked, "Is this one of the yucky secrets? Is this a scary secret? Were you told not to talk about this?"

If a child says he was abused, he's telling the truth. If he says he wasn't, he's lying, seems to be the theory practiced by many social workers. This belief is clearly documented in *The Real World of Child Interrogations*, Underwager and Wakefield, 1990.

Social workers and mental health workers can "train" a child to believe he or she was molested. If the child continues to maintain nothing happened, they may say that other children say it did. They may attempt conjecture: "Do you think it might have happened?" They may use anatomically correct dolls and ask the child to pretend something happened and to show them how it happened. They have now given the child an opportunity to play or fantasize. If that child is at all interested in the enlarged genital areas of the anatomically correct dolls, they have proof of molestation.

The potential of harm for the children involved in these cases was recognized over ten years ago. In January of 1978, the National Center on Child Abuse and Neglect made the following statements in the Federal Register: "Sexual abuse of children, especially in cases of incest, is perhaps one of the least understood and, consequently most mishandled forms of child mistreatment. . .There is often as much harm done to the child by the system's handling of the case as the trauma associated with the abuse. . . care must be exercised, lest the very social intervention employed produce the very outcomes that are feared."

The theory that children don't lie about sexual abuse, because they haven't the knowledge or experience to create such claims, totally ignores the fact that children can be taught to parrot almost anything and coached to relate stories both true and false. This is, unfortunately, why they are such a valuable tool when guided by a manipulative parent and assisted by overzealous and untrained social workers. The child is the victim of the system.

The prosecutor in Larry Spiegel's case made the following statement regarding the validity of his daughter's statement: "If you ask a child the right questions, you get the truth." More accurately, in cases of false allegations involving young children, if you ask the "right" questions, leading questions, closed-end questions, you can get the answers you want.

A child who is being used by a parent as a pawn in the game of custody and child support is daily and hourly subjected to the obsessions and attitudes of that parent as well as to the questions and attitudes of the therapist, who will generally operate from the assumption that the child has been abused. Over a period of time, this type of exposure results in the child either becoming convinced that he or she was, in fact, abused, that something bad happened when they were with Daddy, or the child carrying forever the question, the doubt, about what really did or didn't happen, as we have seen with Mary.

In the case of Mark Doe in Texas, not only was his son subjected to therapy for non-existent abuse, but one of the conditions of his divorce settlement was that his son be placed in a state-approved institution, totally removed from his family, for intensive evaluation and therapy. Mark had a choice: he could agree to the hospitalization of his son or the psychologist for the state would recommend that all three of his children be placed in foster homes. Although the charges of sexual abuse had been dismissed, he was placed in a situation of forcing all of his children into a completely foreign environment, or going along with the requirement of therapy for himself and hospitalization for his son. The child, at the age of three, became an extreme victim of the manipulations of his wife's attorney and the state Social Services system, being placed in an institution designed to treat disturbed adolescent or prepubescent children.

In reviewing Mark Doe's case and the actions and activities of the therapists and hospital involved, Dr. Underwager and Wakefield made the following comment: "When a non-abused child is treated by adults as if the child had been abused and adult pressure and influence is used to produce statements from a child about events that did not happen, this is an assault upon the child's ability to distinguish reality from unreality."

In instances where the child becomes caught up in the agency system, his or her denial may well lead to some well-intentioned but misguided social worker interpreting his play, his dreams, or his behavior on his behalf, depicting that he is, indeed, an abused child. If he continues to deny the abuse, the child will be given more "counseling."

One father, charged with child sexual abuse when he attempted to gain custody of his three-year-old daughter now has supervised visitation, eight hours, every other week. The judge, in ruling on the case, concluded there was insufficient evidence of abuse, but suggested that the girl had been conditioned to fear her father by months of therapy. He ordered the therapy ended. At a recent visitation, the little girl leaned over from her coloring book and whispered, "You put your penis in my bottom."

"No, I didn't, darling," he responded.

"Mama says. We talk about it at home a lot." With that statement, his daughter turned back to her coloring book and nothing more was said.

During a psychological evaluation of another three-year-old, following several months of therapy for alleged child abuse which had elicited more and more sophisticated and wide-ranging admissions from the child, the psychologist at the University of Michigan Family and Law Program made the following observation. "This 'therapy,' although meant to be helpful, has been continually sexually stimulating to her. Each of these charges is the product of continuing interviews and therapy and who knows what." In referring to use of the dolls to determine what had happened, he pointed out that children are curious as well as suggestible and compliant, especially with an adult whom they seek to please.

In the William Smith case, the victimization of the children is on-going. These two children were old enough to realize what was happening and, as they have grown older, have steadfastly denied any wrongdoing on the part of either their stepbrother or their father. In spite of psychological examinations and recommendations to the contrary, the children remain in their mother's custody. Both children are totally baffled by the fact that they must live with their mother and are not allowed to see their father. They are confused by the fact that their mother is lying, they have told everyone that their mother is lying and how she told them to lie, yet no one listens to these two small voices.

In this instance, while there was no physical abuse, Dr. Hill of Ross Associates pointed out that the emotional abuse of having to tell lies, to select one parent over the other and to experience an ongoing uncertainty about their future home and lifestyle may have serious effects on their future mental health. She expressed concern about the lengthy court process to which they were being subjected and the conflicting messages they were receiving from their mother and numerous "helping" professionals who were attempting to manipulate the court system for their own vested interests.

In a review of the children's psychological well being, done two years after the allegations were made by their mother against their stepbrother and, subsequently, their father, Dr. Janice Hill of Ross Associates included the following statements.

"Beginning with the Women Together Shelter experience, Janice and Johnny have been subjected to numerous interviews, physical and mental status examinations with police, physicians, psychiatrists, clinical social workers, psychologists, attorneys and victim advocates. While such investigations may have originated in the best interest of these children, and should have addressed the original complaint of sexual abuse and custody, unfortunately the legal complexity of this case, the numerous vested interests of the parents and the "helping" professionals have resulted in doing further damage to the emotional well-being of these two children. In fact, the Guardian indicated on August 8, 1985 that this therapist's report was essential to the Court's Award of Custody. To date, however, the therapeutic findings of this therapist have not been requested, in spite of well over one and one-half years of consistent and intensive therapeutic involvement with these children.

"To summarize, Johnny and Janice Smith have been subjected to a series of traumatic events:

1. Disruption of their intact family;

2. Changes in temporary custody, living environments, academic opportunities;

3. Intensive and intrusive investigations of alleged sexual abuse by multiple social service, law enforcement and civil justice systems personnel;

4. Parental indoctrination to falsely accuse family members of these serious charges;

5. Parental pressure to establish family loyalty and, most importantly,

6. Child protection service providers, both social services and legal services that have exacerbated their emotional well being rather than protect it.

"It is imperative, then, that a speedy resolution to the custody issue be enacted to truly and finally serve in the best interest of these children. Continued prolongation of this matter on the part of the Court would represent a travesty of justice and simply, but tragically, demonstrate to these minor children that our system to protect and assist children is woefully inept. . .Finally, the best interests of these children could indeed best be served when they are given the opportunity to speak for themselves to the greater authority of the court."

A psychological evaluation was done at the University of Michigan Family and Law Program, involving Bernie, his ex-wife and their three-year-old daughter. Because of an innocent question asked by the ex-wife during a medical examination, the doctor had reported to Social Services that she suspected possible sexual abuse and charges had been filed by the agency. His daughter had been put in sexual abuse therapy for several months to allow her to "deal with" and "provide information about" the alleged abuse. Over a period of months, the child had reportedly alleged a variety of instances of sexual abuse.

At the end of over five hours of evaluation, the psychologist made the following observation: "This 'therapy,' although meant to be helpful, has been continually sexually stimulating to her." He noted the escalating allegations. "Each of these charges is the product of continuing interviews and therapy and who knows what. This evaluator sincerely doubts any of the . . .acts took place, let alone all of them." He also criticized the continued use of anatomically correct dolls in her therapy. "It is important to remember that children are curious. Children are suggestible and compliant, especially with a parent and those adults whom they seek to please and protect."

The preceding evaluations indicate that there may be long term ramifications to the children as a result of being involved in the allegations, the investigation and the almost automatic therapy process. Mary can tell us clearly that these fears are well founded.

. . .I'd had more sex education by the time I was six than you can imagine. With the help of the dolls, I could name every part of the body. They spent all that time talking about it and they'd bring out the little dolls and point to the parts of the body and stuff. . .

And now it's ten years later and Mary should be dating boys and giggling with other girls and exploring the natural curiosity we all experience during our teenage years regarding sex and its fascinating mysteries. Instead, Mary could probably teach her peers almost anything they want to know.

. . .I don't like anything that has to do with sex. I mean, people talk and they say how great it is and I'm, like. . .Yuck!

The physical and emotional effects upon a true victim of sexual abuse are enormous. We have yet to fully comprehend the emotional, mental, and sociological effects upon a child who is coerced into playing the victim of a false allegation of child sexual abuse. Can we, as parents, social workers, mental health care professionals, attorneys, judges, legislators, and caring adults in the general population justify continuing experimentation with our children to find the answers?

Mary's comments clearly illustrate that it is the children who are the true victims of false allegations of child sexual abuse. The agencies and mental health workers win; the attorneys win; one of the parents wins. The children always lose.

Chapter Ten

The Dolls

As Mary pointed out in the preceding interview, children who are alleged victims of child sexual abuse receive an extensive sex education, most frequently with the aid of what social workers refer to as "anatomically correct" dolls. Too frequently, the responses and behaviors elicited in interviews using these dolls are presented to the courts by social workers and child protection team workers as "evidence" of child sexual abuse. There are a number of problems inherent in the use of these dolls as a diagnostic tool.

The Dolls

The dolls are generally twenty to twenty-five inches in length. Pubic hair is simulated with dark embroidery or synthetic fur. The breasts of the mature female doll protrude and both the boy and man dolls have penises, often disproportionately large in the dolls provided by some manufacturers. All of the dolls have representations of oral and anal openings and the female dolls include a representation of the pubic area and vaginal openings. The dolls are designed so the penis fits into any of these openings.

The doll family used in most investigation and therapy generally includes a mature male and female doll and a boy and girl doll, the latter having no pubic hair nor protruding breasts. All are dressed in clothing that is easy to remove. There is no standardization of the dolls' design, some being purchased from various toy manufacturers and some being hand made, nor is there any established standard procedure for using the dolls in investigation or for conducting interviews or play sessions with the dolls.

A serious problem with the standard doll family provided in the interrogations is that it appears to represent a typical nuclear family—mother, father, one boy and one girl. However, particularly in SAID Syndrome cases, the child is frequently dealing with a non-typical family. There may well be Mommy, Daddy, Mommy's boyfriend(s) or second husband, Daddy's girlfriend(s) or wife. There are usually no dolls to represent these additional figures.

In one of the case studies we examined, the mother had remarried and the children were instructed to call their step-father "Daddy," while referring to their natural father by his given name, Rick. In the doll session, there were a number of negative references from the youngest boy referring to "Daddy." The social worker attributed all these negative responses as being directed toward Rick. Rick's attorney asked how the social worker could be sure which man the child was really referring to, given the child had only one male doll to select from and play with.

Scientific Validity of Anatomically Complete Dolls

In the October, 1986 issue of *Trial Talk*, M.J. Phillippus, a psychologist, and Glen V. Koch, a psychiatrist, addressed the use of anatomically complete dolls and their validity in determining sexual abuse. They point out that the dolls, complete but not correct, are manufactured by a variety of companies with no standardization applicable. One manufacturer claims, "They may be used diagnostically to help determine whether incest or molestation has occurred." Without the application of standards, both Drs. Phillippus and Koch contend this is a completely false statement.

These dolls are sold by toy manufacturers, not by standard psychological test distributors. They have been developed excluding the standards set forth in test development by the American Psychological Association (APA). The APA requires that psychological tests are carefully restricted, a licensed psychologist must be a member of APA, and he or she must file a request form before purchasing a standardized test. The doll manufacturers sell their dolls to anyone requesting them and then provide expensive seminars to explain their use. The dolls are then used by social workers and child protection team personnel, who may have no professional expertise in the areas of child play, child development, or diagnostic techniques and standards. Unqualified personnel using non-standard tests are in violation of the tenets of APA. Many judges and trial lawyers seem to be unaware of this. In addition, the dolls do not meet the Frye test for admissibility requirements set forth by the APA.

The anatomically complete dolls were originally used as educational toys in child psychology and schools, and as aids in helping sexually abused children learn to deal with the experience. Today, instead of being used for their intended purpose, they are being used as diagnostic tools by individuals who are often lacking expertise in the areas of diagnosis and interrogation and have little, if any, knowledge of the projection-provoking properties of toys.

Children and Toys

A doll is a toy. Giving a young child a toy is an invitation to play, to fantasize, to engage in make-believe. As pointed out by Underwager and Wakefield in their recent book *The Real World of Child Interrogations*, children's play involves fantasy, pretend, and imagination. The anatomical dolls are routinely used with young and very young children as a means of overcoming their lack of verbal abilities. Yet, research evidence on this issue suggests that children do not reliably distinguish between fantasy and reality until approximately age ten or eleven.

A child is naturally curious. The dolls he or she is accustomed to playing with do not have breasts, a penis, or pubic hair and, in most cases, children have not been much exposed to those parts of the human anatomy. Phillippus and Koch state it is normal for a child between the ages of three and four to be interested in sex and elimination organs, and that the incidence of genital self-stimulation in children of that age is generally high.

Although videotaped interviews with the anatomically complete dolls are often offered as evidence in cases of alleged child sexual abuse, the way a child plays with dolls has not been proven to be indicative of real life. If a child throws a doll on the floor, do we assume that the child throws his or her baby sister on the floor? If a child twists an arm or leg around and around to see if it comes off, do we assume that he twists his brother's arm in the same manner? Dr. T.F. Naumann (1985) pointed out that it is natural for young children to touch and manipulate parts of any toy, as well as to mouth protruding parts of a toy.

Yet, if a child touches the pubic area of a child doll or the penis of the man doll, social workers and child protection workers often view this as proof of the child having been exposed to these actions. In the use of the anatomical dolls, child's play may not be treated as play. Too often, interviewing adults believe they can invite a child to play, to fantasize, to enter a game of "let's pretend" and then use the child's play as evidence of reality.

The Dolls as a Diagnostic Tool

The use of dolls and play sessions is based on the assumption that children who have been sexually abused will demonstrate sexual behavior with the dolls that will not be exhibited when non-abused children are exposed to the same dolls. This theory has been disproven by recent research. In a paper published by the Institute for Psychological Therapies (IPT), William McIver II, Ralph Underwager and Hollida Wakefield explored the characteristics of the dolls and documented the use of the anatomically correct dolls with both abused and non-abused children in a controlled study. Fifty-non-abused children and ten abused children were led through identical exposures and interviews involving the anatomically correct dolls. The average age of the children was four years.

In this study, there were no significant differences between the abused and non-abused children in terms of spontaneous behavior and comments when interacting with the dolls. Sixty-two percent of the non-abused children and fifty percent of the abused children placed the dolls in clear sexual positions and/or played with the dolls in an overtly aggressive manner. Their play activities included placing one doll on top of another in the missionary position and placing the male doll's penis into the oral, anal, and vaginal openings of the dolls.

Fifty percent of the non-abused children and forty percent of the abused children made spontaneous comments, such as, "He did something naughty," "(He) jumped on his bed," and "Daddy went poopy on my head."

A study done by Canadian researcher Dr. R.M. Gabriel (1985) and a report to the American Academy of Child Psychiatry in 1986 both supported McIver et al's findings that there is little difference in the reaction and activities between abused and non-abused children when exposed to the dolls.

Gabriel observed nineteen non-abused children who were exposed to the dolls and to other toys. About half of the children showed interest in the genitals of the dolls and manipulated them. Many of the children exhibited behavior and actions which could have been viewed as indicative of likely sexual abuse if one were in the process of attempting to prove such an allegation. Gabriel stated that, "On the evidence of the dolls alone, when used as part of a 'fishing expedition' exercise, the suspect will almost always be found guilty, especially if the examiner is already biased in that direction."

In the study by Jensen, Realmuto and Wescoe, reported at the American Academy of Child Psychiatry, which involved both abused and non-abused children, some of the non-abused children got the highest rating of "very suspicious" while some of the abused children got ratings of "no suspicion of abuse."

Research has also shown that the assumptions that children will identify the dolls as male or female based on genitals, and use the dolls to symbolize actual people in their lives, is unfounded. The McIver et al study found that most young children were unable to identify the dolls as males or females on the basis of primary sexual characteristics. Only fifteen percent of the children related the dolls to people in their lives. Herbert et al (1987) also found that young children show an inability to identify gender on the basis of the symbolic genitalia.

Sivan, Schor, Koeppl and Noble (1988) found that, overall, the anatomical dolls are of little interest to children and they do not spontaneously choose to play with them. The Herbert et al study reported that the interrogator had to direct the children to approach the dolls. None initiated undressing the dolls, although all accepted the direction of the interrogator to undress them.

Despite their wide use by social workers and child protection team members, there is not, to date, any empirical data that supports their validity as a diagnostic tool. Not only are the anatomically complete dolls not of standard design, there are no protocols or standards established or followed for methods of interviewing and interpreting the responses and activities of the children involved.

In addition to the non-standardization of the dolls, the procedures used by Social Services personnel are inherently suspect, according to Dr. Naumann (1987). Not only are few social workers qualified psychologists, but they usually approach the interview with a plethora of previous information from doctors, relatives, neighbors, and the accuser, which could cause the worker to be biased and to have a set of preconceived notions as to what to expect. Thus, the objectivity, imperative in an interview of this nature, is seriously compromised.

The dolls are not generally accepted in the scientific community and it is the conclusion of McIver et al that nothing obtained from their use should ever be admitted as evidence in a legal setting. A California Appeals Court ruled in 1987 that the use of the dolls was not supported by the scientific evidence and their use did not meet the Frye test for admissibility. Testimony based upon the use of the dolls was therefore ruled inadmissable (*Law Week*, 1987). Recently, the highest court in Holland ruled that evidence gained using the dolls could not be admitted into court, unless the judge could explain why the objections to the dolls did not apply in the specific case being reviewed.

Validity of Evidence

There are a number of questions and concerns regarding the validity of information gained in play sessions with the anatomically complete dolls, questions not only of interpretation but of legality.

Louis Kiefer(1989), an East Coast attorney, points out that if a child is competent to testify—having the ability to receive correct impressions and to recollect and narrate intelligently—the dolls are unnecessary. If the child is incompetent to testify, how does one deem that child's actions with dolls as being credible or competent evidence?

Young children do not have the adult concept of a "lie" or of "justice" and it is unreasonable to expect them to grasp and understand the concept in the time during which the interview is held. It is also important to discover what children can say without it being a lie. In one case reviewed by Kiefer, the child was absolutely certain she had never lied. On cross examination, she admitted to fibbing, unable to see this as a problem. One must establish what is and is not permissible behavior, i.e. telling lies versus fibbing versus telling stories, a somewhat daunting task.

It must be remembered that the child has been invited to play, not to document an event that has actually happened. In a child's mind, make-believe stories are not lies. If the interviewer has helped create the "story" by asking questions, the child often believes this is part of the game.

The Interview

Several issues make the use of information gained in doll session interviews questionable, i.e., the manner in which the interview is conducted, the behavior of the interviewer and the suggestibility of young children. Psychologists and researchers note that children are easily led to model or imitate adults, and normally seek to provide actions and statements that engender positive reinforcement and approval.

Underwager and Wakefield have reviewed numerous videotapes and interview transcripts in which the social worker or child protection team worker has been extremely active in the play session process, asking leading questions, pointing to and touching the "private parts" of the doll and repeating a question numerous times, until the sought-for answer is given.

There are numerous examples of adult modeling behavior that impacts the child's reactions and activities. During the course of the interview, the interviewer may repeatedly touch the genital areas of the dolls, reinforcing the child's curiosity regarding the new and unknown toy. The child will likely follow the adult's example. A statement such as, "Let's pretend this is Daddy and this is you," invites the child to play make-believe. The interviewer then places the dolls in sexually explicit positions or strokes the private parts of the body. Following the interviewer's lead, the child learns to do the same. In the case of false allegations, a child with nothing to report will report nothing. This may be deemed as failure on the part of the interviewer, who wants to *save* this child, having already determined in his or her own mind that the child has been abused, based on information provided by the accuser.

It was noted in several of the studies cited in this chapter that children rarely selected the anatomically complete dolls as the toy of choice, but had to be encouraged or directed to play with them by the interviewer. During the course of an actually doll session interview, children are not allowed to put the dolls aside, but are required by the interviewer to continue playing with them.

Many doll session interviews contain a large number of leading questions and a high degree of reinforcement for desired or expected behavior or responses. Children are highly suggestible and easily led. Analysis of the questions asked and the manner in which they are asked is necessary before establishing the level of credibility attached to the responses. Different kinds of questions will elicit different responses from a child. An open-ended question calls for spontaneous, free recall. "What happened?" might be the question asked of a crying child. If there was no response, the question might be made more specific, "Did you fall down?" The questioner has now begun providing potential answers to the cause of distress. The question can be further altered to provide the child with a potential explanation, as in, "Did Bobby push you down?"

A child's memory in free recall may be quite accurate. However, a response of "Nothing" may not be acceptable, if the interviewer believes that the child has been the victim of abuse. Therefore, the interviewer who receives no definitive response regarding sexual abuse may become more active in the interview, advancing to leading questions in an effort to garner information or evidence. The younger the child, the fewer memories they have, the fewer events they remember. The less a child remembers, the more he or she can be misled by leading questions containing suggested answers.

In his book, *The Battle and the Backlash*, Hechler asked Lawrence Daly, a detective with King County (Washington) Department of Public Safety if, with a young child, it was sometimes necessary to ask what might be considered leading questions to get the story, an account of the case.

Daly responded, "You do. But, I'm talking about where you pick up the doll, an anatomically correct doll, and you say, 'Did your Daddy touch you here? Did your Daddy touch you here?' You can talk to the child and say, 'Are these your feet? Is this your nose? What do you call this? What do you call this? Do you call this anything?'

"But, as soon as you suggest, the child responds because they think that you want that answer. . .It's a suggestive type thing, so you have to be careful. But you can lead the kid a little bit. 'Were you in the bedroom with your Daddy?' Well, if Daddy didn't do anything wrong in the bedroom, the next question's going to be, 'Did anything happen in the bedroom?' That way you can lead, but you don't say, 'Did Daddy touch you there in the bedroom?'"

Unfortunately, that is exactly the type of question too often used by interviewers employing the anatomical dolls.

In addition, the interviewer may provide reinforcement when the child provides desired information. For example, such statements as, "Good girl, you've helped us so much," in response to questions such as, "Daddy touched you here, didn't he?", indicate clearly to a child what type of behavior is expected and rewarded. In addition, repetition of a question which includes the suggested answer will eventually elicit a positive response, in many cases. Often, denial of the abuse or sexually inappropriate behavior results in questions about the validity of the denial, such as, "Are you sure?", or, "Did he tell you not to talk about it?"

When a child is repeatedly subjected to interviews or therapy geared toward identifying or treating suspected sexual abuse, the child is taught, through modeling and questions and reinforcement, to believe something happened, as was the case with Mary.

In the McIver study, six of the non-abused and one of the abused children were intentionally asked leading questions in conjunction with modeling and reinforcing behavior by the interviewer, questions such as, "Can you show me?", and, "How else could they go together?"

All but one child responded by performing the behaviors that were cued or modeled and reinforced by the interviewer. As the interview progressed, the children demonstrated and produced more and more behaviors. Although only one of the children in this group had actually been abused, six of the seven children demonstrated hitting, punching, cunnilingus, fellatio, anal and vaginal intercourse, and the mommy doll sitting on the boy doll's face. In the real world of child interrogation, children are pressured to interact with the dolls until the desired behavior is elicited. They must frequently be encouraged, sometimes almost forced, to initiate play with the dolls. Questions are not asked once and then dropped if the child does not respond as desired. Children are not permitted to put the dolls aside in favor of a preferred activity.

The Interviewer

It has been suggested that, when using the dolls, the interviewer should be unaware of who has been accused and exactly what type of abuse has occurred, in the interest of avoiding leading questions, modeling, suggestions, and prompting which would influence the child. Rarely is this protocol followed.

Interviews with the dolls are most frequently conducted by social workers and child protection team workers, individuals with only undergraduate degrees or less, whose education in the use of the dolls has consisted of one or two weekend seminars or a four-hour in-service training program. These individuals set themselves up as expert witnesses and their opinions and recommendations are accepted and "rubber stamped" by prosecutors and judges.

Mental health professionals generally interpret non-responses as responses of affirmation. If a child does not respond to a question about sexual abuse, it is assumed the child is either ashamed or denying it. Since denial is unhealthy, interrogation continues until a response is elicited that can be interpreted as an admission of abuse and the child can be treated. In the event the adult believes there has been abuse, and the child says "No", the adult may assume the child is keeping it a secret or was told to keep it a secret by the alleged perpetrator. Now the adult must press the child into telling the secret so the child can be saved. If a child answers "No", the questioning continues, the denials often ignored until the desired affirmation is obtained. It is interesting to note that those who most strongly assert that children don't lie are the very individuals who believe that when a child says "No" to questions of sexual abuse, they are not telling the truth about the incident.

Accusations of child sexual abuse are often based on a child's response to an adult's question, not to an actual accusation or statement made by the child. The normal course of events is for an adult to suspect abuse, usually because of a change in behavior, and to question the child. The next step is to contact the police or the social services agency. The first contact is usually a social worker, who hears the adult's account of what they think might have happened. Frequently, this account becomes a statement of fact to the social worker, who now feels responsible for substantiating the claim so they can act to save the child.

The first interview with the child is rarely recorded, only summarized. Thus, there is no indication of what type of questions were asked, whether or not there were repeated denials prior to the affirmation of abuse, or whether the child's accusation was the result of answering suggestible questions or making a free statement. Where audio or video tapes have been reviewed, it has often been found that the interview reports are wrong regarding what the child actually said and what the interviewer actually said. The summary may simply state the opinion of the interviewer, based on his or her recollection of the final outcome of questioning.

In many of the interviews observed by McIver, the interviewer told the child to pretend or imagine. The child did. The interviewer then concluded that the resulting behavior showed that real events happened. The interviewer, now believing abuse took place, continued the interrogation, talking to the child about what started out as pretend behavior but is now represented to the child as real, i.e., "Remember when you told me Daddy did. . ." In this progression, a child may be taught to believe and subjectively experience as real what started out as a response to the adult's invitation to pretend.

Chapter Eleven

The Agencies

The headlines in *The Florida Times-Union* on November 11, 1990 read: **HRS Investigator Finds Baby with Eyes Black, No Clothes—and a Tail**. The *Florida Today* headlines were: **Accused Child-abusers Explain Princess is a Pet**.

The *Times-Union* article began, "James and Mary Seay were surprised yesterday when a state welfare official came to their Westside Jacksonville home to investigate a child-abuse report involving their eight-month-old baby, Princess. Princess, after all, is their pet racoon." The articles went on to explain that the Department of Health and Rehabilitative Services (DHRS) had received reports that the Seays were picking up Princess by the neck and locking her in a bathroom. The Seays introduced the racoon and the investigator talked with their veterinarian. Although the call was obviously a prank, Seay said the investigator told her the agency would have to continue checking to see if the couple has a human baby and that she and her husband would be listed on the HRS central child-abuse registry until the investigation was completed. The middle-aged couple was ordered by other HRS workers to come in the following week for child-abuse counseling. Mrs. Seay, the mother of three teenagers, commented, "I'm just disgusted. This isn't going to be over until Princess is eighteen."

There are many caring and competent individuals involved in social services and mental health care across the country, professionals who are educated and experienced in child development, play therapy, and child interrogation. Unfortunately, due to heavy case loads and frequent turnover in personnel, many agencies are either understaffed or are staffed by individuals who do not have adequate training or expertise to qualify them for the authoritative role they have in areas of child-abuse and, specifically, child sexual abuse allegations.

In recent years, people have begun to question the effectiveness and competence of these agencies, their policies, procedures and personnel. In his book, *A Question of Innocence*, Dr. Larry Spiegel, who was falsely accused of abusing his daughter, relates the following incident:

"I was working with a couple in my clinical practice who had a three-and-a-half-year-old girl. One evening, as a consequence of a series of events, the mother created such a disturbance that the police and Department of Youth and Family Services (DYFS) were called. My business card was on the bulletin board in their apartment, so the police called my office. I went there immediately.

"When I arrived, the DYFS worker was preparing papers to remove the child from the home. I interceded and volunteered to take the child to her relatives out of state, rather than have her placed in a foster home. The DYFS worker said he would check on that, but the child would have to spend the night in a foster home. The following day, I sent Janeen to the DYFS headquarters to request that the child be released into my custody and flown to her relatives in Detroit. As incredible as it sounds, this same agency which pressed child molestation against me—charges which were still pending in court—released this child into my custody. I received a letter from DYFS a few days later, thanking me for my help. Need I say more about the credibility and competence of this agency?"

Ken Pangborn, president of Men International, Inc. tells about his experience with the agency designated to protect innocent children:

His wife had filed for divorce and full custody when their youngest child was a year old. Facing a court that had no interest in what he had to say, Ken didn't fight the decree. However, he later received a call from the state Supervisor of Welfare, telling him horror stories about what his wife was doing to his children and her treatment of them, insinuating that if Ken were any kind of father, he would do something about the situation.

Ken questioned the social worker. "You're telling me I'm a terrible father because I'm not doing anything about this. Let me ask you a question. If I come up with the money to launch a custody fight and go in there after the kids, will you or someone from the agency appear in court, testify to what's she's been doing with the kids and tell the court she shouldn't have those kids and I should?" The Supervisor's response was short and simple. "Why, no, we can't do that."

Anyone who is dealing with a false allegation of child sexual abuse is dealing with some sort of state agency like the above featured DHRS, an agency that believes itself to be acting in the best interest of the children. Whether called Health and Human Services, Department of Social Services or some other variation of that name, there is a state agency that was originally designed to protect children and families. Many of these agencies have some sort of abuse hot line, a telephone number that individuals can call to report child-abuse of any type, often with complete anonymity. This agency, whatever its name, is going to be involved, and probably in control, before you ever know you've been accused.

An allegation of child sexual abuse, whether false or factual, whether placed by an anonymous caller or by an ex-wife, is usually made to the county or state social services agency and sets in motion a relatively standard chain of events.

First the child will undergo a medical examination, to determine whether there is physical evidence of sexual abuse. With young children, rarely is there any such evidence. Next the child is interviewed by a social worker and/or perhaps a police investigator. Subsequent steps vary, depending on the outcome or perceived outcome of that interview. If the child denies the allegations, the next step is often therapy, based on the assumption that the child is too young to understand or too frightened to talk about the experience. This "therapy" may well continue until the allegation can be substantiated.

Many of the agencies dealing with allegations of child sexual abuse include what are called Child Protection Teams, composed of persons representing mental health, social work, medical, legal, and law enforcement disciplines. To date, there is no empirical data to support the conviction that multi-disciplinary teams are more effective or that they increase accuracy of conclusions. Teams are a medical concept, not a criminal law evidence-gathering body. (Schultz, 1989)

There are four types of teams: the hospital-based team (as in my case), the state consultation team, the rural team, and the treatment team. The hospital team is where most criminal charges of child-abuse are initiated and evolve. Most often it will be a hospital-based team that makes the initial decisions that cause further interventions and actions of the state, calling in defense attorneys, prosecutors, therapists, and private investigators. The team approach has some inherent problems, including being so large it bogs down, power struggles within the team ranks, and differing definitions of child-abuse laws among team members. In cases of alleged sexual abuse of young children, there is rarely any medical evidence of penetration. Except for reporting "excited utterances" of alleged victims at the time of the medical exam, pediatricians' opinions of psychological factors are no more valid than laymen's. A physician's opinion or report, when there are no physical findings but a statement is made that abuse is "consistent with," must be treated cautiously. Too often child protection team members tend to give more credence and credibility to medical opinion (versus medical evidence) than may be warranted.

During the trial of a young man accused of molesting children at the Manhattan Ranch Pre-School in California, one of the witnesses for the prosecution was an examining physician, a pediatrician at County Harbor General Hospital. She testified that she had examined one of the child witnesses and that her findings were "consistent with sexual abuse." During cross-examination, the attorney asked the pediatrician if she ever reported findings "inconsistent with sexual abuse." The pediatrician said she never used those words, "because there are no findings inconsistent with sexual abuse." This statement then leads to the conclusion that, if there is no finding inconsistent with sexual abuse, *anything* or *nothing* can be diagnosed as evidence of sexual abuse.

Depending on the attitude and urgency of the accuser, the attitude and ambition of the involved social services agency, the direction of the therapy and conclusions drawn from various interviews, a complaint may be filed with the district attorney's office as the next step. Unfortunately, the accused individual is rarely aware of all this activity and has no idea of the case being built against him until most, if not all, of these steps have been accomplished.

By the time I was aware of the initial allegations, my daughter had already had a medical examination at a local hospital and had been interviewed by social services and a police officer. By the time I was aware of the second set of allegations, she had gone through another series of these examinations. This set of interviews was conducted by social services, the child protection team (who had interviewed her using the anatomically correct dolls), a police detective, and a therapist.

Before the father in the Colorado case study became aware of his ex-wife's allegations at the time of his arrest, all three of his children had been receiving therapy through social services for sexual abuse and DSS had filed a complaint with the district attorney's office. Mark Doe was advised of the allegations against him immediately prior to the family court hearing that was to determine custody. Again, his children had been undergoing social services' directed therapy for sexual abuse without his knowledge.

Once social services has determined that, in their opinion, sexual abuse has occurred, they will usually file a petition for Dependency and Neglect in Juvenile or Family Court. In the case of allegations made by the ex-wife or soon to be ex-wife, the petition routinely recommends that the mother receive residential custody, the accused father be denied any access to the children, at least for the time being, the children receive counseling and therapy for sexual abuse, and the father enter and complete counseling and therapy as an abuser, before any consideration be given to his visitation with the children. In many cases, these recommendations are made before the social worker has even met or talked with the accused father.

Rick's experience in Colorado was not unusual for a father falsely accused of abusing his children. In spite of his ex-wife's recantation and Rick's steadfast pleas of innocence, the family court accepted the opinion of the social services agency that the children exhibited behavior consistent with abuse victims and followed the agency's recommendations. Rick was not to be allowed to see his children until the required counseling and therapy for him had been completed.

The agency-selected therapist advised Rick that he would have to admit to sexually abusing his daughter before he could even attend therapy sessions. He refused to admit to something he hadn't done and requested another therapist. The second therapist selected by DSS was the same one who had filed the accusations against him and who was a good friend of his ex-wife. Unable to trust her, he refused this therapist also and was caught in a catch-22. It appeared that unless he admitted to something he hadn't done, he wouldn't be able to meet the conditions required to see his children.

In a separate case in the state of Colorado, where false allegations were made by the ex-wife during a divorce and custody battle, the two young children and the ex-wife were interviewed by the Department of Social Services. The caseworker's impressions and recommendations were presented as an expert evaluation to the family court. Her report stated that she believed that the child had been sexually abused, that the child presented an advanced knowledge of adult sexual activity. To her knowledge, there had not been any other form of exposure for the child, other than what was described by the children. Therefore, she respectfully recommended that the Court honor the filing of a Dependency and Neglect petition on behalf of this child. In addition, it was respectfully recommended that the physical custody of both children be placed with their mother. Furthermore, this worker recommended that a protective order be issued disallowing physical or verbal contact with the children and their mother by the father. She felt it essential that further investigation and evaluation of the child be done before the father be allowed contact with the child.

The court accepted this individual's evaluation and recommendation and acted as requested, although there had been no professional psychological evaluations done, the father in this case had never been evaluated or even interviewed, and the children had been treated as abuse victims before the allegations were ever made.

Currently, social workers and the mental health care workers within the agencies have a tremendous amount of authority, their opinions being considered as fact, their credibility viewed as unassailable, and their recommendations considered expert testimony and rubber-stamped by judges and prosecuting attorneys, in spite of evidence to the contrary.

More and more studies, investigations and case evaluations are showing that the falsely accused are truly the ones being abused by the social services agencies and the family courts. Over the past several years, many of the agencies responsible for handling child-abuse allegations have grown into sometimes unmanageable bureaucracies, with almost absolute authority over the alleged victim and the alleged perpetrator. Frequently understaffed by individuals who are expected to handle investigative duties for which they have never been trained, the agencies and their employees are, nonetheless, often considered expert witnesses when it comes time to make a determination of custody and guilt in both family and criminal courts. Many of the social workers, investigating allegations of child sexual abuse and making determinations of probable guilt, are totally unfamiliar with the SAID Syndrome and its ramifications. Many have little education or expertise in the areas of child-abuse detection and prevention or child development.

The results of such an approach and the application of such a method are far reaching. First, we have a system so overburdened with false allegations that we don't have the time or energy to do a good job with cases where there is real evidence of abuse. Next, we have children being trained to believe something has happened in such a way they can't tell if it happened or not, as we saw with Mary. The long-term ramifications of this on the children has yet to be determined, but the potential consequences cannot be considered innocuous or inconsequential. The lives of the falsely accused are in ruins, regardless of the outcome of any criminal proceedings or eventual proof of innocence. And finally, we suffer a lack of resources for promoting adequate prosecution of the guilty and adequate protection of the innocence.

Too often, social workers and child protection team members go into the investigative interview with the belief—for whatever reason—that the child has been molested and that their mission is to substantiate that belief in such a way that the family and criminal courts will act in what the worker has determined to be the best interest of the child. Two things occur as a result of this. First, the worker may act as a therapist, instead of an investigator, determined to treat the child. In this case, the child receives strong positive feedback if he or she says something happened and negative feedback, contradictions of his or her statements or encouragement to revise the responses if he or she denies the abuse.

One individual, who was the victim of incest during her childhood, told Mr. Hechler, during the course of an interview for his book, that a child doesn't need "treatment." A child needs solutions, options, an ear to listen, a caring person. How often do the social services agencies get involved in "treating" the child before they have even established the basis of the symptoms, symptoms that have often been relayed by another adult? How often are investigators acting as therapists before they have completed their investigation? Mary provided an excellent suggestion for social workers: "Listen to the kids and help them to deal with it. Don't act like another parent; you're supposed to be a friend, someone to help." In Mary's opinion, the social workers did more harm than good, continuing to push for indications of abuse and raising questions in her mind about what might have happened, despite her repeated denial of abuse from her father.

Lewis Hoffman Esq., an attorney who defends those falsely accused, and Larry Spiegel, a psychologist, author and victim of false allegations of child abuse, argue that much of the problem resides within the social services agencies. Both professionals identified specific issues of concern: a system geared to believe abuse charges; lack of proper training to investigate and assess the charges; the ease with which children can be led by social workers during interviews and investigation; the anonymous reporting system and the convenience of an abuse charge in a custody battle.

Unfortunately, most state agencies that deal in the areas of child protection are primarily autonomous, with little if any supervision from or accountability to anyone. While they can remove children from a home and file a charge without presenting any evidence, they cannot be held personally responsible for their actions—government sovereign immunity protects them. Much of their information and many of their records are exempt from the Public Information Act, making it impossible for the accused or his attorney to obtain the records justifying criminal charges filed against him.

There is often no clear line of command or reporting requirements. The attorney general, public advocate, director of courts, and governor's office exercise no supervision over these child protection agencies, which have awesome powers. In addition, under the aegis of the state, the interests of the accuser, law enforcement, child protection, and allied mental health and prosecutorial personal are advanced and protected. Only recently have some states enacted new laws, sanctioning ex-spouses who knowingly and maliciously file false allegations, making it at least a second-degree misdemeanor.

Today's system for responding to allegations of child sexual abuse is one that in the majority of cases exacts no negative consequences from the individual filing false allegations. An allegation, true or false, immediately elicits interest, attention, emotional and financial support, and legal and investigative services for the accuser and claimed victim.

An accused parent's rights are not uniformly and consistently protected—interrogation by the child protection team is often not preceded by informing you of your rights, and the presence of your attorney may not be permitted. You may be admonished that, if you do not execute a written waiver of rights, you must be guilty since, if you are innocent, you have nothing to worry about. There is nothing further from the truth.

There is the potential for a great deal of monetary reward for those individuals involved in identifying and even more money in treating victims of abuse. An allegation of child sexual abuse inevitably results in evaluations of the alleged perpetrator, the accuser, and the children, as well as required therapy for the children and usually for the alleged perpetrator throughout the process of determining whether abuse has even occurred. The social workers file cases which result in receipt of grant money. State and federal money received by these agencies is dependent on the number of cases they have *filed*. Once an accusation has been made and the social worker assigns it credibility by placing it on file, the agency has its numbers and the individual is placed on the central abuse registry.

To substantiate the case, the child is sent to a doctor for a physical examination, then put through psychological evaluations. The psychologist is paid by the state on a per case or per child basis and, because they are involved in this type of work, become eligible for grants themselves.

Some medical, psychological, and social work professionals appear to have developed large practices by providing affirmation and support of accusations. In some areas, individuals of this nature have been clearly identified and are routinely used by county or state authorities dealing with alleged child sexual abuse. These physicians and psychological agencies can be relied upon to determine that there has been abuse, regardless of the evidence or testimony or lack thereof, as evidenced in the testimony in the California case.

In the William Smith case, an agency-selected physician examined Janice and Johnny, who had allegedly been abused by their stepbrother. In a handwritten note, the physician stated, ". . .Janice exhibited vaginal irritation and stretching of rectal opening, Johnny exhibited reddened throat, end of penis irritated, stretching of rectal opening. Sincerely. . ." While these symptoms may be indicative of abuse, the examination identifying those conditions occurred *five months after the allegation was reported.*

Professionals who do not develop a history of affirmative support may be informally blacklisted.

There is also the danger of professionals who are ready to come to premature closure with minimal information and leap to the conviction that a child has been abused and requires immediate counseling. A premature and swift closure by a mental health professional on an opinion that abuse occurred is recognized as one of the hallmarks of a false allegation. (Klajner-Diamon, Wehrspann & Steinhauer, 1987; Wakefield & Underwager, 1988).

What is most frightening is that often the individuals involved in the case believe they know what happened and work in a heady atmosphere of sincerity and moral righteousness. The prosecutor believes he has charged a guilty man; the social workers believe they have protected a child from more harm; the psychologists believe they have successfully spotted the key signs of abuse; the jury believes—or at least says—that it can be objective and impartial; and the judge, deeming the case indeterminable, errs on the side of caution, doing what he thinks "best for the child."

Almost all prosecutors and social workers claim that statements by children about abuse carry some sort of inherent credibility. However, statistics compiled and released by the American Human Association refute this contention. As of 1978, more than sixty-five percent of all reports of suspected child maltreatment, involving over seven hundred and fifty cases per year, turned out to be unfounded. Of three hundred and twenty-eight sexual abuse cases studied by Underwager and Wakefield over a period of five years, thirty-nine percent were divorce and custody cases. Of those cases which were adjudicated, it was determined by the legal system that in seventy-eight percent of the cases there had been no abuse. (Wakefield, Underwager, 1989). Another, separate study indicated that of each five hundred and seventy-six sexual abuse allegations, approximately two hundred and sixty-seven may be false allegations or very questionable, usually described as "unfounded" (Young, 1985).

There is some feeling of paranoia within the social services agencies. What if they close a case erroneously and there are additional allegations afterwards? It will appear they don't know their business. For this reason, cases are often kept open even after the initial investigation indicates no abuse. The child continues to be watched, perhaps sent to more therapy, while restrictions on visitation remain. In this case, the agency isn't protecting the child. It is actually abusing the rights of the child and the parent while protecting itself. The policies and procedures of these agencies need to be closely and carefully reviewed, while the competency and capability of the social and mental health care officials is questioned.

Agency workers need to be educated in the basics of the SAID Syndrome and have a standard list of investigative questions to be answered before making the automatic assumption of guilt. If the family is not intact, if there are divorce proceedings or a custody battle in process, or if visitation rights are an issue, the investigator needs to establish several facts. Who filed the initial complaint and why? What professionals evaluated the child and when? If the complaint came from the ex-spouse, were other relatives, neighbors and friends contacted and interviewed?

No one suggests that all social workers and psychologists lead children to confess. But, there is no protocol for interviewing children in suspected abuse cases, no rules insisting that *all* members of the family, including the accused, be interviewed before an evaluator decides the validity of an allegation. Because the stakes are so high, many critics say that inexperienced and poorly-trained interviewers are dangerous, that the ramifications of their interview techniques cannot be considered inconsequential or innocuous.

In his book, *The Battle and the Backlash*, Hechler quotes Michael Sands, a Sacramento defense attorney who has handled at least fifty sexual molestation cases over the past twenty some years. "The fact of the matter is that we have documented that the so-called experts—and this includes cops, and the psychologists, and the sex molest support teams—do not do an objective job of questioning the kid. They slant these kids, some of them. I'm not saying everyone."

Often, interviews conducted by therapists and social workers include techniques that are intrusive and suggestive, tainting the interview and rendering the information unreliable and unethical.

Leroy Schultz studied child protection workers recently and presents the following profile: self-righteous, unwilling to admit mistakes, lacking in ethics, naive about children, willing to use hearsay evidence, likely to conduct one-sided investigations, blind to contradictory input. ("The Social Worker and the Sexually Abused Minor: Where are We Going?", 1985)

Several recent studies lead to some disturbing conclusions. Child protection workers often appear determined to find evidence of wrongdoing in order to make themselves look good. Promotions are sometimes given to police officers who have a good record of convictions. An increased case load allows social workers and state agencies to cry for more funds, more staff and greater authority over families, child care workers, and teachers.

In their defense, the number of cases assigned to individual workers may have a strongly negative effect on the ability to properly and thoroughly investigate allegations. However, too often, the job performance of all those involved in the "investigation" of these allegations is measured by the number of "wins" they have in either suspension of parental rights in family court or court judgements of criminal charges. In addition, few social workers are trained in the art of investigation; more often, their background and education is in the therapeutic treatment of abused individuals. While therapy is certainly necessary in cases of abuse, it needs to be separated out from the initial investigative process. Therapy may lead to reinforcement of fiction, causing the child to become convinced the abuse is a fact, since positive reinforcement of expected behavior and actions is what children are taught to respond to. Accordingly, the child in this situation begins to think he or she has actually been abused.

Most social workers have little or no training in the use of the dolls, which are standard equipment for many Child Protection Teams. A social worker usually has a collection of information from the ex-wife, doctors, perhaps relatives, teachers, or neighbors, which would cause him/her to be biased and have a set of preconceived notions as to what to expect from a child suspected to have been abused. Researchers at Case Western Reserve University School of Medicine state that the objectivity of the interviewer is imperative, and advocate that the interviewer receive no prior information relative to abuse and be told only the child's name and his/her birth date.

Schultz (1989) reported on a survey done in 1986, where one hundred questionnaires were completed by individuals who had been acquitted of false allegations made in ten states. Forty-four percent of the respondents felt the social worker was unskilled in investigation of the suspect and in child victim interviewing. Sixteen percent felt the social worker was biased in favor of the charge before the investigation ever took place. Eight percent felt no warrant would have been issued if the first interrogation of the alleged victim and suspect had been videotaped.

The following issues and questions were raised in a motion to amend motion for rehearing, filed by my attorney, that pointed out flaws, inconsistencies, and errors in testimony allowed, hearsay testimony heard and allowed, and denial of constitutional rights to face and cross-examine the witnesses against me.

HRS and child protection team personnel have been often known to draw erroneous conclusions, to use interview and other techniques not scientifically reliable, to use unproven protocols or go outside established guidelines, to unintentionally lead children to desired answers and actions, to fail to examine, explain, or rule out other causes for what they and others observed, and to draw conclusions from incomplete or suspect data.

In addition to these issues, the motion raised a number of questions about the videotaped interview with Diane, the child protection team coordinator and the anatomically complete dolls. Why did the video tape have obvious gaps? What happened during those gaps?

On the tape, the child protection team interviewer refers to a prior interview(s) and session(s) with the dolls. What happened during those prior interviews and doll sessions? Who conducted them? How long did they last? What methods, protocols, and techniques were used? Were they reliable? Were they faithfully followed? Was Diane coached or lead? Intentionally or unintentionally? How many times was her performance practiced before the video was made?

What other explanations exist to account for Diane's behavior on the video tape? Could she, in fact, have been trying to demonstrate innocent or appropriate behavior? Innocent behavior that, with the misinterpretation or contrivance of HRS and CPT, was made to appear inappropriate?

It is interesting to note that, during the course of the Colorado case, the county social services agency failed miserably in a management audit conducted after the County Board of Commissioners received numerous complaints from citizens. The county officials recommended a review, by an outside agency, of all child-abuse and -neglect cases handled by that department, to determine if they were handled properly. Unfortunately, that review was never carried out. However, the county Social Services chief found the staff was not adequately trained, they had not been properly supervised or directed, and the record keeping was inadequate. He also determined that few of the social workers involved in the child-abuse cases were qualified for the work they were doing.

Ken Pangborn, president of Men International, Inc. and a recognized expert in the field of child sexual abuse allegations, is personally aware of the flaws within the social services system. Shortly after his conversation with the social services agency in Wisconsin, Ken learned of the Father's Rights Movement and did file for custody of his three children. His wife's response was allegations of inappropriate sexual conduct which, although nebulous, was sufficient in the midwest at the time. Later allegations made by his wife were more specific.

Chapter Twelve

The Courts

The following quotations are taken from the *Liberator*, June 1990:

Judge J. L., Houston County, GA: "*I feel that everything else being equal, that there is no substitute for a mother, and custody of this child is awarded to the mother.*"

Judge R. J. N., Douglas County, GA: "*I ain't never seen the calves follow the bull, they always follow the heifer; therefore I always give custody to the mamas.*"

Judge I. J., Fulton County, GA: "*Many things change, but some things don't change, and children belong with their mothers, especially younger children.*"

Judge R. W., Gwinnette County, GA: "*I don't believe in joint custody and won't order it. Since both parents are equal, I have no choice but to award custody based upon traditional gender factors, and therefore award sole custody to the mother.*"

Rep. D. G., Macon, GA: "*A bad mama is better than no mama at all.*"

Judge R. F., Cobb County GA: (When confronted with direct evidence of adultery by the mother and the exposure of the child to the mother's conduct) "*These are the eighties and that type of behavior is more accepted now.*"

While these attitudes are not shared by all who serve in our judicial system, these quotations unfortunately represent the prevailing attitude in many of the family/juvenile courts across the country. In spite of the age of liberation and much-touted equality of the sexes, when it comes to children, mothers, and gender bias, our judicial system is not particularly enlightened, it appears. The aforementioned judicial remarks go beyond giving custody to the mother because the child is of "judicial tender years."

Consistently, the case studies reviewed for this book have shown clear indications that neither parent is the perfect parent and that both parents may have some difficulty in the area of proper or adequate parenting skills. However, even when the mother needs assistance from social services and requires parenting classes, it is usually the mother who receives custody and parenting assistance, rather than the father, even when there is no proof or validation of abuse on his part. In Mark Doe's case, the children were placed in the mother's custody, despite the fact that her live-in boyfriend had a documented history of child sexual abuse and the criminal charges against Mr. Doe had been dropped. In my case, the children were placed with their mother, who had been proven, in court, to be an unfit parent.

Child sexual abuse cases can involve one or all of five basic court arenas. Our judicial system provides for more than one type of court and the individual facing allegations of child sexual abuse may well end up fighting on multiple fronts, battling prejudicial judges, biased social and mental health workers, hearsay evidence, and laws that act to his detriment. Each court has a specific purpose, a designated area of authority. Be aware that the findings of one court may have no effect on the findings of another.

The family or juvenile court deals with the settling of custody disputes, visitation rights, and determination of the restriction or removal of parental rights. The criminal courts hold trials, based on an indictment brought against the alleged abuser by a grand jury. Civil suits are filed in state and/or federal court to recover compensatory damages. The appellate court rules on appeals of a criminal court decision or family court ruling. The federal courts deal with complaints regarding violation of one's civil or constitutional rights.

Not only can this system require pursuit of charges on more than one front, it may well mean the necessity of retaining more than one attorney. A lawyer who is skilled in the battles of the trial court, where juries must be convinced and arguments prepared and presented to meet the trial court's official and unofficial protocol, may be totally ineffective in a family court or judge's chamber and vice versa. The time frames and procedures adhered to in civil court and federal court are not the same as those outlined for family or criminal court. An attorney without the experience and expertise required in the particular arena in which you are doing battle can do as much harm as good.

The juvenile court system dawned at the very end of the nineteenth century and remains with us today. This movement was not spearheaded by lawyers, but by social workers who envisioned an environment of informality and intimacy that gathered all kinds of evidence, not strictly evidentiary. Matters of due process and parental rights took on a new meaning within the juvenile justice system; the court's authority was to include determination of the child's welfare and what was in the best interest of the child. A major purpose was to remove the juvenile court from the rigid procedure of the criminal court, thus eliminating the requirement for due process.

The family or juvenile court has a great deal of power. Within our judicial system, these courts often seem to operate differently under the burden of determining the validity of child sexual abuse allegations. In my research, the presumption of innocence appears to be ignored. The right of the accused to face his accuser is brushed aside, in the best interest of the children. Hearsay evidence, usually disallowed in the criminal courts, is sufficient to separate a father from his children for the rest of his life. Interview results, involving anatomical dolls, are often admissible and relied upon by the social service workers who present the information as expert witnesses, in spite of the fact that there is no research to support the validity or credibility of information garnered through the use of the dolls.

The standard of proof in family court is lower than in the criminal courts, which require evidence "beyond a reasonable doubt." Family courts require only that a case be proved prima facie, by a "preponderance of the evidence" or by "clear and

convincing evidence." Hearsay testimony—an out of court statement that is not made under oath, that is repeated by someone to
whom the statement was made and that cannot be cross-examined
in the courtroom—is allowed in the family or juvenile court
system.

These courts often have an unstated agenda for "doing something" about child abuse. If an objective review of the validity
and credibility of hearsay statements were to be instituted, it could
well result in the defendant having a better than even chance of
prevailing. This, however, would produce a result that is inconsistent with "doing something." The family courts, in cases where
there is no definite right or wrong conclusion, i.e., the case is
deemed "indeterminable," will always err on the side of caution,
protecting the child from any possible harm.

Unfortunately, family courts are often not taken seriously by
many in the judicial system, primarily because of the lack of
experience and expertise exhibited by many of the attorneys, the
social workers who offer testimony and even the judges who sit
on the bench. Given the autonomy of the social service agencies
and the looseness of requirements in family court when it comes
to solid evidence, it often appears the scales of justice may be
tipped in the direction of the accuser, particularly if that accuser
is an adult who has the opportunity and motive to influence a very
young child's actions and speech.

Doctors and other professionals, whose reports are used by the
prosecution, are often not available for cross-examination during
juvenile dependency hearings. Videotapes that have never been
seen by the accused, or his attorney, or the court, may be entered
as evidence by the social services agency and are accepted by the
court. For this reason, fighting false allegations in the juvenile
courts is often more frustrating, more difficult, and more time
consuming than fighting charges in criminal court.

Throughout my entire and lengthy ordeal, all motions, orders
and restrictions placed on me were based on hearsay evidence.
The only evidence used to support findings was from the court
recording of proceedings of a dependency hearing, hearsay testimony by an HRS worker, referring to a video tape of a child
interrogation. No admissible evidence was produced at any time,

by any party, at any hearing, to prove by a preponderance of the evidence that my daughter was ever sexually abused or that I was the perpetrator. In actuality, we proved by a preponderance of the evidence my innocence, and the lack of substance to my former wife's allegations.

A further problem often encountered in family courts is the fact that the key or primary witnesses may be social workers with little experience in investigation or courtroom procedures. While we recognize that there are many competent and caring professionals in these fields, there are also many social workers who are not only inexperienced, but overworked and undertrained. This may be due, in large part, to the high turnover in the social service agencies that results from burnout, frustration, low pay, and limited resources. While police officers, who may be called as witnesses, are trained investigators, few of them are knowledgeable or experienced in interviewing young children, or in areas of child development. These witnesses make it difficult for the defense attorney to identify the basic causes, motives, and actions that may be crucial to an objective rendering of a decision by a relatively inexperienced judge.

Law guardians, legal representatives for minors, were not developed until the early 1960s. These attorneys-ad-litem are supposed to serve in the best interests of the children, but time constraints and other outside factors often prohibit this.

In custody and visitation disputes, Guardian ad Litems (GALs) often become involved, especially where there are allegations of abuse, as in SAID Syndrome cases. These individuals are volunteers, trained by social service workers and appointed by the family court judge. Their function is to watch out for the best interests of the children and to act as mediators for the ex-spouses or adversarial parties. One of the functions often served by the GAL is to act as supervisor in cases of restricted, supervised visitation.

As seen in the cases presented in this book, and others reviewed for additional information, the GAL often enters a case with the belief that abuse has occurred. Prior to meeting the accused parent, they have usually interviewed the social workers involved in the case, the child protection team workers who conducted the interrogation, and the accusing mother. Although these volunteers often possess the common sense necessary to cope with the day-to-day aspects of supervision, they usually have no psychological education or expertise. Nonetheless, their opinions and recommendations regarding the accused and the children are frequently rubber-stamped by judges in the family courts.

In the interest of protecting the rights of the falsely accused in the family courts, a court monitor system has been developed by the Family Coalition of Florida and, at last report, is being successfully used in some parts of Florida and other states. The court monitor system places family advocates in the juvenile and family courtrooms and reports observations to the media, giving judges incentive to pay more attention to the needs of the family. The Naples, Florida VOCAL (Valuing Our Children and Laws) reports that after two months, judges were expecting HRS to back up their recommendations and allegations.

Court monitors are volunteers. To institute a court monitor program, call or write to your juvenile judges' office and explain the situation. For example, "I represent (organization name, such as Family Coalition, the Family Rights Committee or VOCAL) that helps families having problems. We understand that the hearings are open unless a child victim will be testifying. We want to begin visiting in the courtrooms during hearings as 'friends of the court.' What is the procedure you want us to follow?" Once you know how the court wishes to proceed, the volunteers can begin their work. Each court monitor should be provided with identifying badges. Monitors should show up at the proper time, properly attired, with pencil and clipboard for taking notes. A prepared checklist is recommended, as the hearings proceed at a rapid rate. A sample checklist is included as Appendix C, at the end of this book. Monitors should follow mandated procedures, observing mandates regarding as no talking during sessions and such. Weekly reports, with no names included, are sent to the media.

There are several advantages to considering the Court Monitor program. First, families get a better shot at judicial justice while the organization(s) sponsoring the program gain more understanding of the judicial processes. This program provides an opportunity to observe which attorneys are working to protect their clients' rights and allows an insight into which HRS personnel, GALs, doctors, and such, are more vigorous in their prosecution of families.

In cases of child sexual abuse, the allegations often result in criminal charges being filed, either by the accusing parent or through the agency doing the investigation and therapy, with the state attorney's office determining the extent and severity of the charges. One of the first problems in being faced with criminal charges of child sexual abuse is the fact that, again, the presumption of innocence doesn't seem to apply. The burden of proof almost immediately shifts to the accused, as opposed to the dictates of our judicial system and the sociological premise of "innocent until proven guilty."

Indictment by a grand jury on criminal charges is accomplished by the prosecutor presenting his case. Only the prosecutor determines what evidence is to be presented and only the prosecutor is present, not the accused nor his attorneys.

Be aware that the prosecutor enters information at *his* discretion, especially when facing the Grand Jury in an attempt to get an indictment. In Spiegel's case, four certifications verifying the events of the weekend of alleged abuse were never shown to the Grand Jury. A letter from the physician, stating that his examination under no circumstances revealed any evidence of child abuse, was never presented. The psychological certification, provided by the doctor seeing Speigel's ex-wife for psychological counseling, was withheld. That certification stated that she had indicated to the psychologist that she had spent two days convincing her daughter to hate her daddy, that she had talked at length about her family's hatred of Larry Spiegel, and indicated that the ex-wife was capable of projecting her own emotional turmoil, doubt, and sexual pathology to her daughter.

In the Smith case in Ohio, the attending psychologist was available to testify at the hearing regarding temporary custody and visitation of Janice and Johnny. Since referral from the state social services agency, the psychologist had seen the children over a period of twenty months, for purposes of on-going counseling and monitoring the progress of the children. She had seen each child twenty-six times on a weekly basis. The judge in the case determined there would be no witnesses, other than a social worker and the agency appointed physician, both witnesses for Mrs. Smith. Worse, he ordered that the children be removed from Mr. Smith's home and live with Mrs. Smith until the trial, having only visitation with Mr. Smith. The children's psychologist expressed concern over the one-sided nature of the judge, stating it would seem more reasonable to hear from professionals on both sides regarding the children's well-being. The best interests of the children were not served by precluding Mr. Smith from presenting any of his witnesses.

A civil court law suit may be filed to recover damages for the alleged victim, the child. In this day of lawsuits for almost any reason, a number of individuals are liable to end up in civil court, including doctors who do not report suspected abuse or exhibit malpractice, social workers who abruptly remove children from their homes (sometimes to foster care when actual physical or sexual abuse occurs), public officials for improper investigation, and the accuser on grounds of slander and libel. The accused may find himself facing a suit in civil court, seeking long-term damages for the emotional and psychological pain and suffering of the alleged victim, invasion of privacy, wrongful torts, etc.

The alleged perpetrator may file a civil suit in state and/or federal court to reclaim damages resulting from the false allegation. And finally, once a father attains at least joint custody, should he notice that the child suffers emotionally and/or physically in the future, he can file a suit on behalf of the child.

Any appeal of a trial judge's decision must be taken to the appellate court for further hearing and decision. This is also the avenue to pursue when appealing rulings in family court. One has thirty days to appeal a trial court order. This appeal involves filing a Notice to Appeal and having the party who is the appellee served with that notice. The appeals process is a slow, grinding procedure. The appeals courts are inundated with what are termed "trivial" appeals, coercing justices to skim by bona fide appeals, rendering them injustices. Ninety-five percent of all domestic appeals heard by the appellate courts in Florida are ruled Per Curiam Affirmed (PCA), meaning that the appellate court has reaffirmed the lower court or trial court decision and the appellant loses. Moreover, the appellate courts usually do not even render an opinion with their PCA order. There is a three-fold reason for this lack of opinion:

1) The appellate courts are inundated with cases and just don't have the time to devote to your appeal;
2) For reasons of politics and prestige, the higher court doesn't like to "muddy the waters" by overturning a lower court's decision;
3) If the appellate court *does* render an opinion along with their PCA order, it allows the appellant information that can be used to appeal that order to the State Supreme Court. A PCA, accompanied by no opinion, usually will not be heard by the higher court.

When an appellant appeals a trial court order, the appellant or his attorney must file an initial brief. The brief can be no longer than fifty pages and it must incorporate statements of the facts, arguments to be made, cited authorities, state statute codes, any errors made, and appellant's conclusions. Of course, the appellee can answer with an answering brief on the merits of the brief and the case.

If one receives a PCA ruling from the appellate court, the next steps you may take include a Motion for Rehearing, a Rehearing En Banc (heard by entire panel of judges), or a Motion for Certification in trying to go to the Supreme Court.

Federal court is the arena to which the falsely accused may turn when lodging complaints regarding violation of one's civil and constitutional rights. When one sues in federal court, for injustices that occurred in the midst of a SAID Syndrome case, one is alleging that he or she was denied "due process of law." One would be alleging that, in the context of the SAID Syndrome case, the child protection team and/or the former wife did not act in good faith and/or that the child protection team acted "ultra vires" or beyond their reasonable authority.

42 U.S.C. 1983 is a very meaningful Federal section being utilized by victims of SAID Syndrome cases today. I am suing my former wife and the HRS under this section, in combination with the Sixth and Fourteenth Amendments. The gist of 42 U.S.C. 1983 is that the plaintiff must show cause that the defendant(s) acted beyond their reasonable authority "under color of state law." Be aware that the federal courts, like the appellate courts, are inundated with a heavy caseload. Again, it's hurry up and wait and seems that justice may be denied, not just delayed.

Federal rulings can be appealed to a higher federal court or even to the U.S. Supreme Court. One must be aware that an Abstinence Doctrine in a motion to dismiss by the defendant can disallow an equitable claim to be heard in federal court and it will go back to the state court. Also, the social services agencies will cling to the Eleventh Amendment in federal court, claiming that they have sovereign immunity. Finally, one must be cautious and diligent and seek and hire an attorney competent in that particular court arena.

In most states, the criminal and family courts have independent functions. Even after the alleged abuser is acquitted in criminal court, the accusing parent can file motions in family court to restrict or prevent visitation. The Family Court is obligated to decide in the "best interest of the child," based upon its own hearings and/or trial. Victims of false accusations seldom realize that, in spite of their acquittal at other levels, the Family Court hearings are necessary before they have their parental rights reinstated, including the right to see their children.

Issues of custody or managing conservator and visitation are determined separately from issues of criminal guilt. Never attempt to predict what a family court judge will do, and never expect them to provide reasons or explanations concerning their orders.

Bear in mind, the agencies and the courts need to cover their backs, make sure that they can justify their actions and their budgets. So what if they appear to lose the case in the criminal court? Because of the different requirements in family court, the accused may well be deemed guilty of abuse there and prevented from seeing his children. Thus, the agency is vindicated in the charges brought against the alleged perpetrator and in their demand for a court hearing regarding the child's welfare.

Bill Dodd, a Miami electrician, has been in and out of court for six years, trying to restore his visitation rights. In 1986, his ex-wife accused him of molesting his daughter. The police cleared Dodd of the charges, and he won a three hundred and fifty thousand dollar slander judgement against his ex-wife. But a family court judge *still* cut off all contact between father and daughter, ruling there was a "probability of abuse."

In SAID Syndrome cases, the majority of the battles will be fought in the family or juvenile court, in an effort to resolve the issues of custody and visitation. It is critical that you locate and retain an attorney well versed in these issues, knowledgeable about SAID cases and familiar with the policies, politics and procedures of family court.

An uninformed or incompetent attorney can cost you the right to see your children for years. In one case study, the accused's attorney advised him to plea bargain, pleading no contest to a charge of physical abuse. The juvenile court used that plea to forbid the father any contact with his children, even thought the criminal charges had been dropped and his ex-wife had admitted to concocting the allegations.

In another case, an attorney who was inexperienced in the area of child sexual abuse allegations, recommended that his client accept a plea bargain offer that included admitting to sexual contact with his three-year-old daughter in the interest of obtaining deferred prosecution. If the client would admit to the allegation, he would receive two years probation and criminal charges would be dropped. However, this action would give the family court all the ammunition they needed to forbid him to ever see his kids again.

In the Mark Doe case, an inexperienced attorney advised Mark that he had no alternative but to meet the ultimatum issued by his ex-wife's attorney in requiring him to admit his son to an institution.

There are numerous instances where the rights of the accused are ignored. The Confrontation Clause is meant to aid in the truth-finding process and protect the right to cross-examine one's accusers. The Constitution requires that a person who has been accused by another has a right to confront his accuser in the flesh, and not through an alternate or substitute. In addressing the problems of an adult substituting for a child witness, a unanimous panel of the North Carolina Court of Appeals stated that where the witness is the principal accuser and the only person, except for the defendant, to have firsthand knowledge of the crime and related events, the appointment of an alternate might deprive the jury of crucial facts which only the witness knows and might reveal in cross-examination.

In 1988, the United States Supreme Court identified a two-part test for determining when the Confrontation Clause must yield to admissibility of hearsay statements. "The proponent (1) must show the necessity for using the hearsay declaration, i.e., the unavailability of the witness, and (2) must demonstrate the inherent trustworthiness of the declaration."

Unavailability occurs when the prosecution has made a "good faith effort" to obtain a witness's presence at trial but has failed. While there may be a number of reasons for unavailability, such as the witness's refusal to testify, memory loss, or death of the witness, in the context of child abuse, several courts have held that a child declared incompetent to testify is unavailable with this ruling. This rationale raises one very important question: If a child is incompetent to testify (i.e., he lacks the prerequisites to be a witness), how can his hearsay statements be said to be trustworthy enough to satisfy the trustworthiness requirement of the ruling?

Because no one is in favor of child abuse and everyone wants to do their part for children, there has been a steady erosion of the accused's right to confront his accuser and a corresponding rise in the use of hearsay.

There is an ongoing controversy surrounding the right of the accused to face his accuser and the potential emotional damage to a child witness. Justice Scalia explained the Confrontation Clause in a recent opinion, Coy v. Iowa, supra, 866: "It is always more difficult to tell a lie about a person 'to his face' than 'behind his back' . . . That face-to-face presence may, unfortunately, upset the truthful rape victim or abused child; but by the same token, it may confound and undo the false accuser or reveal the child coached by a malevolent adult."

Conversely, a recent Supreme Court ruling states that, in alleged child abuse cases, one does not have the right to face one's accuser!

Where analysis of the trustworthiness of hearsay statements is involved, two troubling questions arise: 1) How does a judicial finding of incompetency reflect on the child's hearsay statement? 2) When the statements are a result of some pseudo-scientific procedure, such as a child's play with so-called "anatomically correct" dolls, are those statements accurate and inherently trustworthy?

A young child is called to the stand and, after examination by both attorneys, is ruled incompetent by the judge, based on the child's lack of ability to communicate effectively and not under-standing the difference between truth and falsehood. Is it right to then presume that the story the child related to a doctor or social worker six months ago is inherently trustworthy and satisfies the dictates of the Confrontation Clause? If the term "unavailability" is used to show the child's inability to appreciate the truth, it is difficult to credit anything the child has said earlier as inherently trustworthy. Does a statement made by an incompetent child witness become competent or trustworthy because an adult repeats that statement? The declarant's competency is a precon-dition to admission of his hearsay statements, as are other tes-timonial qualifications.

Child competency and hearsay relevancy hearings are a neces-sity for an alleged perpetrator involved in a SAID case. These hearings can be made reality by the accused's attorney via mo-tions, and will usually be heard by the juvenile court judge, for they are incorporated as dependency proceedings.

The purpose of a trial is to discover the truth. Unfortunately, it may instead become a crusade to get a conviction, manipulate the witnesses and distort the facts for the good of the client. This is too often true of both the prosecutor and the defending attorney, who may feel he has to fight fire with fire. What seems to be lost in the shuffle of legal moves and strategies are the child, the defendant, their emotions, and the resultant psychological effects.

In an article in the Denver *Post* on April 9, 1989, James Selkin made the following statement. "The many people I have known who have been falsely accused of sexual abuse of a child have all agreed that the American justice system, for them, proved a sham. It did not result in the restoration of their reputation, their livelihood or their good name."

Under the heading "search for truth," perhaps the truth to be recognized is that often a lawyer, whether prosecuting or defending, does not, in fact, want the court or jury to reach a sound, educated result or even guess, if it is not in the best interest of his particular client. Where, then, is the best interest of the child truly considered, protected, and defended?

Chapter Thirteen

A Critical Review

In several of the case studies reviewed for this book, the individuals involved provided us with a number of evaluations and analyses that were done during the course of their attempts to regain at least visitation rights, if not custody rights, during and after the divorce.

Many of the evaluations were done by objective, third-party professionals, who documented the situations that had evolved during the divorce and subsequent custody battle. These evaluations, which included review of previous documentation, covered not only the psychological conditions of all parties involved, but the therapies applied, the interviewing techniques used, and the overall scope of events. While much of the information actually identifies problems and suggests solutions, it is important to see what qualified professionals have to say about the manner in which many alleged child sexual abuse situations are handled.

The issues raised and the points made in the following evaluations come from professionals in the fields of child development and child sexual abuse, professionals who are recognized nationally and, in some cases, internationally as experts in their fields.

These evaluations serve to indicate the many problems existing in our current approach to resolving allegations of child sexual abuse and underscore the necessity of properly qualifying and training all social workers who deal with these allegations. They also sound a warning to anyone falsely accused—a warning to secure adequate counsel, to attempt to prohibit therapy and continuing interrogations, to seek expert, outside evaluations and to constantly and consistently assert your innocence, maintain contact with your children and be aware of the people, policies, and procedures against which you are fighting.

Dr. Ralph Underwager and Hollida Wakefield were asked to do objective, third-party evaluations of the doll interview with Diane Tong and the psychological evaluation done by the court-appointed psychiatrist in the William Smith case. Presented below is the transcript from Diane's doll interview, including the actions of Diane and the interviewer, followed by excerpts from the Underwager and Wakefield evaluation of that interview.

Diane was interviewed by a Child Protection Team coordinator and the interview was videotaped. As is usually the case, the interview took place in the child protection team offices, an environment unfamiliar to the child.

Interviewer: Can you remember what my name is? Why don't you sit over here so you can look at me better and look at the camera, too. [Interviewer changes positions with Diane] Okay, you sit right over here. Okay. There. Remember what my name is?

Diane: [nods]

Interviewer: Hmmm? What's my name? Hmmm? Do you remember? [Diane shrugs] Should I tell you again? My name is Susan. And what's your name?

Diane: Diane.

Interviewer: Diane? And how old are you?

Diane: Three and a half.

Interviewer: Three and a half. That's a big girl. And where do you live?

Diane: [no response]

Interviewer: Hmmm?

Diane: I don't live.

Interviewer: You don't live?

Diane: No. My daddy do.

Interviewer: Oh.

Diane: Dean do.

Interviewer: Oh, oh. Is that your daddy's name? What's your mommy's name?

Diane: Carla.

Interviewer: Oh, that's a pretty name. How about your brother? [Diane squirms, wiggles and looks around, moving away] Diane, I want you to sit right here, okay. What's your brother's name?

Diane: Kit.

Interviewer: Okay, Diane, the reason why we're going to talk on the floor this time is so that you don't have to keep talking to people all the time, okay?

Diane: (Unintelligible)

Interviewer: Well, we're going to talk one more time about what happened this morning and it's going to be on this camera so that other people can see it later, okay?

Diane: [nods]

Interviewer: And I'm going to bring these—the dolls—down here again, okay? We'll put them down here this time. Do you want to name the dolls?

Diane: Yeah.

Interviewer: Okay, what's this doll's name?

Diane: [Points to man doll] Dean Tong.

Interviewer: Uh, okay. And what's this doll's name?

Diane: Diane.

Interviewer: Diane, what a pretty name.

Diane: Diane Cook.

Interviewer: What's her last name?

Diane: Diane Cook.

Interviewer: Oh, okay. Okay. Now, Remember where we were when, when we talked about this before, what room that we were in?

Diane: [nods]

Interviewer: What room was, did that happen in?

Diane: [shrugs]

Interviewer: Hmmm? What were you getting ready to do?

Diane: [shrugs]

Interviewer: Was it daytime or nighttime?

Diane: The nighttime.

Interviewer: Nighttime. So what did Diane have on?

Diane: [points at doll] These on.

Interviewer: Okay. [picks up doll] Do you want to show me again. Okay, you can show me with the Diane doll what she had on. Was she sitting up or was she laying down?

Diane: Laying down.

Interviewer: Okay. Want to lay her down?

Diane: [nods] [Interviewer helps arrange doll.]

Interviewer: Her arms move, you have to kind of press her legs down, that's right. Were her arms down?

Diane: [nods]

Interviewer: Okay. Now you show me what she had on.

Diane: [Removes the dolls shoes. Looks at interviewer and points to doll's stomach]

Interviewer: What, what with this?

Diane: With these.

Interviewer: Okay, you take them off. I'll hold her down so she doesn't move. Is that elastic kind of tight? I think if you go like this, boy, she's a big (garbled). There.

Diane: [points at doll]

Interviewer: Okay. This is Diane and you have to, is she sleeping?

Diane: [nods]

Interviewer: Okay. Now, who is this again?

Diane: Dean Tong.

Interviewer: Okay. What did Dean Tong have on? Hmmm? What did he have on?

Diane: This.

Interviewer: Okay, and this is like—what do you call that?

Diane: A shirt.

Interviewer: A shirt. What do you call these?

Diane: Pants.

Interviewer: Okay. Do—what about these?

Diane: Shoes.

Interviewer: Shoes. And he had those on, okay. Why don't you show me then what happened.

Diane: There's a pee-pee and butt.

Interviewer: Oh, there is? Which one's her pee-pee? [Repositions doll]

Diane: [points]

Interviewer: That one? And where's, and where's the butt?

Diane: [points]

Interviewer: That one there, okay. Okay, you show me with the Dean doll what happened.

Diane: [takes Dean doll's hand, places it on the Diane doll's crotch] He put her, his, his finger in there. [Laughter and talking in background]

Interviewer: Okay. Anything else?

Diane: Put his finger in there.

Interviewer: Anything else?

Diane: And I started crying.

Interviewer: Oh no, 'cause that didn't feel good. Any other thing that, that happened?

Diane: Him used other fingers.

Interviewer: Used other fingers?

Diane: [nods]

Interviewer: Okay, you can show me again with other fingers. [Holds Dean doll] Okay. Like that. What about anything else?*Diane:*I don't know.

Interviewer: Okay. Did any other parts touch the Diane doll? Touch Diane here?

Diane: [nods]

Interviewer: Okay. You can show me that. Okay, but any other parts that Dean touched Diane with. Can you show me. . .

Diane: [referring to male doll] What's in here?

Interviewer: Hmmm?

Diane: What's in here?

Interviewer: Well, did Dean have his pants zippered or unzippered?

Diane: Zippered.

Interviewer: Okay, then we'll leave it like that. Okay. You can tell me anything else, is there anything else that the Dean doll did?

Diane: [shrugs]

Interviewer: Hmmm?

Diane: [shrugs]

Interviewer: You can show me.

Diane: [begins undressing doll] What's in there?

Interviewer: Hmmm? I don't know. What is in there? What's in there? What's that called?

Diane: I don't know.

Interviewer: You don't know.

Diane: [shakes head]

Interviewer: Have you ever seen that before?

*Diane:*No.

Interviewer: Okay, then we better close that back up, right? Okay. Can you get that? There, okay. Now, did Dean do anything else to Diane? [Touches girl doll's lower stomach] Anything else, touch her anywhere, bad touches? What?

Diane: [shrugs]

Interviewer: Hmmm?

Diane: [shrugs]

Interviewer: Any other parts of Dean? [Interviewer holds male doll's hand, then sits male doll up between her and Diane]

Diane: [shakes head]

Interviewer: Sure?

Diane: Uh uh [shakes head]. I got to put those back on.

Interviewer: Okay, okay, if you want to put those back on. Okay. Thank you, Diane.At this point, the interviewer stands and starts toward the camera. The camera is turned off, then back on.

Interviewer: [walks on-camera] Okay. Diane, one more thing, another thing I wanted to ask about is this morning, [picks up male doll] you talked to me about something else that Dean did to you. Do you remember any parts of the, any other parts of his body that he put on you? Hmmm?

Diane: [referring to doll] This is the pee-pee and this is the butt.

Interviewer: Right, okay. Do you remember this, this morning when you showed me that Dean put his mouth on Diane?

Diane: [nods] [There is more background noise of talking and laughter]

Interviewer: Can you show me that again?

Diane: [nods, takes dolls]

Interviewer: Let's lie her back down again like she was. [Interviewer positions doll] Okay. Okay.

Diane: [shows dolls]

Interviewer: What part of his body is that, Diane?

Diane: I don't know.

Interviewer: What, do you know what part of the body this is?

Diane: [nods]

Interviewer: What is it?

Diane: A mouth.

Interviewer: So is that the part of the body?

Diane:[nods]

Interviewer: Okay. Can you show it one more time?

Diane: [nods]

Interviewer: Okay. [Moves dolls closer to Diane] With the, with his mouth. Okay, you going to show me again?

Diane: [nods] [Moves male doll so face covers the crotch of the girl doll]

Interviewer: Okay. That's all?

Child: [nods]

Interviewer: Okay, well you've been a real good girl and you've helped me a lot. Okay?

Diane: [nods]

Interviewer: Okay, now you can dress the doll. Let me give you her clothes, Okay.

*Diane:*I can't do this.

Interviewer: Oh, okay, I can. I can help you.

Once again the camera is turned off, then on. The interviewer is sitting beside her desk and identifies herself and her agency as well as Diane, the child's age, the location of the office and the date and time.

The actual tape of the above interview was reviewed and analyzed by Dr. Ralph Underwager, Hollida Wakefield, and the research staff of the Institute for Psychological Therapies, recognized professional experts in the field child sexual abuse and sexual offenders.

The analysis showed that the interviewer was three times as active as the child, providing seventy-six percent of the total statements in the interview. Sixty-four percent of the interview, or almost two thirds of the adult actions, were comprised of leading questions, closed questions, modeling, pressure and/or reward type behavior or questions, paraphrasing of the child's statements by the interviewer and use of anatomically correct dolls. All of these behaviors have been found to introduce error in the information elicited during such an interview.

The analysis stated that this was the thirty-seventh such analysis of interviews. The interviewer in the Tong analysis asked slightly fewer questions of the child, but used anatomically correct dolls twice as much as interviewers in previous studies. The child responded with more affirmations and provided more descriptive statements than children in previous studies. This is not surprising, since the sheer volume of pointed instructions and questions used by the interviewer in conjunction with the use of the dolls may have served to keep the child focused on the task of responding at a very high rate.

The concluding paragraph of the letter that accompanied the analysis bears consideration. "In this particular case, it is clear that this is not the first interview of Diane. The interviewer reminds the child about when they talked about this before. When the dolls are brought out and the interviewer asks, 'What's this doll's name?', Diane immediately replies, 'Dean Tong.' Children, particularly those as young as Diane was in this interview, simply do not spontaneously use the dolls to signify actual people in their lives. Diane's readiness to label the dolls as herself and Dean and to demonstrate with the dolls indicates that she has been taught to do this in an earlier interview. This earlier, undocumented interview was likely much more leading and suggestive even than this one."

This videotape was admitted as evidence and viewed by the family court judge, who subsequently determined that I should not be allowed visitation with my children. The obvious references to previous practices were ignored. ("We're going to talk one more time"; "Remember where we were when we talked about this before?"; "Do you want to show me again?"). When questioning failed to elicit the desired response—exhibits of abuse—the interviewer left the area and the camera was turned off for an undetermined period of time. When the interviewer returned, the first statement included, "This morning you talked to me about something else that Dean did to you." When there was no response from Diane, the interviewer asked, "Do you remember this morning when you showed me that Dean put his mouth on Diane?" After nine attempts to focus Diane, the interviewer succeeded in having Diane position the dolls to indicate the man doll touching the girl doll with his mouth.

The next two evaluations were done in connection with the Smith case. The first is a comprehensive evaluation of the myriad events involved in the case, done by Dr. Rice of Loyola University. The second evaluation, done by Underwager and Wakefield, applies to the conclusions of the agency-appointed psychologist, who is referred to as Dr. Nelson, presented as evidence in the Smith case.

In preparing her evaluation, Dr. Rice used an extensive series of tests and interviews, in an attempt to determine an objective and positive resolution to the ongoing custody problems and their effects on the two children.

Dr. Rice's evaluation included the following statements and information:

"In a city prideful of its Clinic Health resources, with a Child Protection Agency funded by federal and state tax dollars, the appalling mismanagement of this case of alleged sex abuse is worth a review to evaluate the competence of the so-called professional experts."

10/29/84 The teacher acted appropriately in reporting the allegations made by Mrs. Smith, which required investigation within twenty-four hours for the safety of the children.

11/2/84 It was three days later when Ms. L. interviewed Patricia and the children. If, as she stated in a letter to Mr. Smith, she suspected venereal disease or physical damage, why did she not take them immediately to a hospital emergency room, as is routine and mandatory? Why did she not state if she is a state licensed social worker or give her degree or use the official stationary of the County HSA? Why wait six days for a physical examination? This is highly incompetent professional behavior.

11/8/84 The memo from the M.D. is grossly medically deficient for a physical exam. Why were none of the following done, given the allegations of fellatio and rape: throat examination, throat culture, no mention of hymen, no culture or microscopic slide for vaginal irritation, no rape kit and procedure followed. The date of the alleged abuse was not noted. The stretching of rectal opening is a normal function of human beings for bowel movements. If anal intercourse was suspected, why no anal fissures and no culture taken. If Johnny had a reddened throat and irritated penis, why were no cultures taken nor photos taken for court?

11/9/84 The two-paragraph "report" by the psychologist is a professional disgrace. No description of the children is given, no quotations of what each child saw as a problem. "Sustained emotional disturbance" needs careful qualification, as it could be related to the setting, the way the interviewer behaved, the separation from home and their father. In December, this same psychologist gave Patricia an MMPI to complete at home. This is malpractice.

11/12/84 Audiotape with children made by CPT with leading and misleading interrogation.

11/16/84 William was having standard "tickle time" before putting children to bed. Patricia accused him of this being sexual abuse and hit him over the head with heel of shoe. Both children remember this incident. He called police.

12/3/84 William's son indicted for criminal sex abuse, arraigned and released on fifty thousand dollars bail, with help from English relatives in raising money.

12/24/84 Patricia withdrew about ten thousand dollars cash from personal and business accounts, moved herself and the children into a state-supported Battered Women's Shelter. There were no formal charges of battering made against husband. The shelter's criteria for eligibility and accountability should be examined, since this was more than an overnight emergency stay.

12/27/84 Patricia filed for divorce and custody.

01/4/85 Ms. L. of HHS alleged William sexually abused both children. No repeat medical report or psychological evaluation was done for children. Competence again in question.

William filed counterclaims for divorce and child custody. Guardian ad Litem appointed. William expressed concern for abduction as passports were missing. Why did Guardian fail to respond?

1/12/85 Patricia moved into duplex

1/20/85 Patricia approached William at concert box office about clothes, beds, and toys, which he took over to apartment. They dined and made love.

1/22/85 Patricia told him not to visit. William felt hopeless, despondent and suicidal. He began to take pills, but stopped himself and called her. She called police to check on him. After police, Patricia invited William for dinner, afterwards they made love. The next day Patricia tried to contact her stepson at his lodgings, but only talked to landlord's daughter.

1/23/85 Patricia called England and talked for forty-three minutes to her mother. Then told a local woman friend she was going to London via Toronto.

1/24/85 Patricia kidnapped Janice and Johnny to England, in spite of Court Custody and Guardian ad Litem. In London, filed for and was granted child custody by falsely alleging her stepson was found guilty of sex abuse in Ohio. Children became Wards of Court in Britain.

1/25/85 William called England when he found the duplex deserted. Grandmother lied about their presence in her home. William informed local police.

2/5/85 William received summons to be in England 3/4/85 for hearing. Tried to talk to his children in England, but was unable to do so because of interference from Patricia's family.

3/85 A lieutenant with the Ohio police wrote Patricia about leaving unlawfully with children and her availability for local case against her stepson. She requested expenses for return be paid and police agreed. She tried to cash a two thousand dollar check, but check bounced. Wrote to friend with keys and parking ticket for Toronto Airport, requesting her Honda be fetched.

3/6/85 Guardian ad Litem issued affidavit for return of Janice and Johnny to Ohio. Two full months of non-protective guardianship of the children entrusted to her makes it questionable whether this lady is competent or involved enough to deserve this trust.

3/12/85 William went to England, eventually managed to see children with police guard present. Reassured children and said he was trying to get them back home. Returned to U.S. via Toronto where, with police help, the keys and the card, he picked up the Honda.

3/12/85 Ohio Public Prosecutor heard from Patricia that she would not return. He dropped case against stepson as "Nolle Prosequi."

4/1/85 William went to England, certain he could regain children who were feloniously kidnapped, only to learn British Courts could disregard U.S. Jurisdiction. Tried to get help from Social Services to see children and managed a one-hour supervised visit. Children could not leave England.

6/14/85 William asked children if they truly wanted to return to U.S. They flew to the U.S. and immediately reported to police.

6/19/85 The appointed social worker for case recommended counselling for children with Ross Agency.

9/85 Patricia returned to U.S.

9/16/85 Court ruled neither parent was to remove the children from that jurisdiction.

9/27/85 William took MMPI with J M and Patricia repeated previous MMPI with Ross. Visitation conflicts continued.

11/8/85 Court ordered William to pay five hundred twenty dollars a month child support to Patricia, despite the fact the children were living with him.

1/27/86 Patricia submitted affidavit stating William is violent to children. Both children deny statement.

2/1/86 Dr. Nelson's highly biased interpretation of MMPIs showing blatant skew towards minimizing Patricia's pathology. Innuendos given about William with condemnatory, non-applicable opinions were added, as if Nelson were jury, judge, and prosecutor. Technically this is called negative counter-transference to William and positive to attractive young Patricia. Peer review recommended.

3/27/86 Children's psychologist protested to Ohio Court Authorities that hearings were improper. No response from Courts or Guardian ad Litem. Custody established as twelve days mother, two days father.

6/25/86 Both children evaluated by Professor Alice Carl, Univ of Ariz. Her opinion was the children were not molested by their father and she considered him a good candidate for custodial parent. She did not see Patricia.

11/3/86 In a clash with her mother, Janice yelled at her about making them lie. Patricia tried to smother Janice with one hand over her mouth and the other holding Janice's hands on her knee. When Janice asked her father what would happen if she died, he questioned her concern and learned of the above incident. He filed a police report, due to his concern for the safety of the two children if Patricia became desperate about the discovery of her perjury and brainwashing of the children.

11/8/86 Janice wrote a letter to police to give to judge so they could return to their father.

11/22/86 Children sent to Loyola Medical School for evaluation by Dr. Rice.

During the course of the evaluation, two hours of videotape interviews were done, which are available to police, the DA, judge, and other officials and consultants. Dr. Rice points out that "the failure of inept agency mental health professionals" to be even aware that there was a possibility of false allegations is highlighted. Agency personnel behaved as if they subjectively believed (without corroboration or hard evidence, such as confession by the accused, genital injury, venereal disease, pregnancy, or pornographic materials) that, if an accusation is raised, the innocent but accused person must therefore be guilty. The finger of blame was arbitrarily taken as a verdict of guilty. The agency arrogantly preempted the Justice System and, in so doing, abused their power and neglected their own task by being totally incompetent as primary data-gatherers.

Dr. Rice pointed out that the chronological outline makes a critique possible. Child care workers must be trained to have equal suspicion of untruth as well as truth in child molestation allegation cases. They need training in child development and child pathology, to learn that children can be tricked or trained to lie by adults—parents, professionals whom they wish to please or whom they fear—that children can be misled to believe nontruths or to say them. If they were to receive proper and adequate training, professionals then could be open-minded and objective enough to become true "guardians and protectors" of both the children's rights and the family.

Dr. Rice goes on to state the Smith case shows gross insensitivity by workers to both the children and the integrity of their family. There is no record of a family session with father, mother, and children together—why not? William's son was in jail, so this was not a case where perpetrator and child must be kept apart. The father was accused much later, and almost as an afterthought, by his wife. It seems clear the agency women were polarized "pro-Patricia and "anti-William," therefore anti-family and *not* in the best interests of the children. If these were well-trained, child sex abuse professionals, they should immediately have been alert to the fact that false sex abuse allegations to obtain solo custody are "epidemic" in divorce cases as was mentioned by attorney Douglas Besharov, former director of National Center on Child Abuse and Neglect.

Instead of providing exploration, investigation, objectivity, and assistance to the children and family, these HSS workers became antagonists. In reading their documents, Dr. Rice found gross investigative incompetence and misuse of the power entrusted by well-meaning child-abuse laws. There is a question, requiring local investigation, as to whether Patricia was advised by agency personnel to "train" the children in the hotel about what to say about their step-brother's alleged abuse in order to "make a case." Recurrently, the children stated he had *not* sexually molested them, that Patricia had told them to lie about it.

Dr. Rice concluded: "Real molestation must not be missed. False allegations must not be supported."

In his evaluation of Dr. Nelson's conclusion, Dr. Underwager first notes out that it is less than ideal to review testing information without having the raw test data (answer sheets, profile sheets, Rorschach protocol, and scoring sheets). He states that this is the first case in which they've been involved where the attorney was unable to gain access to the case notes, MMPI scores, children's drawings, etc. Many of the issues raised in this evaluation paralleled concerns expressed by Dr. Rice, who recommended a peer review of Nelson's report.

The evaluation further points out that Nelson's performance was in violation of Principle 1 of the Ethical Code and cites the following as not meeting acceptable standards for a psychologist to follow:

(1) The MMPIs were sent home with Mr. & Mrs. Smith and his report did not so state. MMPIs are to be administered in a standardized or controlled environment, particularly in forensic situations.

(2) Dr. Nelson interprets information from the diagnostic interviews with a bias toward interpreting observations about Mr. Smith much more negatively. He appears to have concluded early on that Mrs. Smith's version of history and events was more factual than Mr. Smith's, but provides no support for this assumption. He states that Mr. Smith presented information "with a distinctly personal bias" and says nothing comparable about Mrs. Smith. He states Mr. Smith omitted, denied or dismissed pertinent details, but makes no such comment about Mrs. Smith. He makes no mention of Mrs. Smith taking the children to England against court order, but refers to their return as Mr. Smith spiriting them away. He says she hasn't seen the children, but neglects to state the reason is that she chose not to abide by the court order that she visit them. He states that Mrs. Smith's negative description of Mr. Smith. is born out by test data, but his description of her is not.

(3) Dr. Nelson misrepresents procedures and techniques that do not meet criteria for tests by describing them as tests and offering interpretations based on the non-tests. Animals and Three Wishes are not tests in any sense of the term as defined by the American Psychological Association (APA). There is no empirical evidence to support any of the interpretations of the children's drawings made by Dr. Nelson.

(4) Dr. Nelson's bias is evident in the interpretation of the MMPIs for Mr. & Mrs. Smith. Although we (Underwager and Wakefield) were not provided the test data, it is an over-interpretation, in referring to a within-normal-limits profile, to state that the individual has a "highly assertive and domineering style." In his testimony, Nelson states that Mr. Smith is willful, doesn't

play the game right and that he suspects that the indications of the test scores lead him to believe that Mr. Smith's dominance characteristics have led him to be autocratic. The MMPI Supplementary Scale Manual states that the title "dominance" may be partially misleading, in that the scale reflects taking charge of one's own life more than bossiness. Dr. Nelson characterizes Mr. Smith as an inductive thinker, when in fact neither the MMPI nor the California Psychological Inventory (CPI) measure thinking styles. The CPI is not a measurement of pathology, but a measure of one's strength and sociability.

(5) The statements and conclusions about the children's anxiety are grossly overstated in terms of the data he presents. Again, we do not have the test data, but doubt his interpretations will be supported by that data. He reports the children said nothing indicating problems with their father, generally answering questions with "I don't know." The use of drawings to form conclusions is totally inappropriate. On the basis of the drawings and his interpretation of them, he recommended the children be removed from their father's home and live with their mother.

(6) Dr. Nelson's recommendations are not supported by the data he reports. He states he could not evaluate interaction between Mrs. Smith and children because of recent separation, but depends upon what the agency therapist tells him about Mrs. Smith. However, he makes no attempt to communicate with the children's psychologist, who has been seeing the children regularly for over a year. He states that the children's interactions with Mr. Smith were positive and appropriate. He minimizes the fact that Mrs. Smith has not been seeing the children according to the court-ordered schedule and implies in an affidavit that Mr. Smith or someone has been denying Mrs. Smith access to the children.

(7) Dr. Nelson appears biased against Mr. Smith, inflating psychopathology on Mr. Smith's part, and minimizing or ignoring problems with Mrs. Smith. He acknowledges he doesn't like Mr. Smith, but denies letting this affect his judgement.

(8) Dr. Nelson did not attempt to contact the children's psychologist in order to gather information before forming an opinion. Further, he recommended the children receive treatment

from the agency therapist, despite the fact they were, and had been, receiving therapy from a child psychologist. Later, without ever contacting their current psychologist, he recommended their therapy with her be terminated. Underwager believes this violates Principal 7, Professional Relationships.

Dr. Nelson states that the agency therapist is the only professional who really had an open relationship with the children, ignoring the fact that they had been consistently open with the child psychologist about their concerns and desires.

(9) Dr. Nelson misstates the ethical principles and standards in refusing to provide Mr. Smith's counsel with copies of raw test data. The APA provides that raw psychological data is released only with the written consent of the user or his or her legal representative. Mr. Smith's attorney certainly qualifies as his legal representative.

In the Mark Doe case in Texas, evaluations were done by Underwager and Wakefield of reports issued by the psychologist and the therapist of the Texas CPS and by a mental health counselor at the mental health clinic in which Bill was placed. The following issues were raised in that evaluation.

The Interview:
The videotaped interview with Bill did not meet accepted standards of how such interviews should be conducted. The questions were leading and the interviewer coercive. It was clear that Bill had previously been exposed to the dolls and to similar questions. In spite of the rehearsal, his responses were confusing and not credible. Over sixty-two percent of the interviewer behaviors fell into potentially error-inducing categories such as closed questions, pressure, rewarding/reinforcing responses, modeling, use of aids, and paraphrasing. There was no recognition given to the acrimonious custody battle in progress. In addition, there was no recognition of the fact that Bill was not toilet-trained and his father cleaned his genitals whenever he had an accident.

The Therapist:

No case notes were kept—this is contrary to accepted standards of care and practice. There was over-interpretation of observed behaviors in the absence of empirical support and premature conclusions of alleged abuse. This therapist provides a purely speculative and subjective opinion that depends entirely on her perceptions, biases, and observational skills, with no research reports or child development literature to support her assertions. Using play behavior to support perceptions and conclusions is not acceptable. When adults invite children to engage in play, they invite them to engage in fantasy and pretend behaviors. Research indicates that children who are involved in divorce/custody battles often exhibit behavior problems, but this is not even considered in determining Bill's behavioral problems.

The Psychologist:

There were questions about the competency and training of this psychologist in providing psychological services of the nature she did for the Doe family. Her transcript did not indicate any clinical experience, did not correspond to any American Psychological Association-approved programs for applied specialties, did not show any clerkships or internships or supervised training in any applied activity. It appeared to the evaluator that the total number of credit hours completed (seventy-five) was slightly more than half the credit hours required by APA approved programs.

By the time this psychologist saw Mark, she had already seen Bill several times and had concluded that Mark had sexually and physically abused him. With this conclusion, she interpreted Mark's tests as pathologically as possible. She concluded his "obsessive-compulsive tendencies, high defensiveness and intense need to control. . .his rigidly defensive posture does not adequately bind the underlying anxiety and trepidation of doing poorly." Nowhere is this supported by empirical data, nowhere does she indicate the tests were *not* all performed under supervision and nowhere does she give any allowance for the situation in which Mark Doe found himself at the time of testing.

The interpretations of the Rorschach were personal, subjective and idiosyncratic interpretations. Examination of the actual responses yielded absolutely no evidence for interpreting his Rorschach as pathological, yet she saw "an undercurrent of anxiety, unrequited love, and cloaked sexuality. . .difficulty with relating appropriately to others. . .polymorphous perverse orientation to the environment. . .fantasies (that may include) homosexual, bisexual and exhibitionist feelings. . .hostility toward women. . ."

It appears likely that, from other evidence, she had already made up her mind that Bill had been abused by Mark and his behavior was interpreted in terms of this. It should be noted that a premature and swift closure by a mental health professional on an opinion that abuse occurred is recognized as one of the hallmarks of a false allegation (Klajner-Diamon, Wehrspann & Steinhauer, 1987; Wakefield & Underwager, 1988). While the psychologist recognized the stress of the acrimonious divorce as causing problems for Norman, she concluded that Bill's problems were due to his being sexually and physically abused "most likely by his father."

On her recommendation, Bill was hospitalized in an institution designed to treat disturbed adolescent or pre-pubescent children. He was the youngest there and was exposed to children and therapies more advanced than his age. Hospital notes suggest that the statements about abuse by his father were encouraged and reinforced in the hospital.

The Mental Health Institution:

The diagnosis, after three months of observation and treatment, does *not* meet the diagnostic criteria of DSM-III-R. Bill was not toilet-trained at the age of three years, yet was diagnosed as having encopresis (which cannot be diagnosed before age four) and enuresis (which cannot be diagnosed prior to age five). However, because of the diagnosis, an inordinate amount of attention was given to soiling and wetting. This attention (a reward) reinforced the possibility of repeated instances of the same. It appears that, once the decision was made that Bill was abused by his father, the observations, interpretations, and diagnoses were made with the goal of supporting that conclusion.

Studies by Underwager and Wakefield indicate that when a non-abused child is treated by adults as if the child had been abused and adult pressure and influence is used to produce statements from a child about events that did not happen, this is an assault upon the child's ability to distinguish reality from unreality.

Throughout the videotaped interview done with Bill, the interviewer had to repeatedly ask the questions to get the desired responses. When desired responses were finally attained, and the interviewer tried to confirm them, Bill responded with "I don't know." Using the anatomical dolls, the interviewer routinely touched or pointed to the "private parts" of the doll when asking where Daddy had touched Bill. At the end of the interview, when asked if he told the truth or a lie, Bill said, "A lie." He repeated this assertion three times.

Chapter Fourteen

Fighting Back

This is a war. It requires money, personnel, a will to fight, strategic and tactical planning. Ken Pangborn of Men International, Inc. counsels, from his own experience, "Take no prisoners."

False allegations of child sexual abuse, especially when levied in a divorce and custody battle, are a declaration of war and need to be treated as such. The offense has been taken by your accuser and his/her attorney, and it is critical that you mount an immediate and aggressive defense.

The issues at stake are varied. First is your access to and relationship with your children, and then your freedom, which can be restricted or denied as a result of these allegations. Second is your reputation and your future in the community. As long as these allegations remain unresolved, there are many who will immediately question your innocence and your name will remain on the child-abuse registry, negatively affecting any of your attempts to work with children or the elderly. Third is your livelihood. The attitudes of your employer and/or customers and co-workers aside, these allegations produce feelings of shock, inertia, and self-pity in the accused that, if allowed free rein, will most certainly impact concentration and job performance. Fighting false allegations of child sexual abuse will require strengths of character, mental and emotional depths that have never been required of you before.

Your enemies appear to be legion, as you have seen throughout this book. The accuser, of course, is number one, but her backup troops will cost you the most in time, money, and frustration. You will be battling social workers and child protection team members who firmly believe that children don't lie, who view hearsay evidence as gospel, who believe it is their responsibility to substantiate—instead of investigate—the allegations. You will be battling prosecutors whose salary and advancement are predicated on successful prosecution and confirmation by the courts of your guilt. You will be facing family courts where inexperienced judges, with little if any knowledge of child development or the SAID Syndrome, generally rubber stamp conclusions and recommendations from social workers, child protection teams and Guardians Ad Litem. You will fight against medical and psychological reports—sheets of paper that can not be cross-examined. And, throughout the entire ordeal, you will often have little if any advance notice of what you will be fighting next nor any opportunity to prepare for it.

The initial defensive action is two-fold. Hire an experienced, competent attorney, one with expertise and a track record in fighting child sexual abuse allegations and begin educating yourself. Rick, William, Mark, and I were all prepared to fight the allegations, to prove our innocence and be reunited with our children. There is no way of knowing the difference it could have made had each of us started with an attorney who was an expert in this field, but it is likely that our cases would have progressed in a more positive and rapid manner.

Do *not* agree to anything until you have retained a competent attorney who can advise you on the ramifications of your actions. Do *not* allow a public defender to represent you. Good attorneys are expensive; I am well aware of that fact. There are Pro Bono (for free) attorneys available, but they are few and far between, particularly in this area of expertise. However, an incompetent or inexperienced attorney may well lose your case in either family or criminal court or both. This will result in loss of contact with your children and the potential of twenty-five years in jail. Either situation results in years of court appeals with the attendant court costs. The financial consideration becomes small when compared to the forced separation of father and child, and the loss of freedom and reputation.

With the steady increase in allegations of child sexual abuse over the past years, many of which are now occurring in the context of divorce and custody battles, there are an increasing number of professionals developing the needed skills to specialize in this area of defense. Lewis Hoffman, Esq. and his "A" Team are an example of expert defense, recognized nationwide. If you have a local attorney, he may be familiar with someone experienced in this area. If not, contact your nearest VOCAL office (see Reference Section of this book) and your state bar association.

Interview your attorney carefully. You are placing your future and that of your children in this individual's hands. Be sure he or she is familiar with the SAID Syndrome and aware of how the child protection and juvenile court system works.

Knowledge is power and nowhere is that any more true than when facing false allegations of child sexual abuse. The more you know, the fewer unpleasant surprises there are to deal with. While knowledge of what is, or is not, causing problems, restrictions or delays does not lessen the pain, it can reduce the amount of energy spent on frustration. Knowing your rights and your options makes it easier for you to help your attorney defend you, as you can provide input and information to build your case against the allegations.

I strongly encourage you to become actively involved in your own defense. Learn as many facts as you can, as quickly as possibly, even though it may be a difficult and frustrating task. The more you know about the allegations, the supporting evidence and the methods used, the better able you will be to question or refute the information. Research other cases, using the Law Library at your county courthouse; there were striking similarities among the SAID Syndrome cases we studied.

Examine any and all information and evidence, testimony, evaluations, or court filings for indications of inconsistency, error, or flaws. This may reveal that, for some reason, the child's story is impossible, based on when it happened or where it happened for example. This immediately places the child's credibility in question and allows you to investigate where the alleged comment may have come from. You may find that the abuse was alleged at a time when you hadn't seen the child or that the description of his/her surroundings apply to her mother's home instead of your own.

In my case, there were several inconsistencies or flaws. First, Diane's initial physical examination, the night she returned from visiting me, showed no evidence of sexual abuse. However, a second exam, done two hours later at a different hospital, one known to cooperate fully with the child protection team, did indicate abuse. She had not been with me in the interim; she was with Carla and her live-in boyfriend during this time.

In the Smith case, it was discovered that the physician's examination resulting in a finding of evidence of sexual abuse had occurred five months after the allegation was made.

The videotaped interview with my daughter had obvious gaps, with no indication of what had occurred during those gaps. It appeared that the video had been electronically altered and doctored. Thus, the family court saw the video "not in its original form." The child protection team worker conducting the interview routinely referred to previous interviews and doll sessions to remind Diane of what the answer to a question should be. None of the previous sessions were videotaped or documented.

One of the best means of catching discrepancies is through the use of depositions taken from the adversarial parties. Depositions are merely interrogatories in which the person deposed answers questions from an attorney, while under oath and with a court reporter present. These can be vitally important in identifying discrepancies which may later surface in court.

Obtain copies of your files, in their entirety, from the social services agency and the Guardians ad Litem, if possible. It is difficult to defend yourself against statements of which you are unaware. In most cases, you will be unable to get your files from the child protection team without a court order. In Florida, recent legislation states that, unless the case is closed as proposed confirmed, you must have a court order to get any files from HRS.

In an interview with Ken Pangborn, he stated that this type of education was a major turning point for him. He finally saw that, if he were to educate himself, if he went out and found out how to deal with the system, he could win. And he did. He got the right kind of legal representation, he learned what needed to be done and he made sure his attorney did it. It took some time, but things started turning around and, in the end, Ken was awarded sole custody of his children.

An immediate counterattack is essential. The best chance the falsely accused has to counter and overcome the allegations exists at the first hearing. While the accuser strikes the first blow and is clearly on the offense, a swift and aggressive counterattack demonstrates to the court and the accuser that you are prepared and capable of fighting and defeating this attack.

Unfortunately, false accusations of child abuse are so devastating that often both the accused and his attorney are rendered speechless and ineffectual. An attorney may recommend that they wait until the first hearing and see how things go. **This is a mistake.** Get another attorney!

If you cannot acquire some control of the litigation at this first hearing, you are doomed to wallow through weeks, months, or years of court hearings, motions and evaluations, all of which are destined to be stressful as well as emotionally and financially devastating, while the child is repeatedly interviewed and programmed, whether by accident or design, to embellish the story.

There are four fundamental objectives recommended in preparing for the first hearing: (1) shift the court's focus from the alleged conduct of the accused to the psychological functioning of the accuser; (2) have an independent psychologist appointed to evaluate the *entire* family, while prohibiting interrogation of the child until the evaluation is completed. Split the cost with your ex-wife or pay for the evaluation yourself, to assure access to the results; (3) attempt to regain custody or visitation immediately, with the understanding that such custody or visitation will include constant adult supervision by a third party, preferably someone outside the social services agency; (4) persuade the court that any delay in addressing the issues raised is detrimental in the extreme to the child, who is the focus of the protection. (Clauss, 1989)

After the first hearing, opportunities to gain control are few and far between and must be created by the defendant. Because of the perception of immediate guilt in allegations of child sexual abuse, it is critical to shift the court's attention to the real perpetrator of abuse—the falsely accusing parent and inept/unqualified investigators and therapists.

In reviewing the allegations and reports of the Child Protection Team, defense should identify the following and determine if they affected team judgement:

☐ Did the crisis nature of team deliberation cause distortion in assessment?

☐ Does the team have too many cases to hear, inciting premature judgement?

☐ Were key participants unable to attend or give their contribution?

☐ How are new members broken in or given time to jell as team players?

☐ Did visitors to team cause distraction?

☐ Was confidentiality of alleged offender, alleged victim protected?

☐ Did examining physician "deputize" anyone?

There are a number of questions to be posed regarding the team decision-making process and the conclusions reached. A few of these include:

☐ Gender determined aspects of team judgement;

☐ Poor medical judgement or poor analysis of findings;

☐ Too much reliance on opinion of the family-involved social worker;

☐ Member(s) possible bias in favor of child.

Some important questions to bear in mind when formulating defense include:

☐ Was fantasy erroneously interpreted by the alleged victim?

☐ Is the right person being accused by the alleged victim?

☐ Does the alleged victim wish to punish a particular adult?

☐ Is the alleged victim guilty about something else connected with the sexual events?

☐ Can the alleged victim distinguish between reality and fantasy?

☐ Was the allegation part of a divorce, custody or visitation battle?

☐ Did the alleged victim get anatomy lessons from agency social worker?

☐ Did the alleged victim make prior complaints of molestations? With what results? Is the victim addicted to victim's role?

☐ Did the alleged victim experience any sex education at school, Scouts, day care, or at home, which may account for graphic nature of sex act description?

☐ Were inappropriate and unproven techniques used, such as anatomical dolls or children's drawings?

☐ How does the team deal with allegations of innocence?

The answers to these questions can have a substantial impact on the credibility and value of the team conclusions and report.

It is critical that your attorney take depositions from the adversarial parties, including court-appointed psychologists and other professionals, prior to the hearing and trial.

Where a divorce and custody situation is involved, under no circumstances should you agree to have the matter continued, unless visitation of some sort can be obtained. If you lose contact with your child, the mother is in complete control of all that the child hears and says. As long as you maintain contact, the child may find it more difficult to believe what others are saying, because it conflicts with his or her first-hand experience. In addition, visitation rights may afford you the opportunity to have your own psychological evaluation of the child done. In the event you obtain visitation with the supervision of an objective third party, the nonverbal reactions of the child toward you may well discount the credibility of hearsay evidence and testimony.

After you have established a consistent and logical basis, file a responsive pleading. You must determine that there has been no abuse or that abuse has occurred, but by someone else. Be sure you have done adequate research and the grounds for your pleading are well defined and can be defended. Changing your theory after filing the pleading may lead the judge to believe you will grab hold of anything that may aid your case.

Filing a responsive pleading allows you to present your side of the argument, with supporting facts, to balance the prosecutor's file of allegations, hearsay evidence, non-expert opinion, and statements the child supposedly made.

Do everything possible to prevent any further therapy or interviewing that may enforce the child's confusion or belief regarding the allegations of abuse. Too often, these activities serve as a teaching tool where modeling, suggestion, and repetition result in a young child learning to act the part of a victim. If any interviewing is to be done, require that your attorney be present.

If you are falsely accused of child sexual abuse, it is recommended that you immediately motion for a competency hearing for the child victim and for a hearsay relevancy hearing. These two hearings will surface in juvenile or dependency court.

Most children, under the age of seven, will be deemed incompetent by the court because they simply can not distinguish a truism from a lie. The alleged perpetrator should be aware that a child's out of court statement to an authority or a child protection worker can be used against him in juvenile court, where the Rules of Evidence do not apply.

A dependency proceeding is not, in law, what is termed an adjudicatory proceeding. To the contrary, juvenile court judges retain a great amount of latitude. Hearsay evidence is allowed. However, the defense can ask for a Hearsay Relevancy Hearing, which entails a pleading by the defense asking that only certain relevant or material statements be allowed, ones that come in the context of good faith.

In Florida, for example, one can argue on Florida Statute 90.803(23) to challenge the trustworthiness of the child's statement and how it was obtained. I used this rule, but to no avail. Regardless, it is pertinent that the defense strenuously object to any hearsay statements that are made in juvenile court.

Because witnesses and physical evidence are rare in child molestation cases, defense attorneys must go to great lengths to challenge the credibility of the victims. They may check out the child's school records for disciplinary problems. They may interview classmates, neighbors, and relatives to learn of any psychological problems. In one Florida case, the defense attorney discovered a child had exposed himself at school before his client was accused of sexually molesting him.

Again, you and your attorney are constantly battling the belief held by social workers, child protection teams and many of the judges that small children never lie about something as serious as sexual battery or abuse. Defense Attorney Robert Pope of St. Petersburg asks, "If they can tell the stories about the elephant that lives in their room, why is it so difficult to believe that they made up that story about rape or abuse?" One of your best defenses is the ability to disprove the probability of the child's alleged accusation.

Make no statements unless your attorney is present and do not waive any of your rights, especially to a hearing. Refuse any attempts at plea bargaining. If your attorney even looks like he might consider or encourage plea bargaining, or even suggest that you plead nolo contendere to *any* charge brought against you, find another attorney immediately. Plea bargain offers are almost always one of the attempts made during the course of this type of battle.

The prosecutor may try to convince you that if you will plead guilty to a lesser charge, this will soon be over and behind you and you will be able to see your children. Bear in mind, it is always in the prosecutor's best interest to get a conviction, even if it is to a lesser charge. Therefore, at some point, when you, the victim, are perceived to be physically, emotionally, and financially drained, they may approach you with an answer to all your problems. If you plead guilty to a lesser charge, they will drop all the criminal charges and you won't have a felony conviction on your record. Unfortunately, taking advantage of this offer will put you right back in Family Court, facing a judge who now is looking at a man who has admitted to inappropriate behavior. What do you figure that does to your odds of unsupervised visitation or custody? It may well result in an order separating you from your children permanently.

If you are forced to accept evaluations by a court-appointed psychologist (as opposed to the outside, objective evaluation of the entire family that is recommended), ask the following questions: (1) What protocol will be used during the evaluation? (2)

Will the father be examined in the presence of his child? (3) Will the mother be interviewed? (4) Where will the interviews take place and when can the report be expected?

Dr. Lee Coleman, a forensic psychiatrist in private practice in Los Angeles, California, strongly discourages the use of psychologists and psychology for anything. Recognized nation-wide for his expertise in the field of child abuse and false child sexual abuse allegations, he believes that the more evaluations presented, the less likely it is that the judge and jury will hear the facts and use their common sense. If the court orders an evalua-tion, naturally, you must take it, but Dr. Coleman recommends you go on record as taking the evaluation under protest, because you question results received from questionable methods.

There are a number of tests and evaluation methods which may be required by the court or recommended by your attorney in an attempt to prove your guilt or innocence. Standard evaluations require between six and eight hours, and include an extensive interview and the administration of psychological and psychosexual testing.

Traditional clinical interviews allow defendants to provide information about their backgrounds and allow the mental health professional to evaluate the mental status of the defendant, in-cluding his appearance, behavior, emotion, and thinking patterns. During this time, a complete psychosexual history is elicited in detail. Psychological testing provides relatively standardized in-formation about different aspects of a defendant's functioning, identifying factors associated with learning style, planning ability, concentration, and memory. Personality testing provides information on the presence or absence of other psychological problems, preferred personality styles, any aggression or violence in the individual's life, and comparison with known offender test protocols. The MMPI provides overall information about the defendant. While MMPI results may indicate negative reaction and behavioral traits, it must also be realized that certain reactions and responses may be the direct result of the feelings of paranoia, helplessness, hopelessness, resentment, and anger engendered by false allegations of child sexual abuse and separation from one's children. At best, an MMPI is an *adjunct* only to diagnostic endeavors. While The Multiphasic Sex Inventory has been developed to assess psychosexual functioning, the penile plethysmograph may be used to assess the sexual interest patterns of the defendant. Physical arousal is measured in response to the presentation of audio and/or visual stimuli.

The most important weapons you have for fighting back are your attitude and your presence. You yourself can be your biggest advantage or your worst detriment. It is critical to project a positive manner and attitude.

Facing false allegations of child sexual abuse engenders a range of emotions from self-pity to frustration, from anger to desperation, from aggression to defeat.

The way you present yourself to social workers, Guardians ad Litem, prosecuting attorneys, and judges, has a subtle, but definite, effect on their perception of your guilt or innocence. An angry man is seen by them as being unable to control his emotions and therefore unable to control his actions and probably capable of unacceptable behavior. While this thought progression is not particularly logical, given the situation and the normal emotions one would experience during this type of circumstance, it is often present.

It is imperative that you develop the ability to control your emotions and project a picture of calm, caring, cooperative interest. Co-operate with the social workers and child protection workers, while recognizing that their goal is to build a case against you. Displays of bad temper, impatience, or anger will inevitably place you in a poor light and cause negative comparisons of you with the custodial parent. Be congenial but firm.

Be courteous in dealing with prosecutors and judges. In formal settings, such as the courtroom, a professional appearance in slacks and a jacket and an attitude of cooperation and calm will do much to convince a judge that he or she is viewing an average, intelligent, and "normal" individual.

The angry-young-man stance will do little to further your case, as I learned from personal experience. When I finally gained unsupervised visitation, in August of 1990, the judge commented on the positive changes in my attitude. It almost seemed that, since I was no longer angry, I was no longer a child abuser!

In any war, innocent bystanders become casualties of the battle. In this instance, those casualties are your children, and one of the hardest facts to accept is that there is little you can do about it. The children are inevitably confused. Why is Daddy suddenly a bad person? Why do strangers constantly ask the same questions, over and over again? Why can they no longer see their father?

The alleged perpetrator may easily make mistakes in judgment, thinking he is acting in the best interest of the children by shielding them from their mother's actions, by fighting a "clean" fight and not dragging her name in the mud through the courts, by believing the children may benefit from therapy, or that interviews with the children will prove his innocence.

The biggest favor you can do your children is to obtain an order preventing any further interviewing of the children and ceasing or preventing therapy. If an allegation has been brought, it should have been based on the child's accusation which is already on record. Further interrogation would only be for the purpose of either fishing for more accusations or substantiating the first, if it appears to be on shaky grounds. Either way, additional interviews serve only to enforce the child's confusion about or belief in the allegation.

Providing a small child therapy for sexual abuse, when there is no proof of such abuse, has far-reaching effects, as we learned in our interview with Mary. It provides excessive and unnecessary education in anatomy and sexual areas. More importantly, it teaches the child to act the part of a victim. If a child is told something often enough, it becomes a fact to them, whether true or not.

In this instance, it is in the best interest of the child that *nothing* be done in the areas of interrogation and therapy.

The sudden disappearance of his or her father may be the most distressing issue for the child. In cases where there are allegations of child sexual abuse, the social workers, child protection team, and the accuser push hard and fast to deny contact of any kind between father and child. It is not uncommon for the mother to explain to the child that Daddy is bad, Daddy is mean, Daddy doesn't love them anymore, Daddy will never come back. The actions of a manipulative custodial parent may well result in the child suffering from some level of the Parental Alienation Syndrome. This is a factor you and your attorney should be aware of.

Richard M. Gardner, M.D. has studied this condition extensively and points out that there are essentially three categories of the Parental Alienation Syndrome, each requiring different methods of treatment and resolution.

In severe cases, the mothers are often fanatic, obsessed with antagonism toward their husbands and, in many cases, paranoid. The wife often sees in her husband many noxious qualities that actually exist within herself. By projecting these unacceptable characteristics onto the husband, she can consider herself an innocent victim. These individuals will use every mechanism at their disposal (legal or not) to prevent visitation. The children are subjected to a constant and consistent bombardment of denigration of the father, which results in perpetuation of the syndrome. Court orders that seem to be recognizing only the child's dislike of the father make it possible for the mother to intensify the alienation, improbable that the father will be able to reestablish a positive relationship with the children and impossible for a qualified therapist to treat the children, or for the issue to be resolved.

In moderate cases, the parent is less fanatic and paranoid, often exhibiting the rage-of-the-rejected-woman. However, there is still a constant campaign of denigration and a significant desire to withhold the children from the father as a vengeance maneuver. A wide variety of excuses interfere with or circumvent visitation. Many times, this form of alienation leads to decisions by the mother that she needs to relocate. Her rationale for this move may be that she is suddenly "homesick" for the state she left ten years ago, she needs to get away from the scene of the (custody) conflict, she needs to "start over." Regardless of the excuse, in the context of a recent or ongoing custody battle, an informed court will advise the mother that she is free to leave the state at any time, but if she does so, it will *not* be with the children.

In mild cases of alienation, usually seen in instances of joint custody, the mother is generally acting out of anger and perhaps some degree of vengeance, but is more concerned with cementing her position with the children. These parents realize that prolonged litigation and actual alienation of the children from their fathers is not in the child's best interest. These cases are generally "cured" by a court order providing primary custody with liberal visitation, thus removing the child's obligation to take sides.

Your ultimate goal is to prove your innocence and regain unrestricted access to, if not custody of, your children, while acting in their best interest. It is a staggering commitment, but I encourage you to fight back with every means available.

I asked Mary how she felt about her father's actions, about what he did in fighting the false accusations that had been made by her mother.

"He did the right thing, he fought against the allegations." Mary was very emphatic about encouraging fathers to fight the allegations, to fight for their right to their children.

We asked Mary's father if, with 20-20 hindsight, he would have handled things differently.

"Yes, I would have come out from the gate and destroyed her. Playing by the Marquis of Queensbury rules is not doing your kids any favors. My kids would have had four fewer years of hell to live through, destruction of their minds, their self-image. If I had recognized that...

"The thing is, it's the kids who take the beating. I, in my misplaced nobility, tried to stay away from going after my ex-wife, but that's what I should have done."

Chapter Fifteen

A Summary of Problems and Solutions

According to Douglas Besharov, the original director of the National Center for Child Abuse and Neglect and now a law professor, seventy percent of child-abuse cases are unfounded. A national study done in 1986 by the Child Welfare League showed that sixty percent of child-abuse allegations were proven false. To reach a judgment of unfounded, in cases of child sexual abuse, often takes months of juvenile and, perhaps, criminal court time, thousands of dollars in attorney fees and results in the disruption of the family, the accused's career, and his entire lifestyle. Wouldn't it seem logical that any system producing a sixty to seventy percent error rate should be examined for deficiencies?

As we have seen in the case studies presented and others researched, there are a number of problems surrounding the entire question of child sexual abuse allegations, beginning with the credibility of the alleged child victim and running through the social services agencies, the mental health profession, the court system and the issue of individual rights.

I make no pretension of having the answers to all these problems, nor do I propose to offer a quick solution. This is not a problem that began yesterday and can be solved tomorrow, but an intricate network of issues and attitudes that must be approached in a careful, consistent, conscientious, and compassionate manner. Indeed, the pervasive problem of false allegations of child sexual abuse has resulted from actions that were initially presented as a solution to the concerns engendered by abuse of children. The solution has become a problem itself, a not uncommon occurrence when the long-range ramifications of decisions are not considered.

In this chapter I will attempt to first define and summarize the problems surrounding false allegations of child sexual abuse that I have discovered. It is hoped that this summary will provide a map of potential obstacles for anyone who is falsely accused. It is further hoped that this presentation will encourage agencies, legislators, lawyers, judges, and individuals in the mental health care professions to carefully analyze the manner in which our current system operates, with an eye toward developing a system that better serves the best interest of the child.

I will then examine some potential solutions to these problems, in the hopes that involved agencies, legislators, and individuals may begin to fashion a system whereby true perpetrators are properly identified and prosecuted, while innocent victims of false allegations are exonerated and allowed their full rights to their children, their good reputation, and a full life. These solutions have been proposed by various experts in the field of child development and, in some cases, include legislation that has been passed or is pending in various states. Unfortunately, the list of solutions is much shorter than the list of problems. . .

Problems:

☐ Definitions of child sexual abuse, like most other definitions of abuse and neglect, are ambiguous at best and most often non-existent in the statutes that address the issue. During Dr. Spiegel's trial, a physician was asked if it was sexual abuse for a father to kiss his two-year-old daughter on the tush. The physician responded "Yes," but qualified the response by adding, "Yes, if the mother is out of the room." During a supervised visit, I kissed my daughter on the cheek and was told by a horrified social worker, "Mr. Tong, that is inappropriate behavior!"

☐ Not only are definitions of abuse ambiguous, but the definition of "evidence" is equally flexible. In cases of child sexual abuse allegations, which generally involve young children, there is rarely any medical evidence. A physician's statement that behavior is "consistent with abuse" is an opinion, not evidence. A mother's contention that the child said it happened, particularly when the child will not repeat the accusation or, in fact, denies the abuse, is not evidence; it is a statement made by the mother. A social worker's statement that he or she believes the child's behavior is indicative of abuse is, again, an individual's opinion, not evidence.

☐ The submission and acceptance of hearsay evidence in the family courts, with judges accepting the statements and opinions of social workers and child protection team members as expert opinions, is a distortion of the laws and the constitutional rights of the victim and the accused. The current trend in using hearsay testimony makes it too simple for a prosecutor to resort to hearsay in lieu of live testimony, in order to gain a tactical advantage.

☐ The automatic acceptance of self-proclaimed "experts" by the courts needs to be closely examined. Many social workers, child protection team members, agency therapists and law officers have little, if any, education or training in the areas of child development, play therapy, or play projection. Few of these individuals have qualifying clinical experience. The individual investigating the allegations of child sexual abuse may be untrained, incompetent, or personally biased.

Hechler's book included a case study in which the state called an "expert witness." This expert witness was a police officer who had taken a forty-hour course in child maltreatment. This witness had no other credentials, no associated degrees, no advanced psychological courses. The witness introduced information on pedophiles and homosexuals and stated that, although the accused had done nothing but hug the child, there was always an escalation of activities in the seduction of children. He further advised the jury that, if the accused hadn't been arrested, he might have gone on to perpetrate all manner of heinous crimes on the children he supervised. (The accused individual was convicted.)

☐ There is a noticeable difference in the treatment of the accused and the accuser. State statutes and procedures almost always act to the detriment of the falsely accused. An allegation of child sexual abuse brings immediate concern and support to the accusing parent, who is afforded belief, therapy, sympathy, and legal counsel by the state. The accused is rarely made aware of what's occurring until the case is built and then has no where to turn for support, objective and helpful counseling, or funding for the legal counsel necessary to prove his innocence. Rarely are the accused and accuser afforded the same opportunities to present their side of the issue, the accused often not even afforded the courtesy of an interview by the child protection team. The alleged perpetrator must pay for his own attorney, evaluations, and any court costs, while providing child support and sometimes alimony, even though he may be denied any contact with the children he is supporting.

There is a startling lack of effort or interest in interviewing/investigating the accused. Often, the accused is unaware of the allegations until the state agency and prosecutors office have had time to build their case. Particularly in cases where there is the potential of a SAID Syndrome situation, the omission of interviews with the accused parent shows a glaring lack of objectivity in gathering pertinent information.

The accused is denied access to his own records, in regard to allegations made by the social services agency or child protection team. In most states, these records are considered strictly confidential and it requires a court order for the accused to learn the exact nature of the allegations and its source, the results of interviews, evaluations, and allegations, and exactly what he is defending himself against.

☐ Given the way the system currently operates, it is all too easy for an individual to manipulate it to their benefit, particularly in cases of custody or visitation. The accusing parent may exaggerate a nonexistent or inconsequential sexual contact. The child, in order to ingratiate himself with the accusing parent, or feeling the necessity of approval from the custodial parent bringing the accusation, goes along, not necessarily even understanding, if they are quite young. It is a widely known fact that, in the instance of a sexual abuse accusation, custody is almost instantly awarded the other parent and, in most cases, visitation of any sort is denied the accused parent.

☐ There remains, throughout much of our judicial and social services systems, the automatic assumption that the mother is the best parent, regardless of her ability to function adequately in that role. This gender bias provides parenting classes and HRS supervision and instruction to a mother, but rarely is this considered for the father. This bias resulted in Mark Doe's children living with a convicted abuser, the man to whom their mother is married. This bias resulted in my children living with my ex-wife, even after she was proven to be an unfit mother.

☐ Many of the so-called "standard tests" are in violation of the tenets of the American Psychology Association. Judges and lawyers need to be aware of this.

☐ There is some question as to the value of psychological evaluations done on parents where allegations of child sexual abuse have occurred as an add-on to a divorce and custody battle. There are many "experts" whose qualifications are miles apart and whose methods of testing and manner of interviewing are diverse enough to result in different results from the same type of test. These experts are seeing the individuals at a time when they are hurt, angry, confused, frustrated, and frightened, yet attempt to draw a profile of how these individuals think and act under "normal" circumstances.

☐ Often, the individuals involved in substantiating and treating the abuse are not acting in the best interest of the children. It appears we have a bureaucracy that perpetuates the problem, combined with the subtle establishment of a system of experts who can be relied upon to substantiate allegations of abuse.

☐ The child-abuse industry is an extremely lucrative one, pumping vast amounts of money into various agencies in the mental health field, whether state or federally-funded or private. There are too many payoffs involved in the levying of false allegations. Attorneys receive large fees, the ex-wife obtains custody of the children, state agencies receive grant monies and larger budgets, and evaluators, therapists, and mental health professionals and institutions receive large fees for unnecessary treatment. One individual has pointed out that if we were to take the profit out of the children, where child-abuse allegations are concerned, the problem would go a long way toward correcting itself.

☐ The effect of the accusation on the falsely accused is not often realized. An allegation of child sexual abuse automatically makes you guilty until proven innocent in the eyes of the public, society, and social workers. There is frustration, anger and anxiety. Through the court battles and investigations, there is tremendous financial expense. All of these build to a level of depression that makes the falsely accused begin to question the sense of continuing the fight. It would be much easier to give up. Support groups for the falsely accused are appearing across the nation, but all too often there is nowhere for the individual to turn.

☐ The proposed conditions for allowing the accused to see his children again too often include a requirement that he attend child sexual abuse counseling or therapy. This condition is frequently imposed before there is any valid evidence of abuse and is often stipulated even after criminal charges have been dropped or the individual has been acquitted and creates a no-win situation. If you want to see your children, you must enter the required therapy. To be accepted into therapy, many therapists require that you admit to child sexual abuse. If you do not, there will be no therapy and therefore no contact with your children. If you do admit to the abuse, you're admitted to therapy, but the family court has reason to deny you any contact with your children.

☐ Use of the anatomically complete dolls encourages the child to fantasy, which is then treated as fact.

☐ In too many states and counties, social workers are dealing with two to three times the recommended number of cases. With the tremendous increase in allegations, false and valid, this overload prevents a thorough investigation and evaluation. In addition, burnout resulting from this situation leads to high turnover among social workers. As a result, many social workers, agency mental health workers, and child protection team members are untrained and inexperienced, resulting in a high degree of incompetency, particularly in areas of comprehensive and objective investigative techniques and skills. In a number of agencies, the social worker's job performance is measured by the body count of cases discovered or convictions gained.

☐ Case workers may see a great deal of real suffering on a daily basis. As a result, objective analysis and reaction are replaced by emotional decisions. When the same caseworker who is responsible for emotional therapy is also responsible for investigative work on the case, there is inevitably a crossover of efforts and information that should have been uncovered during an investigation is smothered in the immediate desire to "help" the victim. A lone social worker, whose interest is primarily therapy, cannot conduct a qualified, objective investigation, looking for answers to the question, "What is the basis of this allegation?"

☐ In regard to investigators serving as therapists, Hechler's book, includes this insight. "To avoid this very conflict, the *Federal Standards for Child Abuse and Neglect Prevention and Treatment Programs and Projects* suggests that Social Services departments 'assign specific staff for the purpose of *intake* (receipt and evaluation of child abuse and neglect reports) when the Local Unit has two or more child protective service workers,' and 'assign specific staff for the purposes of *treatment* (provision and/or obtainment of services and resources to meet the needs of the child, individual members and the family as a unit.)" (Emphasis in original.)

☐ The manner in which the system currently treats allegations of child sexual abuse provides that only the accused has accountability responsibilities. The individual making the accusation has historically suffered no legal or financial ramifications if the allegations were false. This is slowly changing in some states. "Expert" witnesses, who use unproven testing or interviewing techniques and who provide biased opinions of test results, suffer no legal or financial ramifications. Social workers and child protection team members operate under the protection of "sovereign immunity." The lack of checks and balances, the absence of accountability to legislators, heads of state or the court system, guarantee that HRS agency workers can dictate the lives of the falsely accused and his family. The establishment of anonymous hot line reporting of child abuse allows an individual to make the allegation without identifying himself/herself, therefore making it impossible to hold that individual accountable for the devastation that may result.

☐ The theory held by most social workers is that "children don't lie." Even though the statement is made by the mother, it is held that the child must have said it and so it is truth. When the child denies the allegations during an interview, the theory shifts to the fact that he or she is now ashamed or frightened of repeating the accusation. Consequently, the child's recantation is often ignored.

☐ The practice of placing the young child into therapy as soon as an allegation is filed is not in the best interest of anyone involved except, perhaps, the therapist. This therapy too often teaches the child more about the accusation and the role they are to play. In many cases, we are treating young children for a condition that doesn't exist.

Solutions:

☐ A review of the type of evidence and testimony that is allowed and accepted by the court is a necessary initial step. Today's technology provides various means by which hearsay testimony can be avoided and the child witness can provide actual testimony without undue stress or trauma. The use of closed circuit television, either one-way or two-way systems, provides the defendant the right to face and cross-examine the alleged victim without subjecting the child to an adult courtroom filled with strangers. Another option is the possibility of using videotaped testimony, taken in the defendant's presence. All initial and subsequent interviews of the alleged victim should be video recorded.

☐ Laws need to be passed that protect the right of the accused and include consequences for a false allegation. The 1990 Ohio legislature passed House Bill 44, assessing liability against anyone making false and malicious allegations of child abuse. Currently, a bill introduced in Ohio would forbid agencies to override a judge's decision or the decision of one's peers. It will also address appropriate access to one's own records and will contain a penalty clause making agencies and caseworkers accountable for their actions. The 1989 Arizona legislature passed a bill amending their Section 6, Title 13, Chapter 36 to provide that a person acting with malice, who knowingly and intentionally makes a false report of child abuse or neglect, or a person acting with malice who coerces another person to make a false report of child abuse or neglect, is guilty of a class three misdemeanor.

☐ Social workers, child protection team members, attorneys and judges need to become familiar with the signs and potential of the SAID Syndrome when handling allegations made during the course of custody/visitation battles. Social workers and mental health care professionals should also be cognizant of factors that may be indicative of the Parental Alienation Syndrome.

☐ In the context of divorce and custody battles, when allegations of child sexual abuse are made, particular attention must be focused on the accuser's psychological make-up, psychological needs, hidden agendas, and his/her influence on the child's allegations.

☐ "Experts," such as social workers, child protection team interviewers and policemen, need to be closely examined as to their actual "expertise" and qualifications before their diagnoses, opinions, and recommendations are considered or accepted. Many juvenile courts run forty cases through each hour, relying solely on the social services recommendations and rubber-stamping those recommendations.

Regarding social workers as expert witnesses, we should ask the following questions about the individuals and their interviewing techniques: What are the social worker's qualifications? How are those qualifications defined? What are the interviewing techniques? When are there enough questions, too many questions? How many times must the child go through the same questions in order to satisfy everyone's requirements for expert testimony? What are the results of this repetition?

☐ Child care workers need to be trained to have equal suspicion of untruth and of truth in allegations of child molestation. They need training in child development and child pathology to learn that children can be tricked or trained to lie by adults—parents, professionals whom they wish to please or whom they fear.

☐ Before a case moves into the courts or criminal charges are filed, each situation should be reviewed for outside factors that may be indicative of a motive for false allegations. Is there a divorce or custody battle in process? Does this case have any of the red flags of the SAID Syndrome? Is the family intact? Which parent filed the complaint? Did the child actually indicate there had been abuse or did the complaint come from a parent or other adult? How was the investigation handled and what professionals were involved? Were all individuals directly interviewed, as well as friends, neighbors, relatives, and so forth?

☐ Initial interviews must be videotaped, to identify the credibility of the information acquired, the circumstances in which statements were made, the manner in which the interrogation was conducted, and the competency, if any, of the professionals conducting the interviews.

☐ Child competency and hearsay relevancy hearings should be used to determine the effect of the child's age, the ability to communicate, and to discern truth from falsehood at the time the out-of-court statements were made. This may shed light on the child's competency and the trustworthiness of his/her hearsay statements. Guidelines must be established, determining when a child witness crosses the line from merely being uncommunicative to unavailable.

☐ Any investigation of child sexual abuse should be done by a team of qualified individuals, preferably a designated task force. A responsible team should include individuals trained in objective investigation, psychiatric/ psychological intervention, medical evaluation, social work, and logical legal work.

☐ The court monitor system, discussed under "The Courts" in Chapter Twelve, could serve as an excellent informal research system to identify areas of concern regarding types of evidence and investigative techniques that do not serve in the best interest of either the alleged perpetrator or the alleged victim.

☐ It is essential that the validity of using the anatomical dolls be closely examined. With no standards for either the production of the dolls as a testing mechanism or for the manner in which they are used, this protocol is not accepted by the scientific community and considered highly suspect by the majority of expert professionals involved in the areas of child development and play therapy. If the dolls were used to gain "evidence" from the child, *both* sides should be allowed to speak to the validity of the use of such methodology.

☐ Judges and attorneys need a better understanding of the various tests, such as the Minnesota Multiphasic Personality Index, the California Psychological Inventory, various play and drawing tests, to be able to identify biased reporting, invalid uses of the tests, or too much reliance on any one given test. The various psychological tests available measure different facets of the individuals personality and psychological makeup and need to be used as a *set* of tools to reach valid conclusions.

☐ Consistent and objective actions by support groups, such as VOCAL, National Congress for Men and Children, Family Rights Committee, CASA, and other similar organizations can identify the problems within the system and work towards forming and proposing solutions that will protect the innocent as well as the children.

As stated in a report filed by an investigative committee reviewing the actions of a child protective services agency in Texas, "Regrettably, an infusion of resources alone will not be sufficient to address these problems. Judgment, ethics and attitude cannot be purchased or legislated. Money cannot buy common sense. . ."

Chapter Sixteen

An Attorney's View of Some Essential Elements of Pre-trial Preparation and Litigation

By: Charles Jamieson, Esq., A-TEAM Counsel
Introduction

When Dean Tong requested I write a chapter in his book regarding "Defending Against False Child Abuse Allegations" I was at first somewhat dismayed. This is a subject matter that one could write several books about and still not fully and comprehensively cover all the aspects of litigating a false child abuse allegation case. Consequently, in this short chapter, I have not tried to provide a comprehensive overview, but rather I have attempted to discuss some important aspects that must be confronted by an individual litigating a false child abuse allegation, regardless of what form it may occur: divorce court, criminal court, juvenile court, or civil court.

Many of the comments contained in this chapter may seem, at first review, to be based on nothing more than a common sense, assertive approach in defending a client. However, it is amazing how many times a lay person or an attorney will apparently become confused and discouraged, and not act in an assertive fashion in the defense against a false child abuse allegation. Because of this dynamic, one should never overestimate an attorney's ability to devise even what appears to be the most common sense and simplest response to a child abuse allegation. As an educated consumer of legal representation, a lay person should always assume that his attorney is open to suggestions and should always proceed, during any interview with your attorney, with the attitude you have certain things you wish to discuss or suggest to your attorney. Inevitably, you will find that the attorney is willing to sit back and speak to any individual about any alleged grievances, which they may have.

Most cases are won or lost prior to the commencement of trial. Consequently, I have focused my presentation on important pre-trial issues which the falsely accused must confront in the context of preparing for trial.

Like any attorney, I begin this chapter with a disclaimer. This should not be viewed by any individual as a "paint by the numbers" method of defending against a false child abuse allegation. Every case must be tailored to its own facts to fit its own facts and dynamics. Consequently, the suggestions made in this chapter, should not be followed blindly by any individual in forming or instituting a strategy of defense against a false child abuse allegation.

Negative Impact of the Allegation

No issue stirs such emotions in our society today as the issue of child abuse. It is an issue that is in the forefront of society's media, be it newspapers, television or radio. It is easy to comprehend why child abuse evokes such an overwhelming negative reaction. We are socialized from the time we are quite young to be protective of children. It is a message that is communicated to us in many forms on a daily basis throughout our entire lives. Consequently, it is not unreasonable to expect that an allegation of child abuse will evoke a uniformly negative response. The negative reaction associated with child abuse allegations cause many individuals to forget rational thought, and results in an atmosphere of hostility and prejudice towards an individual falsely accused, which must be overcome in order to preserve the principles of justice and due process. As attorneys and lay people involved in these types of cases, we cannot forget that this is a powerful dynamic which caused an individual falsely accused of child abuse to have to overcome the major unspoken, underlying premise in such cases: "An accused is presumed guilty until proven innocent."

The most effective way to counter this dynamic is the planning and implementation of a comprehensive and assertive legal strategy. The watch words for the strategy to counter the opposition's case should be: "object, object, object;" and "limit, limit, limit." The watch words for the implementation of a defense should be "educate, educate, educate;" and "explain, explain, explain."

Choosing Sides

Despite their protestations to the contrary, Americans, by their nature, choose sides in any controversy. It is part of our national ethos. Almost every person, in traveling, has turned on a television set and found themselves gazing idly at a sports event about which they know nothing, which involves players of whom they know nothing. Inevitably, within the first few moments of watching this sport, the viewer will start consciously or unconsciously rooting for one side or the other. This "rooting" may not be of the obvious, boisterous kind, but it will always inevitably occur.

In the same fashion, do not believe the statement that people will not choose sides in a child sex abuse allegation. Every significant person in the accused's life either consciously or subconsciously will determine which party they will side with: the accuser or the accused. Even if they do not verbally state a preference, many people will state "I don't wish to become involved." Even by this apparently neutral statement, the individuals are in fact stating a preference because they are not going to support the accused.

Because of this dynamic, it is absolutely important to immediately reach out and obtain a written statement from those individuals who may be potential witnesses on your behalf. As soon as possible, it is important to try and have these individuals commit their support to you in some form of a written statement. This statement can be obtained by an attorney, or more preferably, by an investigator. Any investigator who attempts to obtain these statements should be educated as to the themes of your case so that the appropriate questions can be asked.

An investigator is also useful in attempting to obtain statements from potentially hostile witnesses. Unless there is a specific Court order entered that prevents your side from having contact from the opposition's witnesses, then it is appropriate and essential that your investigator attempt to contact these individuals to learn what they have to say about the issues in this case. If an individual refuses to talk to your investigator, then the tactic of sending them a certified, return receipt requested letter requesting that they permit your side to ask them questions about what they may know about the case. Inevitably, those individuals, who have been instructed by the opposition's attorney that they don't have to talk with your side, will ignore the letter. If that occurs, then a second, similar letter should be sent. Such letters create the opportunity whereby you can have potent cross-examination of this witness before a judge or jury by creating an innuendo that these individuals had something to hide. At the very least, it permits the opportunity to have your attorney pose the closing argument: "What do these individuals have to hide, and why did they refuse to cooperate on a very simple request regarding the knowledge they have of the case?"

Chronology

Among other things that the O.J. Simpson trial brought to the national spotlight was the importance of timelines or chronologies.

A chronology is one of the most important devices that a falsely accused individual, or his or her attorney, can create in the preparation and presentation of a defense. Chronology is a documentary procedure of organizing the information available in a child abuse case in a chronological or time oriented fashion. A chronology can be used to organize consistent and/or conflicting information concerning how an incident or accusation occurred; the events that preceded and occurred after the allegation occurred; how the investigation was conducted after the allegation occurred; what potential effects or influences various events may have had on the child or other major characters involved in the allegation; and it also produces an insight as to how an allegation occurred and/or escalated.

A chronology is a standard method of organization which can help your attorney establish his or her themes of the case; and bring out causal links between seemingly related, and sometimes seemingly unrelated events.

There is no easy way to prepare a chronology other than rolling up your sleeves and write down all the important facts and incidences which have occurred in the case in a painstaking fashion. This requires that the creator of the chronology obtain information from every source available, including, but not limited to: the accuser's recollections; friends of accuser's recollections of events; all possible records of the alleged child victim (including medical, school, and mental health); the section notes and evaluation reports of any mental health professionals involved in the case; civil case records from dependency or divorce court; criminal records if appropriate; and the views of all witnesses. Chronology is not a one time task. It should be consistently and thoroughly updated with the production of each new piece of information and/or report. It should be reviewed from beginning to end on several occasions by both the accused and the attorney, and their impressions should be carefully compared and discussed.

A chronology should be kept for each child in a multiple child case and for each defendant in a multiple defendant case. As the chronology is being generated, it has several uses. It can help the attorney create a trial strategy and theories of defense. In addition, it can be used to help generate emotions; discovery requests; develop material for the jury; and help develop the opening and closing arguments of the attorney.

Learning About the Child Victim

It is important to discover everything one can about the child victim or victims involved in the case. What are their favorite movies and books? Once identified, it is absolutely essential that these books and movies be carefully reviewed. Sometimes the children's allegations will mirror particular themes contained in children's G rated movies. In addition, particularly with young children, the fantasy elements contained in movies sometimes generates their own fantasy and may cause them to make allegations about things which have never occurred.

It is also important to find out what sources of potential sexual education and/or stimuli to which the child has been exposed. Has the child victim ever had any playmates that were sexually abused. What kind of sexualized stimuli has the child been exposed to in the form of X rated films, cable television shows, daytime soap operas, in what child abuse awareness or educational programs has the child participated (be sure to obtain a copy of the curriculum of each presentation), adult magazines (such as Playboy or Penthouse), and R rated movies. These may all provide explanations as to why a child may be acting or stating things in a sexualized fashion, but yet has not been sexually abused.

In preparing for litigation, one must also obtain all records concerning the minor child. This includes all medical records, all educational records, and all mental health records. These records should be obtained through a direct request by the alleged perpetrator (if the alleged perpetrator is a parent of the alleged child victim) and through discovery requests and motions. The medical records are critical in attempting to ascertain if there are other medical conditions or incidents in the child's life which may have created a physical condition, which may offer a benign or non-abusive explanation for the physical findings at issue in the case. School records are often vital in exploring whether the child has disciplinary problems or behavioral problems which may lead to development of a possible theory for the defense. Mental health records are critical in reviewing whether appropriate procedures have been followed in the evaluation of the alleged child victim and the subsequent therapy sessions. In addition, a review of the mental health records are useful in determining whether evaluation and/or therapeutic techniques of mental health professionals have led to memory contamination, particularly in the case of younger children.

An extensive knowledge of the child's background, as well as their likes and dislikes, is essential for an attorney to be able to create an appropriate form of cross-examination of the alleged child victim needs. Children have different levels of maturity, sophistication, and articulation. Those developmental levels differ between children of the same chronological age, as well as children of different chronological ages. Consequently, in order to formulate a successful cross-examination, extensive knowledge of the alleged child victim is important.

Contextual Defense
In formulating a defense during any child abuse case, it is

absolutely critical to determine if the alleged child victim is really indicating that something inappropriately happened to him or her. The proverbial sixty four dollar question is "did something really happen and if so, what was it?"

The seemingly simple question is critically important. In today's society, males are encouraged, more than any other time in our recent past, to become actively involved in all aspects of child rearing. Those aspects include bathing, diapering, and administering medication to anal/genital areas of babies who have rashes, urinary tract problems and other medical problems. Despite this change in child rearing practices, it is surprising the number of times a child will say that their father has touched them in their genital or anal areas and the investigating agency automatically assumes that the child is talking about being sexually abused. Consequently, it is critical in the review of the history and materials in an investigation of child abuse to ascertain if there was an exploration into the context in which the alleged abuse occurred. If the touching occurred in a situation where the alleged accused has participated actively in child care, then a potential defense may be created on the basis of the agency's misconstruing a benign or appropriate action.

In contextual exploration of an allegation, it is also important to ascertain whether the allegation is a by product of other parties. This may be a stereotypical coaching of an estranged parent or mistakenly aggrieved relation or acquaintance of the accused. Although not frequently, children are sometimes brainwashed into making allegations.

Expert Witnesses

It is a sad fact that without the assistance of expert witnesses, the falsely accused stands a good chance of being found to have committed child abuse. Attorneys are trained in law school, in legal logic, in the formulation of legal questions, and how to research and find the applicable statues and case law regarding legal questions. Attorneys are not trained in the areas of psychology, sociology, and medicine, which factor prominently in most false charges of child abuse. There is a common expression among individuals who are experienced in child abuse litigation:

"A mediocre attorney can win a child abuse case with a good expert; however, a good attorney will have a hard time winning a child abuse case without the assistance of an expert witness."

An explosion of research has occurred in the past few years in the fields of medicine and psychology concerning the issues of child abuse. An expert is useful in helping educate the falsely accused and their legal counsel as to current accepted principles within the fields of medicine and mental health, regarding child abuse. Such current knowledge is critical in attempting to expose some of the commonly held myths which were created approximately ten years ago and which have entrenched themselves in some areas of the medical and mental health field. An example of such an outdated myth would be: Children do not lie about sex abuse; or a relaxed anal tone is a diagnostic sign of child sexual abuse. Expert witnesses are also essential in helping to formulate areas of cross-examination of the opposition's experts at the time of trial. Experts will also indicate information as necessary to be acquired in order to adequately review your case and help formulate themes for the defense.

Finally, experts are critical in helping to explain some of the critical questions that occur in any child abuse trial (whether by judge or jury). Some of those questions include:

1. Did the child suffer from any medical conditions or incur any kind of injury which would result in the physical condition which is similar to a condition resulting from child physical or sexual abuse?

2. If the accused did not sexually abuse the child, then why is the child claiming that the accused abused them?

3. Has there been an overreaction or misinterpretation of a benign incident or statement?

Experts are also useful in educating the attorney and the trier of fact as to what research has been done to establish what behavior or findings are normal. For example, there is surprising little data as to what is the normal base rate for children touching their genital or anal areas. Although most parents are aware that all children touch themselves in this area, there is little knowledge as to what should be considered normal touching and at what age.

Any experts you can retain will help neutralize the opposition's experts and will provide valuable assistance in the preparation and presentation of your defense.

Another useful purpose for an expert is to educate the trier of fact. Most people do not know the true facts about child abuse. Their beliefs and ideas concerning child abuse have been molded by the media and by myths which may have been accepted as being fact by mere repetition. This shortcoming affects both judges and many potential jury members. By the use of your expert, you can obtain research and data by which you can construct an aggressive, defensive strategy that can help counteract the prejudice that is inherent in a child abuse charge and the "myth and folklore" espoused by the opposition.

Collateral Proceedings

The importance of the institution and active participation in collateral proceedings cannot be underestimated. In the event you are falsely charged in a criminal action of child abuse, then a collateral action might be some kind of civil action whereby you could participate and involve the same allegations. The advantages of doing so are many. In the majority of the states in this country, discovery which is permitted in criminal proceedings is quite limited. However, the discovery which is permitted in a civil action, such as a divorce case, is far more liberal. Consequently, in the event the former spouse brings a false accusation of child abuse, a collateral post final judgment motion for modification action could be utilized to engage in discovery and find out information which would not ordinarily be available to you and your attorney in a criminal case. For instance, most states do not allow depositions in criminal proceedings. To circumvent this "road block" to be able to use this powerful engine of discovery, institute a collateral or corresponding civil case and take the depositions in the civil proceeding.

In those jurisdictions where the family court may try to limit your criminal attorney's involvement in a proceeding, it may be appropriate to hire a separate attorney to pursue the modification proceeding in divorce court. However, your criminal attorney would continue working actively in the background to help direct the discovery strategy in the civil case and to make available to you any information which could be gleaned from this matter.

Pre-trial Practice

One of my first legal mentors taught me that in any case, no matter how strong it may appear, has weaknesses. It is the job of any good defense attorney to probe constantly in every case to discover those weaknesses in an attempt to wedge them open to the advantage of his or her client. This is the basic attitude an attorney defending against false allegations of child abuse should take. Essentially, the attorney should raise every objection that he thinks appropriate and must move to limit the majority, if not all, the evidence offered by the opposition in their case.

Both the medical and mental health fields have undergone a revolution in recent years. Research has indicated that many of the "sacred truths" held by these professions, regarding issues in child sex abuse cases, have either been modified or been found to be erroneous. However, there has been an uneven distribution of these developments throughout the medical and mental health fields. There is no child abuse case in which it is not appropriate to file motions to suppress, motions in limine, or motions to limit the introduction of evidence. For instance, such motions can be filed regarding the suppression of evidence concerning anatomical dolls, child sexual abuse accommodations syndrome, and sex offender profiles, just to name a few. However, the need to file such motions only highlights the critical need for attorneys to be educated in the medical and mental health aspects of defending false child abuse allegations.

There is a more practical aspect regarding the effect of an active pre-trial practice in terms of obtaining discovery and filing motions. The underlying approach should be to "paperwork the opposition to death." This is not just a vehicle of harassment. Prosecutors, for the most part, are understaffed and overworked. They have heavy case loads that prevent them from spending a great deal of time on any case. In a similar fashion, the majority of attorneys in private practice carry a rather heavy case load in order to maintain a volume of income to meet the ever increasing demands of overhead expenses, and their own individual salaries. In some cases, prosecutors may provide a better plea bargain if they see they have a major fight on their hands. In family court matters, you may get a better settlement if the opposition believes they have an unduly expensive and aggressive fight on their hands. Aggressive pre-trial motion practice and discovery practice is the most effective tactic to be utilized by those individuals who cannot afford to hire a battery of experts and may not have the financial wherewithal to withstand a protracted and lengthy trial.

The focus of your pre-trial motion practice is to move to object and/or limit the evidence of the opposition and to ask for everything pursuant to discovery, including "the kitchen sink." An attorney representing an alleged perpetrator should understand from the beginning that many, if not the majority, of his motions will be denied. However, unless a vigorous motion practice is pursued, those few "breaks" that the falsely accused may obtain from the legal system will not be granted.

Conclusion

Child abuse allegations immediately stir negative emotions in nearly everyone, including attorneys and judges. The only way to counteract the assumption that "an accused is guilty, until proven innocent", is to carefully plan and institute a comprehensive, defensive strategy. Such a strategy must include obtaining all the information you can about the "players" in the development of the child abuse allegation, obtaining experts to assist you, instituting an aggressive strategy to obtain all the possible information you can, and to object and limit in any way possible the opposition's case. If one follows this basic strategy, then you will maximize their chances for a successful outcome if they find themselves falsely accused of child abuse.

Charles D. Jamieson is an attorney in the law firm of Glickman, Witters and Marell, P.A., 1601 Forum Place, Suite 1101, West Palm Beach, Florida 33401, telephone number (407) 478-1111. His practice is focused in the area of child abuse issues.

Chapter Seventeen

What You Need to Know

By: Kenneth R. Pangborn, Trial Consultant

Eighteen years as a Trial Consultant dealing with cases of alleged sexual misconduct have taught me a few things about these cases and the people accused of such acts. Chief among those things are the mistakes that people make when confronted by the allegations. When people first hear the hint of the coming allegations their reaction is to disregard them as silly and laugh off the possibility of actually being in trouble. This is their worst mistake, but only the first of several they will make. When you do finally become concerned about the allegations invariably you select the wrong attorney and squander precious resources in bottomless holes. You will face a confusing set of circumstances that few lay people are equipped to understand much less deal with correctly. Instead of finding one attorney who is able to handle all aspects of their case, many people wind up with several lawyers, one for the divorce case, one for the juvenile case, and one for the criminal case. Most frequently this lawyer committee works at cross purposes with each other, and seldom are they more than a rabble. In my eighteen years we have been able to work out ways of handling sex cases that results in the vast majority of the cases we handle being closed unfounded and dismissed before trial. This means a profound financial saving for our clients. The big money in these cases comes in the trials. Which is why others who claim expertise in this field stress the trial. It's in their interest to see your case go to trial, not yours!

Most people get their ideas about how the legal system works from television and the movies, so we come to a situation like this with expectations that are not realistic. People cling to immature beliefs in "truth, justice, and the American way." People often believe that they are innocent and everyone will somehow see that the allegations are all one big lie. Over the years, I have received thousands of letters from people in prison, who violently insist that eventually people will just see that they are innocent. It just does not work that way. They stay in prison a very long time. Their bitterness builds. There is no "magic" cure. There is no "fairy godmother" who will sprinkle fairy dust on you and make it go away.

What you need to know more than anything else is what you will be really facing. In the legal system you will face many people who have agendas that often have nothing to do with the truth. You will encounter strident activists. You will encounter poorly trained case workers at social agencies. And you may face experts who are complete frauds. Over the years we have encountered quite a few people who have claimed to be psychologists who in point of fact were impostors, in illustration. One of the more celebrated of these was Dr. Dennis Harrison of Baltimore. Harrison was a media darling, acting as a consultant to the Geraldo Rivera television show and Oprah Winfrey's television show. Harrison even testified before Congress. Harrison became most famous over the Elizabeth Morgan - Eric Foretich case in Washington, D.C. in 1985. Harrison, however was not a psychologist even though he had obtained a license in the State of Maryland by fraud. Harrison was cited with multiple counts of perjury.[1] He had testified as a psychologist in hundreds of civil and criminal trials.

Few lawyers know enough about the mental health sciences to recognize when they are being snowed by a good conman or conwoman. Some are outright frauds like Harrison, still others merely misrepresent or exaggerate their credentials. Others misrepresent the facts (truth) in a case, some to a small but deadly degree and others will tell whoppers. But they get away with their scams for years because nobody seems to catch their lies. In a recent case in Texas we worked on, the "Psychologist" has been that local region's "expert" for almost 8 years in child sexual abuse cases. While she did have a Doctorate degree, it was not in psychology per se, but an offshoot branch of psychology dealing with substance abuse. One day she decided that she was an expert in sexual abuse and hung her shingle. She was accepted as the local authority for 8 years before we began to question her. Her credibility suffered a complete meltdown. She is no longer regarded as a reliable expert witness.

You will confront a great many issues in dealing with the legal system. You should begin by understanding that there are essentially two questions you will face in a child sexual abuse allegation;

1. Are you a pervert?

2. Why would the child say you did something if it weren't true?

If you fail to prove the answers to either of those questions to the satisfaction of the judge or jury, or others in the system, you will face things going from bad to worse. You need to know that proving the answers to those questions will not be cheap or easy. There are no K-Mart blue light specials. You will get exactly what you pay for. That being said, I can't tell you that if you do nothing the worst will happen. There is, after all, such a thing as dumb luck. Yes there have been cases that have gone away. Most of the time they come back in a few months or years. But some just resolve themselves. Not many, but some. You can have all the justice you can afford, if you can't afford justice you won't get justice. This is the sad truth you face at the opening to your case.

You will encounter strident opposition from child abuse investigators and police investigators. They begin with a mindset that most people are guilty. They also have been sold a volume of clichés such as "children never lie about abuse." Well in simple truth, they sometimes do. And often they are wrong! And often they are wrong because despite what the extremely strident voices say, children are suggestible. Current research clearly indicates the serious problems that exist with the most common forms of interviewing that are being used. Extremists within the mental health community banded together a number of years ago to form the American Professional Society on the Abuse of Children (APSAC) which is strident in its denial that children are at all suggestible. They discount the foundational research by Dr. Stephen Ceci of Cornell University and Dr. Maggie Bruck of McGil University. Since their original work, a mountain of evidence has been building to show the process whereby children's perceptions of events can be altered by inept interviewing and by parents or others influencing children for ulterior motives. According to Ceci and Bruck, "in light of the full corpus of data that we have reviewed, these extreme opinions are not supported by the available research. This research shows that children are able to encode and retrieve large amounts of information especially when it is personally experienced and highly meaningful. Equally true, however, is that no good will be served by ignoring that part of the research that demonstrates potentially serious social and cognitive hazards to young witnesses if adults who have access to them attempt to usurp their memories. Inattention to the full corpus of empirical data will only forestall efforts to improve the way child witnesses are treated and delay needed research into ways of optimizing young children's testimonial accuracy through better interviewing techniques and judicial reform."[2]

Eighteen years ago when I began my work to assist lawyers in preparing cases for trial all the cases involved allegations against men. Today there is a growing body of allegations against women. Representing women in such cases is much more difficult. The tools to defend women are mostly still in development. But there are answers. Ten years ago allegations of sexual misconduct against women were laughed off as an impossible notion. Today the system seems to be trying to prove something by being even more vicious in its attacks on women. There have been many noted cases of women being sent to prison on flimsy evidence. Kelly Michaels in New Jersey comes to mind. The women in the "Little Rascals" case in the Carolinas is another. The Sousas also come to mind. Hundreds of women have been accused in cases of alleged ritualistic satanic sexual abuse. Yet, according to Dr. Kenneth Lanning of the FBI, there has never been even one documented case of satanic ritual abuse proven.[3]

Central in the problems faced in preparing a successful strategy for dealing with sexual abuse allegations is the problem you face with adversarial experts who claim to have validated the allegations against you by their scientific means. It is simple when as previously mentioned the adverse expert is a patent fraud. Often, it is not that easy. You find the individuals have valid academic credentials. In so many of the cases I have reviewed I seldom see any effort at pre-trial discovery. It is essential to have notes of these "therapists" as well as audio or video tapes for intense review. Essential for your ability to evaluate the process children have been subjected to is the amount of information you can obtain on the process that was employed.

What we often see is poorly trained case investigators and therapists who use techniques that more resemble prisoner of war interrogation reminiscent of the Korean War than of methods appropriate for small children. We also encounter the passionate "true believers" who subscribe to the idea that the ends justify any and all means. In many cases these individuals are acting out their own life drama using the children as puppets on the stage of their own life. Faulty investigations of child abuse are common. What you encounter is a strident belief among some professionals that every accused is guilty. Or as others have put it; "Many professionals have difficulty accepting the possibility that some alleged offenders are innocent, that some children give inaccurate accounts of abuse, or that faulty evaluations can lead to the misdiagnosis of abuse."[4] This is the area where traditional defense is so utterly lacking in the requisite expertise. Being able to sort through the useful from the waste. All too often some of those who defend these cases, and who think of themselves as expert in this issue, rely on some experts who have become well known defense experts. Sadly, in many cases a bit too well known. The last thing you want is someone who is easily identifiable as a "defense whore" who always finds for the defendant, and who has a narrow span of experience. These folks, while often people of stellar character, are more harm than good. Also a word to the wise is that these cases are decided on the "weight" of evidence. A slight "weight" advantage to the other side and you lose! So I generally recommend experts of the highest reputation in the belief that it is much better to be safe than sorry. You don't get to do it over if you lose.

Developing a winning strategy is something that comes from lots of experience and lots of hard work. A winning strategy isn't an accident. And it doesn't come from a "formula." I see others who claim to be the best at defending sex cases claim they can reduce the problem to a "syndrome" from which they can apply quick, easy and cheap solutions. On some occasions they work. Most often they are disasters. These folks won't tell you of the cases where their patients died! Also, winning strategies can't be "phoned in." These are hands-on type problems.

The problems that you face if you are accused of sexual transgression largely have to do with the choices you make when you first learn of them. The *only* appropriate response is "*panic!*" This is the time to have a clear head. You need to be careful on the selection of a lawyer, as I said before. Make _sure_ you have an expert. If you can't get the best, then you will definitely need a trial consultant to help the marginal lawyer handle the case. You want your case worked hard from the very start. The "let's wait and see what happens" strategy is from the old school of thought, and today leads to disaster. These cases don't just blow away like they did 20 years ago. Judges who flippantly dismiss such cases are removed from the bench.

Naive people facing accusations of sexual misconduct are terrified, as they should be, when they finally come to realize the seriousness with which the allegations are being taken by officials. There are many "experts" who employ methods for interviewing children that are problematic for us in preparing your case. Dr. Henry Adams of the School of Psychology at the University of Georgia says this; "This tragedy often occurs in therapy where investigation is confused with therapy. The major justification for much of this coaching or 'child brainwashing' is that they must prepare the child for court."[5] The problems in this regard can be systemic. Even to the degree that in one American community it was so out of hand the issue became one for the Grand Jury in the community.[6] It is important to note the many influences upon children that distort their memory. It is also important to know how to answer that situation without alienating a jury or a judge. You cannot get away with "beating up" a kid on the witness stand. Clever words with children almost always backfire. There needs to be a careful employment of science to unravel the ball of mis-information that often permeates these cases. Misinformation that more resembles primitive superstition than science. It is the job of a good defense team to bring the truth to this kind of case. Some practitioners believe that you can shade the truth or should in these cases. I strongly disagree. As the accused, the *BEST* tool you have to take into a courtroom is your credibility. If you destroy that, all the clever banter from a "mouthpiece" in the world won't help you. Again this is not an area for cleverness. It is an area for hard work. Lots of self proclaimed experts on "False Abuse cases" offer cheap and easy solutions. You would do well to understand that in this situation, perhaps more than any other, if it sounds too good to be true....it IS! There just isn't any *real* cheap and easy solution to this kind of case! I wish there were. This is an area, sadly, where if you're broke, you're screwed! A successful defense isn't cheap.

One of the keys for you to judge your defense team is by how they approach your case. Do they attack your case with a sense of urgency? Or do they approach it with an attitude that it can be done tomorrow or next month just as well as today! You should feel like your case is the only case they have, like you are their most important client and your case is an "emergency." Because, my friend...IT IS! If you take any other attitude it'll cost ya!

You've got lots of choices to make. Another key point you need to know, as I close this part of the chapter, is where do you fit in within the strategy of your case. It is essential that you are central to the case strategy. There can be no really successful defense without your intimate involvement in the decision making process. You need to be kept informed and involved. The more leg work you can do the better our plan works in defending you and getting you back with your children and your life.

As an aside I have often mused about the hearsay exception that is given such wide berth in child sexual abuse cases. This exception allows into evidence the statements of children made to social workers and others regarded as statements of abuse. An issue I see as ripe for legal discussion is just how some experts believe that a child who does not understand the difference between the truth and fantasy has their credibility magically transformed by merely telling the story to a social worker instead of under oath in court. I fail to see how the child's testimony is magically transfigured from incompetent to competent merely by it being related to a social worker instead of a jury or judge. The present system is too ripe a field for the harvest of mischief by mental health professionals with an agenda other than the truth of the matter of abuse. The legalisms that the debate is couched in steer clear of the magical thinking that this transmutation process has any real validity to it.[7] I would also commend the scholarship of Cornell University psychologist Stephen Ceci who says; "An emotional battle is being waged today in our nation's courtrooms, Universities, and livingrooms. This battle revolves around the credibility of children's testimony, particularly in sexual abuse cases. To listen to one side, you would think that everything that a child tells a social worker or therapist must be believed, no matter how bizarre the allegations, no matter how suggestive or coercive the techniques used to elicit them.."[8]

The problem I have encountered with people who initially contact me is that I tell them what is needed, and many people just find it hard to believe that if they don't do the things I suggest that the problems I describe are likely to come true. A percentage of the people get lucky and things blow over. But, most of the people come back to me with their worst nightmare having come true, and now destitute asking me what I can now do for them in their forthcoming criminal trial. Like others who have less than cheerful stories to tell, I can lead a horse to the water's edge, but I cannot make you drink! If you think a sexual misconduct case can be handled on a McDonald's budget you are living in Disneyland. The process of defending yourself will be expensive (5 figures), it will be demeaning and in general not lots of fun. You can, of course delude yourself. Lord knows there are many unscrupulous people who will take your money and aid you in your delusions that "everything will be okay." No strategy is worse in these cases than the old "let's wait and see what happens" mentality that permeates 99.99999% of the defense bar! Sometimes the cases just blow away. Rarely today. But almost always they come back in a few months and each time they blow away and blow back they become more difficult to dispatch and more expensive. Whining about the situation won't solve it for you. You have the choice to be a victim, road-kill, or to put an end to your torment. No matter what anyone says there is no cheap and easy solution. No quick fixes. But this is one of life's events when people's judgments are at its worst. Most people just refuse to believe the system is as corrupt as it is and that you will be PRESUMED GUILTY! You will be required to prove yourself innocent beyond a shadow of a doubt, and even then, MANY people will refuse to believe you didn't do what you are accused of. Think of when you read the morning newspaper and saw the story on John Jones accused of molesting 22 children. Remember what you said? Pretty intolerant, wasn't it! Your eyes are opening now. But if you are in that group of people who just refuses to believe that life as they have known it has ended, and that they must act or drown, no life preserver will work for you. Some people refuse to believe their Titanic is sinking even as their lungs fill with sea water! Sadly it doesn't have to be that way. Some people learn easier than others.

I can't impress on you enough the importance of acting quickly. The sooner you attack the allegations and demolish them the better it will be for everyone. The difference in final cost is usually tremendous. Spend a few thousand dollars at the beginning of a case or face the need for many tens of thousands of dollars because of neglecting the allegations. And for most people, doing nothing results in being eventually faced with a fait accompli, and either having to accept a plea bargain (guilty plea) or ending their relationship with their children because they don't have any hope of raising the funds for a full blown trial.

Oh yes, let me correct one piece of deceptive advice. Many people are encouraged to accept a "Nolo Plea." (Nolo Contendere, or no contest.) If you are told that this is not a "Guilty" plea, you're being lied to. It is a guilty plea, and once you have accepted it you have forever waived any right to appeal whatever verdict follows. Despite what you are told, a judge does NOT have to agree to the terms you were promised, and in about 40% of the cases they do NOT! Over the years I have spoken to hundreds of men in prison who keep crying on the phone to me "but they promised me that I wouldn't have to go to jail." One of the men who followed the advice was given a life sentence without the possibility of parole, and since his sentence his lawyer has refused to return phone calls.

[1] Hillary's Psychologist Loses License
Michael Hedges
Washington Times, AP Wire 9-13-90

[2] Suggestibility of the Child Witness: A historical Review and Synthesis
Stephen J. Ceci, Maggie Bruck
Psychological Bulletin, 1993 Vol 113 No. 3 403-439

see also

The Suggestibility of Children's Recollections
John Doris, Ed.
American Psychological Association, 1991
ISBN 1-55798-118-3

[3] Ritual Abuse: A Law Enforcement View or Perspective
Kenneth V. Lanning
Behavioral Science Instruction and Research Unit FBI Academy, Quantico, VA.
Child Abuse and Neglect, Vol. 15, pp 171-173, 1991

[4] Assessing Child Maltreatment Reports
Michael Robin, Ed.
Page 26
Haworth Press, New York, 1991
ISBN 1-56024-161-6

[5] Child and Family Abuse by Child Advocates
Henry E. Adams
Presidential Address South East Psychological Association, 3-26-93

[6] Child Sexual Abuse, Assault, and Molest Issues
Report, San Diego County Grand Jury
June 29, 1992

[7] State of Florida vs. Jack Timothy Townsend
635 So. 2d 949

[8] Jeopardy In The Courtroom
Stephen J. Ceci, Maggie Bruck
American Psychological Association, 1995
ISBN 1-55798-282-1

THE A-TEAM
BETTER THAN EVER!
What is the A-Team?

The A-Team is a referral list of attorneys and other professional resources assembled to meet the unique needs of your case
and others who have been wrongfully accused of child sexual
abuse, child abuse, rape or other related offenses. The A-Team
concept brings the best of modern technology and strategies to
help resolve the legal problems of the wrongly accused.

A-Team History
In 1982 I and several other professionals became aware of an
explosion in the number of allegations of child sexual abuse in
contested divorce and child custody disputes. This was almost
immediately followed by an explosion of allegations against day
care center employees and teachers at all levels. By 1983 we
learned that the massive increase we were seeing in the accusations of child sexual abuse were no accident. We learned of the
existence of a publication being circulated through a few women's
shelters entitled; "The Mother's Child Custody Combat Manual."
Since then a newer, more advanced booklet has been distributed
nationally now titled; "How to Avoid The Custody Battle." Also
in 1983 we began getting feedback from father's rights groups and
individuals all across America as our interest in this subject
became well known in that movement. We began our research
into resources and general information that could be used to
assist men caught in this bind. As we assembled information we
became alarmed at a number of things. The first was the geo-
metric increase in the number of cases. America went from a
scant 3,000 reported incest cases in 1980 to over 132,000 in 1987.
And nearly one half million by 1990. This is a growth industry!
And this phenomena has hit other countries as well. Neither this
problem nor our services are limited to the United States. We can
help you if you are in Europe or almost anywhere. We also were
disturbed by the legal trends that resulted in more and more
divorced parents being sent to prison because of these allegations.
We soon detected four clear problems:

1. The men themselves were naive about how the system would work in their case. They were also giving off erroneous signals that made others believe them guilty.

2. Local attorneys were unprepared to handle this kind of situation and legal advice was almost universally bad!

3. People in the "Child Protective Services" welfare establishment had been largely infiltrated by militant activists and resulting investigations were largely biased against fathers.

4. That women were also being wrongly accused.

In an effort to confront the overwhelming burden of wrongful allegations, a multilayered resource system was designed to cut through the bewildering web of lies with special emphasis on stopping the "fast track" to criminal court. We found competent lawyers who REALLY know how to deal with these kinds of cases and, who can take the side of the accused into court and prove what is needed. We recruited a tough highly effective team of America's finest academic minds in law, psychology, psychiatry and other disciplines and pieced together a program that WORKS! In addition, continuing development of new, efficient methods remains a priority. Since we began the "A-Team" in 1984 we have had several imitators. Some claim to be "better" than we are. None have been able to match track records with us.

Since we formed the A-Team concept it has become a topic of derision in several extremist viewpoint books and in numerous articles. Needless to say, the vigilantes dealing with these subjects don't like us much. (See "Kiss Daddy Goodnight, Ten Years Later." Louise Armstrong, 1987, p. 281). We think that it is significant that our "A-Team" is the only operation that has drawn such overwhelming venom from the Incest Vigilantes!

Better Than Ever
Today we competently handle a broad range of issues, including:

    A. Child Sexual Abuse Allegations.

    B. Child Abuse and Neglect cases.

    C. Rape (sexual assault) Allegations.

    D. Interstate and International Child Custody cases. (Parental

Kidnapping)
>   E. Interstate visitation cases. (Concealment of children)
>   F. Sexual Harassment.
>   G. Establishing (proving) REAL child abuse!

It's No Laughing Matter

Too many people STILL don't take allegations of these kinds seriously until it's too late. People often have immature notions based more on television than on reality. This leads many people to believe that the truth will eventually come out. It doesn't, and it WON'T unless you MAKE it come out. The FIRST thing you NEED is to understand you are in REAL TROUBLE! That you need our help! Do not count on the system being fair. It won't be unless it is made to be fair. Don't be a victim of fabricated abuse allegations. Victims are losers! We can help you be a winner!

Also, most people when first confronted with these kinds of allegations lack effective communications skills to convince those in the system that CAN be persuaded of your innocence. We KNOW what the problem is! We also know HOW to correct it so that you will present yourself as you will NEED to! You need to be REPROGRAMMED to WIN! VICTIMS ARE LOSERS! We can help you become a WINNER!

What To Do If You Face Trouble

First, don't panic! Help is a phone call away. Organize yourself. Give us a call at the number below. Then have a COPY of your file ready to send to us by express mail. Prepare a "Time Line" OUTLINING the events from the start so we can have some idea of what has happened to you and why.

Our initial phone consultations are NO CHARGE! (Long distance phone calls are returned collect.)

Contact The "A-Team"

Kenneth Pangborn
Trial Consultant
3980 Orchard Hill Circle
Palm Harbor, FL. 34684
(813)786-6911

Chapter Eighteen

Self-Help Guide

This chapter contains the "dos" and "don'ts" for anyone who may be in a position to face false allegations of child sexual abuse and for anyone who is already embroiled in the battle against such false allegations. It incorporates all the suggestions and recommendations that have been discussed throughout the book, as well as additional recommendations from psychologists, attorneys, support groups, and other individuals who have been victims of false allegations. I have grouped the information by category, i.e., relationship with the children, emotions, attorneys, expert witnesses, and court appearances. At the end of the chapter, I have included a listing of support groups of which I am aware, to assist you in finding help during your battle to prove your innocence and regain the right to your children.

If You Suspect the Potential of False Allegations: If you are in a high risk situation, i.e., in the process of filing for separation or divorce, involved in or anticipating a custody battle, or considering an attempt to get a change in custody or visitation schedules:

If the marriage or separation has been stormy, watch out for over-cooperativeness or friendliness as a behavioral change. This may be a prelude to false allegations.

Document everything throughout the divorce/custody suit. Note what the kids say during your visits (particularly anything out of the ordinary), anything your spouse/friend says that is rash or unusual, whether there's a male friend in the picture.

If something smells rotten in Denmark, have an eyewitness present at all visits with your child to corroborate your testimony, if needed. Don't be alone with your child if you have any suspicions about your spouse's actions or potential actions.

If the child seems irrational or psychologically/emotionally/physically wrong, take the child to an independent expert M.D./Ph.D. *before* you bring the child back from a visit with you. This may alert you to factors or events in the child's home environment of which you are unaware.

If you foresee a bitter divorce/custody battle ensuing, hire an expert attorney who is familiar with SAID syndrome cases and who will litigate in your and your child's best interest. This may help you avoid making mistakes in dealing with your spouse's demands or proposed conditions of divorce and/or custody.

If you suspect your wife is going to file for divorce and you live in a no-fault state, file first, seeking an ex-parte order granting you temporary custody, effective immediately.

Close joint accounts and cancel credit cards. It's going to take every cent you have to fight the allegations.

Remain in the house, unless ordered to move out by the court or advised to do so by a professional you trust. Once you leave the house, your wife or ex-wife has full control of the children.

If You Are the Victim of False Allegations, Do the Following:

Treat the accusation very seriously. This accusation will affect every area of your life.

Hire a competent and qualified lawyer immediately, one familiar with false allegations of child sexual abuse and, preferably, with the SAID and Parental Alienation Syndromes. Recommendations may be made by VOCAL or other support groups or the State Bar Association. Get multiple opinions on your case from seemingly objective, competent individuals.

Find the money to defend yourself properly. Inadequate counsel, due to financial constraints, may result in your losing your children or in a longer than necessary court battle.

Immediately retain a civil rights attorney to sue for damages against false allegations. The accuser and participating state agencies may be liable for damages you suffer as a result of the false allegations.

Do everything possible to halt any further interviewing or treatment, unless there is some guarantee the individuals involved will avoid teaching the child that he/she has been abused. Continuous interviews and/or therapy may be used to train the child to give desired responses or tell pre-programmed stories.

Attempt to require that all further interviews will be videotaped. This assures the ability to check for objectivity and validity of questions asked and methods used.

Have an independent psychologist appointed to evaluate the entire family.

Pay for all evaluations yourself or split the cost with your ex-wife. This assures you have access to the results.

Prohibit interrogation of the child until the independent evaluation is complete. Again, this is to avoid training the child to give desired responses during interrogation.

Attempt to regain custody or visitation immediately, with the understanding such custody or visitation will include constant adult supervision by a third party. This reduces the potential for parental alienation syndrome.

Shift the court's focus from the alleged conduct of the accused (you) to the psychological functioning of the accuser. This may show the accuser fits the typical profile of a SAID Syndrome case or specific type of accuser.

Go immediately on the defensive and demand accountability.

Persuade the court that any delay in addressing the issues raised is detrimental in the extreme to the child.

Maintain contact with the alleged victim. This will make it more difficult for the child to believe what others are saying because it will conflict with their first-hand experience.

Steadfastly maintain your innocence.

Learn about the judges who might sit on your case. Request a different judge if you are assigned one with a history of being prejudiced.

Keep detailed records of everything. Document the children's visits or reasons visits were canceled, conversations, comments and actions.

Maintain files of all documents and review them often for inconsistencies. You may be better able to spot inconsistencies than an attorney unfamiliar with your family.

Keep a daily journal of events. This shows where you were and what you were doing and may pinpoint inaccuracies of statements made by the accused.

Keep records. If it is legal in your state, buy a teletaper to record any conversations with your wife, your ex-wife, social worker(s), or anyone remotely connected with the case. A calendar, diary, expenses, photographs, and video tapes may show inconsistencies.

If you are denied a normal visitation, note when and why, where you were and what you were doing. This may contribute to raising questions as the good faith efforts of your wife on the part of the children and their best interests.

Track past, present, and future events on the calendar and in the diary, noting where you were, whom you were with and what you did, whether you had your children or not. This may prove that you were at a ball game with a friend when the alleged abuse or any future allegation was supposed to have occurred.

Obtain evidence that is admissible in court. . .affidavits from friends, children, character references. This can be used to indicate that there has been no previous indication of problems and again point interest to the accusers personality profile.

Have a reliable witness at all meetings, interviews, phone conversations. This assures accuracy and credibility in a their word/your word situation.

After all meetings, interviews and phone calls, write to the person with whom you spoke, listing the main points discussed and asking that if you have misinterpreted anything they respond by return mail to your letter. Mail the original

certified, return receipt requested, and keep a copy. This forces accountability from the other party involved.

Obtain and keep transcripts of all proceedings. These should be reviewed for inconsistency or inaccuracy.

Be careful what you say—it will be used against you. Your (ex) wife and those working with her are looking for anything that can be used to cast suspicion on your denial.

Scrutinize all prior statements on the subject by the complainant. You may be able to identify discrepancies regarding the allegation.

Attempt to ensure that child is not being coached. This frequently occurs in the home or during successive interviews.

Educate and be helpful to social/agency workers investigating. Be firm, but cordial with social workers and CPT members. This attitude projects a positive, cooperative image of you as an individual. They will be expecting anger that they can use to place you in a negative light.

When and if an HRS home study is ordered, be sure studies are the same in all respects. If they view two different sets of circumstances, they cannot make a valid comparison.

Get depositions of anyone and everyone involved in working with the child and the prosecution. If nothing else, this establishes the qualifications, protocol and techniques used, the basis upon which the professional came to the conclusion of abuse.

Recognize the social worker is trying to build a case against you, no matter how they try to impress you as being helpful.

Get involved—help yourself and your attorney.

Where flight to another state takes place, make use of the Uniform Child Custody Jurisdiction Act.

Try to win the case "before going to court" by pointing out weaknesses to the investigator's attorney.

When you've won the case, follow up immediately, e.g., get court orders, certify them, serve them.

File appeals immediately when your constitutional rights are violated.

Motion to recuse the judge or motion for a change of venue if you're being treated unlawfully by the court.

Be sure your attorney is kind and gentle with the child witness. Badgering a child has negative impact on judges and juries.

Take a lie detector test, paid for in cash. Invite social services to attend this "public" polygraph.

Learn as many facts as possible and keep them in manageable form. The more you know, the better able you'll be to fight statements and allegations.

Be prepared and willing to go to court.

Learn as much as you can about the laws in your state and the requirements child protection agencies must fulfill to receive their funding. This may indicate funding is based on number of cases filed or successfully convicted.

Assist in researching cases that may be of help to you and your attorney. There may be precedents you can apply or motions that you could use in your own case.

Require child competency and hearsay relevancy hearings. This may prevent invalid or suspect evidence from being presented.

Check to see if the accuser has levied allegations against any other individual or organization. If so, the accuser's credibility may be in question.

Have a family doctor with whom you can substantiate any injuries.

If possible, have the child examined. Do not consent to the child being examined by a doctor associated with social services.

Request through the courts an independent psychiatric and/or psychological evaluation of the victim be done immediately. This will counterbalance any subjective evaluations the agencies may attempt to use against you.

Get professional medical and psychological help. Don't try to battle the stress and depression by yourself. You must be strong for yourself and your children.

If possible, have your own psychological evaluation of the child done. This negates the need to rely solely on a state-selected psychologist.

Obtain expert psychological /psychiatric review.

If you are forced to accept a court-appointed psychologist, establish what protocol will be used, if you will be examined in the presence of your child, if the mother is to be interviewed, where the interview is to take place and when the report can be expected. This establishes your expectation for accountability from all involved.

Question the use of anatomical dolls. Hire an expert, such as Dr. Underwager, to assist you in rebutting the validity of the dolls and results of any interviews involving their use.

Have videotaped interviews analyzed by nationally-recognized experts in the field of child development, interrogation, and sexual abuse. This analysis may point out the leading questions and modeling behavior that would call the results of the interview into question.

Reach out for support from family, friends, doctors, psychologists, VOCAL. This allegation will cause frustration, anger, and depression that is almost impossible for one to bear alone.

Become an activist in family rights and for the rights of the falsely accused. Be objective and be an advocate for the children and the entire family.

Expect the unexpected.

Channel your anger into constructive methods of fighting back.

Allow yourself to grieve, for the loss of time with your children, for your loneliness, for your child's current circumstances.

Accept as normal your feelings of anxiety and depression and find an individual or support group with whom you can talk through your emotions and concerns.

Forgive yourself for mistakes you have made or may make and apply what you have learned to all future situations.

If supervised visitation is required, attempt to have supervision by a third party who is not from social services.

Upon consent from your attorney, use the media to your advantage.

If You Are a Victim of False Allegations, DO NOT Do the Following:

Accept a public defender. Few, if any, are qualified or experienced in this area.

Accept an attorney who is inexperienced in such allegations and who knows nothing of the SAID Syndrome. He will be unaware of the machinations of a typical accuser.

Be afraid to change lawyers if you feel your current is unable to defend you adequately against the charges that have been brought. This charge could lose you your freedom and your children.

Expect "common sense" in the activities of the child protection workers, prosecutors, or the courts. Their motivations and objectives are often misguided.

Admit to anything you have not done.

Be over trusting and open yourself up to vulnerable weak spots.

Offend the child protection workers. They will be looking for anything that can be used to cast you in a negative light.

Sign anything without legal counsel being present or notified.

Agree to a plea bargain or enter a plea of *Nolo Contendere*. Either of these qualifies you as guilty.

Never take your spouse/friend for granted and succumb to naivete. Do not underestimate them, particularly if jealousy, insecurity, adulterous threats/actions, and arguments persist.

Interrogate your child at all about the mother's intentions/actions or the child's acute transformation of behavior if any. You must prevent the child from becoming a pawn or tool for your own wishes.

Be nonchalant. You *must* be aggressive and nip any potential problems in the bud ahead of time.

Act guilty.

Make any concessions. Doing so will be looked upon as evidence as guilt.

Waive any rights, especially to a hearing.

Underestimate the effect of the initial pleading against you.

Underestimate the effect your responsive pleading may have.

Hesitate to advise your attorney and the court of attitudes, practices and behaviors that would help prove your wife unfit.

Play the gentleman. Pretending the accuser is still the woman you loved and married can get you a jail sentence and lose you the children. At best, it will lengthen the process of disproving the allegations and being reunited with your children.

Submit to a psychiatric/psychological evaluation for yourself before discussing this with your legal counsel.

Succumb to the Parental Alienation Syndrome. Utilize this syndrome to your advantage to aid you in your custody endeavors.

Allow the situation to drive you into self-imposed isolation. You need support, assistance, and understanding at this time.

Attempt to influence the children by telling them horror stories about their mother. The children will resent this and may well become confused.

Agree to have the matter continued, under any circumstances, unless some sort of visitation can be arranged. It is important that your children see you regularly to counteract the negative information they may be receiving from others.

Be afraid of the media. Work with your attorney to work with the press.

Give up. Your life and the lives of your children depend on you.

Appendix A

The following questionnaire was developed by J. Petty as a suggested guide in identifying valid versus false allegations of child sexual abuse.

Identification of False Allegations

1. Relationship of reporter to perpetrator:
2. Was there any evidence that the abuse/neglect reporter:

   A. Was generally hostile or resentful toward the perpetrator for reasons not *directly* related to the abuse?

   B. Had something of personal value to gain if the abuse was substantiated (such as gaining child custody, eliminating visitation or parental rights, financial gain, etc.)?

   C. Suffers from post-traumatic stress disorder?

   1. History of being abused themselves?
   2. Stressors that would evoke significant symptoms of distress in anyone?
   3. Response numbness to external world?
   4. Recurrence of recollection of trauma via dreams or intrusive remembrances?

   [NOTE: Mothers who have been abused tend to over-identify with their child and believe abuse has occurred.]

   D. Had a serious psychiatric disorder and had a pathological symbiotic relationship with the child?

   1. Histrionic Personality
   2. Borderline Personality
   3. Schizophrenia
   4. Paranoid Disorder
   5. Munchausen-by-Proxy
   6. Other.

   E. Appears to be an over-concerned professional who has prematurely committed themselves to believing the allegations and has influenced others to believe the same?

F. Tended to offer progressively more elaborate versions of the original story?

3. Did the child repeat the story consistently to more than one person?

4. How many?

5. Did the child repeat the same story to the same person over tme?

6. Was the story consistent with information gathered from other mediums, such as drawings or dolls?

7. Did other involved children repeat the same story? If so, how many?

8. Does the child tend to make up stories, exaggerate or fantasize excessively?

9. Has the child progressively offered more elaborate versions of the story with unexpected adult words and phrases?

10. Does the child have any reasons, other than having been abused by the perpetrator, to be resentful, hostile, or revengeful toward the perpetrator?

11. Is there any evidence that the child has been influenced by others through leading questions or threats?

12. Were stories told by the child challenged to determine whether the child is consistent or suggestible to adult influence?

13. Did the child maintain consistency following challenge or leads?

14. How influenced by suggestibility does the child appear to be (highly, moderate, not influenced)?

15. By whom? Relationship?

16. Did the child go beyond expected details by telling sensible, credible stories?

17. Is there evidence of the accommodation syndrome?

A. Has the child substantially diminished or withdrawn the allegations?

B. Has the child stated that he/she has been told what to say?

C. Has the child been threatened with harm or loss if they don't withdraw the allegations?

D. Have you directly observed anyone attempting to get the child to change their story?

E. In the presence of particular reporters the child appeared:
Guarded?

Intimidated?
Ambivalent?
Frightened?
In whose presence?
18. Did the mood or effect on the child match what would be expected during disclosure?

Appendix B

Fake or Factual? Speedy Identification
of Child Sexual Abuse Allegations
by The Joint Custody Association, Los Angeles, California

Bona fide sexual abuse:

    Mothers will generally be upset, secretive, and embarrassed;

    Child will be fearful and timid in presence of abusing parent;

    Description of abuse will be consistent, real, serious.

Fabricated sexual abuse:

    Mother has need to tell the whole world, expresses no shame;

    Child also wants to tell the whole world;

    Child is comfortable in presence of the accused, may even scream the accusations in the face of the accused parent;

    Descriptions often have preposterous scenarios.

Children from four to seven:

    Tend to overgeneralize;

    Fabricate in an effort to fill in the blanks;

    Will begin to believe what they have said.

Common problems among individuals involved in parent-child abuse:

    Impulse control problems;

    Difficulty monitoring or directing emotional reactions;

    Excessive self-centeredness;

    Strong dependency needs;

    Poor judgement.

Divorced women who accuse spouses of incest:

    Usually overzealous and dishonest;

    Histrionic or combative;

    Aggressively demand the decision-makers act quickly;

    When questioned for specific details, can provide little information and are reluctant to have their children interviewed alone.

*Mothers who are child-focused and not fabricating
or exaggerating:*

> Express remorse for not protecting child sufficiently;
> Willing to consider other possible explanations for behavior;
> Willing to have child interviewed without their presence;
> Concerned about impact on child if child testifies;
> If allegations can't be verified, willing to let go of the
> investigatory process as long as child's well-being can be
> monitored.

Mothers interested primarily in attacking fathers:

> Insist on being present when child is interviewed, and
> prompt the child;
> Are unwilling to consider other possible explanations for
> child's statements;
> Are eager for child to testify at all costs;
> Shop for other professionals who will verify her suspicions;
> Involve the child in multiple examinations;
> Demand the investigation continue, irrespective of
> impact on child.

*Three types of data, in assessing the child, to be
considered are:*

> Child's verbalizations;
> Child's test responses and play interviews;
> Reports of parents, teachers, and others knowing child.

Appendix C
Family Rights Organizations

VOCAL (Victims Of Child Abuse Laws)
7485 E. Kenyon Ave.
Denver, CO 80237
ATTN: Donna Smith
1-800-745-8778

Florida VOCAL
ATTN: Larry McAlexander
1-800-297-6985

FMS (False Memory Syndrome Foundation)
3401 Market St.
Suite 130
Philadelphia, PA 19104-3315
ATTN: Pam Freyd, Ph.D.
1-800-568-8882

COP-AFN (Coalition Of Parents-American Family Network)
ATTN: Mike Neligh
1-800-478-9410

CRC (Children's Rights Council)
220 1 St. N.E.
Suite 200
Washington, D.C. 20002
ATTN: David Levy, Esq.
1-800-787-KIDS

NCFC (National Congress for Fathers and Children)
P.O. Box 171675
Kansas City, KS 66117
ATTN: Travis Ballard, Esq.
1-800-733-DADS

Worldwide Christian Divorced Parents
4504 Skyline Court N.E.
Albuquerque, N.M. 87111
ATTN: Roger Saul
1-800-MY-DADDY

AAFA (Alliance Against False Allegations)
P.O. Box 6561
Arlington, VA 22206
ATTN: Tom Vail
703-444-4519

VOCAL New York
P.O. Box 4295
Utica, N.Y. 13504
ATTN: Rev. Wm. Wendler
516-671-0534

VAST (Victims and Advocates Start Talking)
6007 Hillside Ave. East Drive
Indianapolis, IN 46220
ATTN: Lawrence Newman, Esq.
Beverly Newman, Ed.D.
317-255-9395

National Child Abuse Defense and Resource Center
P.O. Box 638
Holland, OH 43528
ATTN: Kim Hart
419-865-0513

Reidline Research
427 Ascot Court
Sanford, FL 32773
ATTN: Reid Kimbrough
407-328-7685

Family Advocates
2124 N.E. 123 Street
Suite 205-36
Sans Soucs Plaza
N. Miami, FL 33181
305-895-7461

NASVO (National Association of State VOCAL Organizations)
11625 E. Old Spanish Trail
Tucson, AZ 85730
ATTN: George & Leslie Wimberly
520-722-1968

The Justice Committee
2737 28th St.
San Diego, CA 92104
ATTN: Carol Hopkins
619-285-9973

G.R.I.N.S. (Grandparents Rights In New Strength)
0689 CR 5
Corunna, IN 46730
ATTN: Kay & Ray Berryhill
219-281-2384

MERGE (Movement for the Establishment of Real Gender Equality)
10011 116th St.
Suite 501
Edmonton, Alberta
Canada T5K 1V4
ATTN: Ferrel Christensen, Ph.D.
403-488-4593

Virginia Coalition of Concerned Parents
P.O. Box 366
Lacey Spring, VA 22833-0366
ATTN: Rick Thoma
540-896-4270

DADS (Dads Assisting Dads)
150 174th Terrace
Reddington Shores, FL 33709
ATTN: Bob Zeller
813-393-9647

National Fatherhood Initiative
16049 Copen Meadow Dr.
Gaithersburg, MD 20878
ATTN: Wade Horn, Ph.D.
301-948-0599

Mens Defense Association
"The Liberator" Mens Newsmagazine
17854 Lyons St.
Forest Lake, MN 55025-8107
ATTN: Dick Doyle
612-464-7887

FAPT (Fathers Are Parents Too)
Rt. 2 Box 42
Soperton, GA 30457
ATTN: Paul Bridges
912-529-6293

Fathers' Rights Newsline
P.O. Box 713
Havertown, PA 19083
ATTN: Don Middleman
215-879-4099

Coalition for the Preservation of Fatherhood
14 Beacon St. Suite 421
Boston, MA 02108
ATTN: Tom Rettberg, Ph.D.
617-649-1906

Children's Rights Coalition
12103 Scribe Dr.
Austin, TX 78759
ATTN: Eric Anderson
512-454-4797

National Black Men's Health Network
250 Georgia Ave.
Suite 321
Atlanta, GA 30312
ATTN: Dr. Jean Bonhomme
404-524-7237

Children's Rights Council of Japan
P.O. Box 583
Max Meadows, VA 24360
ATTN: Walter Benda
540-637-3576

Washington Families for Non-Custodial Rights
P.O. Box 33509
Fort Lewis, WA 98433-0509
ATTN: Robert Eier
206-582-8440

ATTN: Ms. Ursula Ofuatey-Kodjoe
Gartenweg 1
79194 Gundelfingen
Germany
011761585906

Appendix D
Attorney Referral List

From this writer's knowledge and opinion, the following American defense lawyers have concentrated their practices in the areas of child abuse and custody. Some litigate in criminal court, only. Some litigate in family court, only. Others specialize in handling appeals, only. These are America's finest defense lawyers for those that have been **wrongly** accused of child abuse. I suggest you retain any attorney **only after** you have perused the lawyers Curriculum Vitae. Be certain the lawyer has defended similar clients to your case scenario, albeit, alleged sexual or physical abuse, alleged munchausen syndrome, alleged repressed memories, alleged failure to thrive, etc.

Disclaimer: This writer does **not** receive any monies for refer ring potential clients to any of the following lawyers. Moreover, this writer is **not** responsible for any negative ramifications that may ensue out of litigation from representation of the following lawyers. Consult the book **Martindale-Hubbell** at your law library for attorneys who specialize in family law issues.

Charles Jamieson, Esq...A-TEAM Counsel
The Centurion
1601 Forum Place
Suite 1101
West Palm Beach, Fl. 33401
407-478-1111

Robert Van Siclen, Esq...Wenatchee Witchunt Counsel
4508 Auburn Way N.
Suite A-100
Auburn, WA 98002-1381
206-859-8899

Friedman & Manning, P.C.
2 Norman Skill Blvd.
Delmar, N.Y. 12054-0069
518-439-0375

Janson Kauser, Esq.
2107 NAD Road, Unit D
N. Charleston, SC 29418
803-569-1125

Jerry McDougall, Esq.
P.O. Box 50898
Amarillo, TX 79159
806-355-1202

Dennis Levin, Esq.
One Commerce Park Sq.
Suite 345
23200 Chagrin Blvd.
Cleveland, OH 44122
216-831-3939

Travis Ballard, Esq.
President, National Congress for Fathers and Children (NCFC)
4511 Marathon Heights
Adrian, MI 49221-9240
1-800-KID-N-DAD

Paul Wallin, Esq.
2020 E. 1st St.
Suite 300
Santa Ana, CA 92705
714-571-0227

Romanow & Fuller, P.A.
Attorney C. Clifton Fuller, III
7 Market St.
Belfast, ME 04915
207-338-1311

Rowe Stayton, Esq.
13140 E. Mississippi Ave.
Aurora, CO 80012
303-745-5578

Bruce Lyons, Esq.
600 N.E. 3rd Ave.
Ft. Lauderdale, FL. 33304
954-467-8700

Jay Milano, Esq.
600 Standard Building
Cleveland, OH 44113
216-241-5050

Michael Oddenino, Esq...General Counsel for CRC
444 E. Huntington Dr.
Suite 325
Arcadia, CA 91006
818-447-8084

Charles Suphan, Esq.
3 Silver Burch Ct.
Little Rock, AR 72212
501-227-9490

Patrick Clancy, Esq.
1600 S. Main St.
Suite 185
Walnut Creek, CA 94596-5431
510-256-6884

Jeffery Leving, LTD.
123 W. Madison
Suite 300
Chicago, ILL 60602
312-807-3990

Mark Mestel, Esq.
3221 Oaks Ave.
Everett, WA 98201
206-339-2383

Kathryn Lyon, Esq... Wenatchee Witchunt Researcher
4909 Shellridge Rd. NW
Olympia, WA 98502
360-866-8157

Toby Thaler, Esq.
P.O. Box 1188
Seattle, WA 98111-1188
206-622-8103

John Finn, Esq.
49 Main St.
Yarmouth, ME 04096
207-846-1429

Tom Ryan, Esq... Defends those accused of
Munchausen Syndrome, wrongly
1600 W. Chandler Blvd.
Suite 220
Chandler, AZ 85224
602-963-3333

Joel Thompson, Esq.
4500 N. 32nd St.
Suite 100
Phoenix, AZ 85018
602-957-2010

Robert Storrs, Esq.
45 W. Jefferson
Suite 803
Phoenix, AZ 85003
602-258-4545

Danny Davis, Esq...Lawyer for Ray Buckey in McMartin case
P.O. Box 3516
Beverly Hills, CA 90212
213-659-5800

Louis Kiefer, Esq.
60 Washington St.
Suite 1403
Hartford, CT 06106
203-249-3600

Roy Black, Esq...represented William Kennedy Smith in
rape trial
201 S. Biscayne Blvd.
Suite 1300
Miami, Fl. 33131
305-371-6421

Lawrence Braunstein, Esq.
11 Martine Ave., Penthouse
White Plains N.Y. 10606
914-997-6220

Eliot Clauss, Esq.
291 Broadway
13th Floor
New York, N.Y. 10038
212-349-6775

Dr. Mel Guyer, J.D.
1500 E. Medical Center Dr.
Ann Arbor, MI 48109
313-763-0174

James Murdoch, Esq.
131 Main St.
P.O. Box 363
Burlington, VT 05402-0363
802-864-9811

Sverre Staurset, Esq.
725 Yakima
2nd floor
Tacoma, WA 98402
206-572-8880

Appendix E
Case Law and False Accusations

The following listing of cases is not meant to be comprehensive, but to identify major decisions related to evidence issues; the interpretation of the confrontation clause, hearsay issues and child competency, the admissibility of expert testimony and the questionable acceptance of anatomical dolls and play therapies and repressed memories in the scientific community in sex abuse cases. Also, there are cases which address the accused's right to redress, duty owed to a third party, and immunity issues and the government.

Disclaimer: This writer takes no responsibility for the use or misuse of the following citations, by in pro per litigants, public defenders, or retained counsel. If you question the proper usage of a given citation albeit, appellants brief or motion accompanied by a memorandum of law in Federal Court, etc., **consult a qualified attorney.**

Santosky v. Kramer, U.S. Sup. Ct. 88-5889 (1982). Held that there must be conclusive evidence beyond a reasonable doubt (not merely a preponderance of evidence) to terminate a parent's right of access to their child.

Felix v. State of Nevada, 109 Nev. 151, 849 P.2d 220 (Nev. Sup. Ct. March 18, 1993). The High Court reversed the convictions, finding the trial court erred in not properly establishing child competency, in disregarding the lack of medical evidence, and in allowing a lack of spontaneity in reporting by the children and leading questions to be admissible.

Hellstrom v. Commonwealth of Kentucky, No. 90-SC-262-Mr (Kentucky Supreme Ct., 1992). The High Court reversed and remanded, holding that "neither child sexual abuse syndrome nor the symptoms that comprise the syndrome have recognized reliability in diagnosing child sexual abuse as scientific entity and thus testimony on the syndrome and the symptoms is not admissible.

People of New York v. Knupp, 579 N.Y.S. 2d 801 (N.Y. Sup. Ct., App. Div. 1992). Held that accused was denied right to a fair trial by the improper admission of mental health testimony. Admission of expert testimony of a "validator," who had previously testified in several other cases that children suffered from "intrafamilial child sexual abuse syndrome" was held improper. Undue prejudice outweighs probative value. Upon retrial, Knupp, who had served two years in prison, was acquitted of sexual assault charges.

State of Idaho v. Wright, 497 U.S. 805, 110 S.Ct. 3139, 111 L. Ed. 2d 638 (1990). A child sex abuse conviction was reversed because hearsay statements made by the child and reported by the physician did not bear adequate indicia of reliability. The doctor failed to videotape the interview, asked leading questions and had a preconceived notion the abuse took place.

State of New Jersey v. Michaels, 136 N.J. 299, 642 A.2d 1372, 1994 N.J. LEXIS 504, (N.J. Sup. Ct., 1994); previous history-264 N.J. Super. 579, 625 A. 2d 489, 1993 N.J. Super. LEXIS 174 (N.J. Superior Ct., 1993). Kelly Michaels, a nursery school teacher at the Wee Care Day Nursery was convicted by a jury of 115 counts of sexual assault of children in 1988. After spending 5 years in prison her convictions were reversed by two higher courts, which held that to reprosecute the defendant the state must prove by clear and convincing evidence that the statements and testimony extracted from the children were done so by proper interviewing techniques and reliable at pre-trial. In December 1994, the state decided not to retry the case.

United States v. Tome, No. 93-6892 (U.S. Sup. Ct., argued Oct. 5 1994); decided January 10, 1995. Reversed a conviction of a New Mexico man for allegedly raping his 4 year old daughter.

The High Court of the land considered the admissibility of hearsay statements made by a child complainant "of recent fabrication or improper influence or motive." In a 5-4 decision, the Court held that Federal Rule of Evidence 801(d)(1)(B) rendered inadmissable hearsay statements of accusations made to others after the alleged motive or influence first arose.

Ward v. State of Florida, 519 So. 2d (Fla. App. Ct. 1988). The Court held that "child sexual abuse syndrome is an area sufficiently developed to permit an expert to testify that the symptoms observed in the evaluated child are consistent with those displayed by victims of child sexual abuse." However, the court noted that the testimony of the syndrome is circumstantial evidence and may not be received as corroborating evidence that the defendant committed the criminal act charged on the specific occasion.

White v. Illinois, 112 S. Ct. 736 (1992). The U.S. Supreme Court considered requirements for assessing the reliability of a child's accusatory hearsay statements made against a defendant before their admission into evidence. The unavailability analysis is a necessary part of a Confrontation Clause inquiry only if challenged out-of-court statements are made in course of prior judicial proceedings.

Coy V. Iowa, 487 U. S. 1012 (1988). The U.S. Supreme Court reversed a sexual child abuse conviction because the trial court permitted the prosecution to use screens to block the children's view of the defendants. The Court held that, without a finding of necessity, such a procedure violated the Confrontation Clause.

Maryland v. Craig, 497 U.S. 836 (1990). The Court held that shielding child witnesses from sexual abuse defendants is constitutional, but only if the lower court finds: 1. One-way closed circuit television is necessary to protect the child's welfare. 2. The child would be traumatized in the presence of the defendant. 3. The emotional distress suffered by the child witness in the presence of the defendant is more than **de minimis.** The defendant's right to cross examination is upheld. And the Court, jury and defendant have the right to observe the child's demeanor.

Ohio v. Roberts, 448 U.S. 56 (1980). The High Court of the land ordered a two-part test for determining when the right to confrontation must yield to the admissibility of hearsay: The proponent 1. Must show the necessity for using the hearsay declaration (witness unavailability) and 2. Must show the inherent trustworthiness of the declaration.

State of Florida v. Townsend, 635 So. 2d 949 (Fla. 1994). The Supreme Court held that the competency of a child is a factor that should be considered in determining the trustworthiness and reliability and thus the admissibility of hearsay statements.

Frye v. United States, 54 U.S. App. D.C. 293 F. 1013 (1923). People v. Kelley, 17 Cal 3d 24 (1976). "The Kelley-Frye Rule of Reliability." Stipulated that novel scientific testimony is admissible if generally accepted by the relevant scientific community.

Daubert v. Merrell Dow Pharmaceuticals, 113. S.Ct. 2786, 125 L.Ed 2d 469 (1993). Here, the High Court of the land expounded upon Frye and applied the Federal Rules of Evidence. The Daubert opinion, written by Justice Blackmun, specifies that under Rule 702 an expert's testimony pertaining to 'scientific knowledge' must be grounded in the methods and procedures of science and derived from the scientific method. In order to be admissible, the trial judge must examine the scientific validity of the underlying methodology. In addition, under Daubert, the criteria underlying methodology. In addition, under Daubert, the criteria for admissibility is:

1. Whether the theory has been tested.

2. Whether the theory has been subjected to peer review and publication.

3. Whether the theory or technique has a known rate of error.

4. Whether the theory has attained **general acceptance** within the relevant scientific community.

Several judicial decisions reflect the view that evidence generated by the use of anatomically correct (detailed) dolls lacks a sufficient scientific basis to be admitted into evidence:

In re Amber B, 236 Cal. Rpt. 623, (Cal. App. 1 Dist. 1987), 191 Cal. 3d 682 (1987).

In re Christine C, 191 Cal. 3d 676 (1987).

U.S. v. Gillespie, 852 F2d 475 (9th Cir. 1988).

State of New Hampshire v. Hungerford, Superior Court of Hillsborough County, N.H., Case No. 94-S-045 thru 94-S-047, May 23, 1995. After a Frye/Daubert hearing and factual review, the Court held that repressed memory testimony was not sufficiently reliable under Frye or Rule 702 to be admitted as evidence.

Hunter v. Brown, Tenn App. LEXIS 95, 1996 WL 57944, Feb. 13, 1996. In this case of first impression, the Tennessee Appellate Court declined to apply the discovery rule to toll the statute of limitations in repressed memory cases. "We find that there is too much indecision in the scientific community as to the credibility of repressed memory."

S.V. v. R.V., Supreme Court of Texas, 1996 Tex. LEXIS 30, March 14, 1996. The Court held that because Plaintiff relied on the discovery rule, the evidence must have met a higher level of proof. This case did not survive as the Court ruled against the discovery rule.

Engstrom v. Engstrom, Superior Court, Los Angeles County, CA, Case No. VCO16157, Oct. 11, 1995. The court granted a motion to exclude the testimony regarding repressed memories, repression, or dissociation, finding that the phenomenon of memory repressions is not generally accepted as valid and reliable by a majority of the scientific community and that the procedures used in the 'retrieval' process have not gained general acceptance in the fields of psychology or psychiatry.

Hafer v. Melo et al, 912 F. 2d 628, 636-37 (3rd Cir. 1990), U.S. Sup. Ct. 90-681 (Nov. 5, 1991). The High Court of the nation held that a plaintiff can sue a governmental official in his/her personal or individual capacity.

Wilkinson v. Balsam, DC VT. 4/95...No.2 94-CV-375, 4/17/95. The Federal Court rejected the claims of a psychiatrist and two state social workers that they were cloaked under a shield of absolute immunity. The Court based its findings upon shoddy investigatory work of the social workers and deceitful behavior by the doctor, in that the reporting physician overstepped his bounds in going beyond simply reporting a case of child abuse.

Montoya v. Bebensee, 761 P. 2d 285 (Colo. App. Ct. 1988). A Colorado Appeals Court reinstated a father's negligence and outrageous conduct claims against his daughter's therapist for her behavior in a SAID case. The court held that a therapist who counselled a child **owed a duty of care** to the father because the harm he suffered from unfounded child abuse charges was **foreseeable.**

State of Minnesota v. Huss, 506 N.W. 2d 290 (1993). High court of Minnesota overturned a father's conviction for criminal sexual assault, concluding the child's accusations were 'improperly influenced by a highly suggestive book on sex abuse, which was shown to her repeatedly by a therapist.

Caryl S. v. Child Adolescent Treatment Services, Inc., 614 N.Y.S. 2d 661 (N.Y. Superior Ct., 1994). The court found factual basis for the grandparents' claim of negligent misdiagnosis and denied defendants' motion to dismiss. The Court further found that a duty of care was owed to not only the child, but also the alleged abusers, the grandparents.

James W., et al., v. The Superior Court of San Diego County, Kathleen Goddfriend, et al, 17 Cal. App. 4th 246 (Calif. App. Ct. 4th Dist. July 1993, modified August 16, 1993). Therapists' activities went far beyond the intent and spirit of the statute. Court recognized when counselors 'abuse' a therapeutic relationship with family members they are liable to both the child and the parents. The case was settled out of court for 2.5 million dollars in May '94.

Appendix F
Internet On-Line Resources

The following list of World Wide Web and E-Mail addresses will help you tie into a plethora of information on false accusations of child abuse, that is available over the super information highway. Of course, you must own or have access to a computer system and be on-line to do so.

Disclaimer: This writer is not responsible for the dissemination of inaccurate information that is transmitted over the Internet. Because information can be intercepted and altered, due to lack of safeguards, I urge you to proceed with caution when on-line. If you have questions, call Ken Pangborn @ 1-813-786-6911.

WORLD WIDE WEB ADDRESSES

http://bsd.mojones.com/mother_jones/JA96/levine_jump.html
    A Question of Abuse

http://user.aol.com/doughskept/witchhunt/cases.html
    Alleged Witchhunt Cases

http://www.vix.com./men/index.html
    Men's Issues Page

http://www.dadnkids.com/ncfc/
    National Congress for Fathers and Children

http://www.bayou.com/ncfc
    National Congress for Fathers and Children-Louisiana

http://www.tiac.net/users/sbasile/CPF/
    Coalition for Preservation of Fatherhood

http://www.onedaly.com
> Lawrence Daly, Expert Private Investigator

http://www.A-Team.org
> Future Home Page of the A-Team

http://www.ncfm.org
> National Coalition of Free Men

http://www.ini.net/otpf
> Of the People Foundation

http://www.sconet.ohio.gov/
> Supreme Court of Ohio

///cl~jlaigle.aol.com or ///cl~jlaigle/home.htm
> Fred Dever, A man wrongly convicted of sexual child abuse in Ohio, and his story, as told by the National Center of Men.

http://www.vix.com/crc/aboutcrc.htm
> The Children's Rights Council

http://www.vix.com/pub/men/falsereport/child.html
> False Allegations of Child Molestation and Abuse

http://www.protocom.com/protomall/mensdefense/index.html
> Men's Defense

http://www.vix.com/pub/men/falsereport/resources/
> False Accusations of Sexual or Physical Abuse in Custody Cases

http://www.vix.com/pub/men/falsereport/childabuse/brott94.html
> A System Out of Control: The Epidemic of False Allegations of Child Abuse

http://www.vix.com/pub/men/falsereport/commentary/ass-law-jhtml
> Recent Escalation in Child Abuse Charges Tied to Divorce

http://www.vix.com/pub/men/falsereport/wsj-witchhunt.html
   Modern Witch Hunt

http://liquid2-sun.mit.edu/fells.html
   Junk Science

http://liquid2-sun.mit.edu/witchhunt.html
   Witch Hunt Information Center

http://www.dhs.state.tx.us/tdprs/homepage.html
   PRS Home Page

http://www.primenet.com/~dean/
   The Divorce Page

http://www.aa.net/~nw-fact/
   Northwest Feminist Anti-Censorship Taskforce

http://users.aol.com/cclawa/
   CCLA Home Page

http://www.law.indiana.edu:80/law/other.html
   Other Legal Servers and IU Servers

http://www.ccsi.com/yeeha/index.html
   YeeHa! Texas Website & Resource Directory

http://thomas.loc.gov/home/c104query.html
   Search Full Text of Legislation - 104th Congress

http://www-physics.mps.ohio-state.edu/government-addresses.html
   Government Internet Addresses

http://www.igc.org/fair/media-contact-list.html
   FAIR'S Media Contact List

http://www.vix.com/pub/men/media/address.html
   Addresses for Major Media

http://www.usc.edu/dept/law-lib/legal/topiclst.html
   Legal Resources on the Internet

http://www.mediainfo.com/edpub/e-papers.us.html
   Internet Services/U.S.

http://www.rutherford.org/
   The Rutherford Institute

http://www.efndfn.org/~srl/
   In the Pursuit of Justice?

http://www.tribal.com/
Tribal Voice

http://www.state.tx.us/
   State of Texas Government World Wide Web Server

http://www.ojp.usdoj.gov/bjs/
   Bureau of Justice Statistics

http://accused.com
   Accused

http://www.lawlib.uh.edu/handi/
   HANDI Home Page

http://www.w3.org/hypertext/DataSources/bySubject/Overview.html
   The World-Wide Web Virtual Library: Subject Catalogue

http://www.newslink.org/menu.html
   Newslink

http://wwwl.trib.com/NEWS/APwire.html
   Wire Services

http://link.tsl.texas.gov/
   Texas State Electronic Library

http://forensic.nova.edu/
    CCADE Web

http://www.customcpu.com:80/personal/mneligh/afn/
    The American Family Network

http://lawlib.wuacc.edu/washlaw/
    Washburn University School of Law - Washlaw www

http://204.65.48.6
    State Auditor's Office - Texas

http://www.llr.com/
    LawGroup Network

http://www.handsnet.org/cwla/
    Child Welfare League of America

http://www.fie.com/www/justice.htm
    Department of Justice Servers

http://www.rnc.org/
    Republican National Committee

http://guide-p.infoseek.com/Titles?qt=Federal+child+abuse+
grants&col=ww&sv=N2&Seek+Now.x=52&Seek=Now.y=3
    Infoseek Guide : Search Results - Child Abuse Grants

http://www.kosone.com/people/ocrt/cps_vict.htm
    Parents Victimized by CPS

http://www.acf.dhhs.gov/ACFPrograms/index.html
    ACF Programs and Services

http://wwwl.primenet.com/~nolawyer/
    Bad Judges and What To Do With Them

http://www.realtime.net:80/~matriod/
    Texas Family Law

http://members.gnn.com/eztherapy/index.htm/index.htm
    False Allegations of Child Sexual Abuse

http://www.ethics.state.tx.us/
    Ethics Commission's Home Page

http://child.cornell.edu/APSAC/apsac.home.html
    APSAC Home Page

http://38.240.82.11/public/
    Crime Data Bases

http://www.sbaonline.sba.gov/ignet/internal/hhs/hhs.html
    HHS Office of Inspector General

http://www.lbb.state.tx.us/
    Legislative Budget Board (LBB) - Texas

http://www.lbb.state.tx.us/lbb/members/reports/fiscal/FSHHS\
FSHHS.htm
    Dept. of Health and Human Services - Texas</A>

http://www.chron.com/
    Houston Chronicle Interactive

http://www.sos.state.tx.us/
    Secretary of State - Texas

http://www.vocal.org
    Victims of Child Abuse Laws - Florida

http://www.os.dhhs.gov:80/
    U.S. Department of Health and Human Services

http://www.sbaonline.sba.gov/ignet/
    IGnet -- Federal Inspector General's Office

http://www.tc.umn.edu/nlhome/g012/under006/
    Institute for Psychological Therapies

http://www.access.gpo.gov/gao/index.html
    General Accounting Office

http://ccwf.cc.utexas.edu/~suefaw/texas.html
    State of Texas Sources of Information

http://www.fbi.gov/
    Federal Bureau of Investigation

http://www.quitam.com/
    The Qui Tam Information Center

http://www.ljx.com/cgi-bin/f_cat?prod/ljextra/data/external/
9512021.c05
    Texas Confrontation Clause

http://www.ustreas.gov/treasury/bureaus/usss/usss.html
    U.S. Secret Service

http://www.flash.net/~badger/
    The UTOPIA Foundation

http://www.gao.gov/index.htm
    GAO Home Page

http://www.Latimes.com/HOME/NEWS/APONLINE/
    Los Angeles Times AP Online

http://www.bcm.tmc.edu/psych/child.html
    Division of Child & Adolescent Psychiatry

http://www.WashTimes.com/index.html
    The Washington Times

http://www.emrkt.com/books/deantong.html

http://www.emrkt.com/books/dbmd.html

http://www.os.dhhs.gov/search
    Health & Human Services Search Engine

http://www.hg.org/hgname.html
    Hieros Gamos - The Comprehensive Legal Site

E-MAIL ADDRESSES

Pangborn@A-Team.org....
Ken Pangborn, Trial Consultant

cpf-l-request@stormy,salem.ma.us....
Coalition for Preservation of Fatherhood

tdawson@accesscomm.net
Terry Dawson, President of Houston Texas VOCAL

hohme@dcci.com
Herm Ohme, Internet Surfer

flyzz@indirect.com
Linda Donewald, Interner Surfer

smiller@cap.gwu.edu
smiller@CapAccess.org
afc@CapAccess.org
American Fathers Coalition & Stuart Miller

mensnet@cap.gwu.edu
Men's Health Network

ncfc@bayou.com
National Congress for Fathers and Children, Louisiana

donlewis@tmn.com
Virginia Fathers Alert

onedaly@onedaly.com
Lawrence Daly, Expert Private Investigator

mensdefens@aol.com
Mens Defense Association

FISHMANH@allegheny.edu
Howard Fishman will testify as an expert witness **"pro bono"**
in termination of parental rights cases.

vail@erols.com
Alliance Against False Allegations

cclawa@aol.com
Concerned Citizens for Legal Accountability

George.Hero@nopc.org
George Hero on False Accusations

pjf@cis.upenn.edu
False Memory Syndrome Foundation

Milton_Cunningham@msn.com
National VOCAL

AFN@customcpu.com
American Family Network

gerimc9525@aol.com
Florida VOCAL

ChipnClara@aol.com
Kriseya Labassida case

alt.dads-rights
Fathers Rights Newsgroup

PangK@aol.com
Ken Pangborn, Trial Consultant

INGRAMORG@aol.com
Ingram Organization

pzd.apa@email.apa.org
American Psychological Assn. Final Report of the APA
Working Group on the Investigation of Memories
of Childhood Abuse.

reid.kimbrough%77@satlink.oau.org
Reidline Research and Reid Kimbrough Research in Domestic Relations.

Appendix G

Investigative Intake Process- Flow Chart

Used with Permission from Systematic Investigations, Lawrence Daly, President @ 10725 S.E. 256th, Suite 1, Kent, WA 98031

I. Multiple Sources of Referrals
- **Case Referral**

II. Case Received
- **Assign Account Number-Enter In MC Database**
    - Accountability Process
        - Copying, • Long Distance, • Backgrounds

III. Create Computer Client Files
- Create Client Folder   • Create Clients Notes File

IV. Case Organized

A. Police Reports	I. Witness Contact Database
B. C.P.S. Records	J. Timeline of Events
C. Police/Other Agencies	K. Case Breakdown
Statements	L. Background Investigations
D. Legal Documents	M. Notes To File
E. Medical Records	N. ODC Statements
F. Correspondence	O. Case Assessment Form
G. Case Analysis	P. Miscellaneous
H. Case Action Plan	Q. Case Status Report
	R. Witness Statement Interview Notes

V. Reviewing Case File
- Identifying Issues   • Preparing Witness Contact Database
- Preparing Allegation Breakdown • Identifying Missing Discovery

VI. Client Interview - Witness Interview
- **Meeting with Client**
    - Reasonable & Logical Explanation to Allegations
    - Determine Validity of Response
    - Counseling - Referral to Sexual Treatment
        - Evaluation, • Treatment

VII. Case Analysis
- **Identifying**

• Alleged Victim(s)	• Teachers
• Relatives/Children	• Medical Personnel
• Other Witnesses	• Daycare Provider
• Child Protective Services	• Records
• Police Personnel	• Suggestions (Case Action Plan)
• Councilors	• Notes/Comments
• Foster Homes	• Motions

VIII. Case Action Plan
- Initial Plan   • Summary   • Milestones

IX. Timeline Of Events
- Preparing Timeline From Discovery
- Identifying Missing Time/Dates Of Relevance
- Create Initial Hypothesis

X. Backgrounds
- **All Parties, Including Client**
  - Complete Criminal, Civil, Domestic Checks
  - JIS - Public Access
  - Other Agencies - User Services
- Searches Should Be Done By Computer First
  - Conduct Follow-up With In Person Check
- Federal Criminal and Bankruptcy Checks
- Analyzing Background Findings
  - Searching For Criminal History
  - Searching For Personal History Information
  - Searching For Additional Witnesses

XI. Preparing For Interviews
- Prepare Questions For Interviews
  - Who, What, When, Why, Where, Which, How
  - Tape
  - Court Transcriptionist
  - Shorthand
  - Summary

XII. Conducting Interviews
- **Decision Making - Value Of**
  - In Person
    - Summary Prepared By Investigator
    - Transcription Prepared By Typist
    - Telephone
    - Summary Prepared By Investigator
    - Transcription Prepared By Typist
    - Deposition
    - Transcription Prepared By Transcriptionist

XIII. Analyzing Findings To Date
- Reviewing Documentation To Date
- Prepare Case Status Report To Attorney
- New Case Action Plan
- Revise Initial Hypothesis

XIV. Receive and Review Discovery Requests
- Organize And File Into Case File (On Going Process)
- Identify Any New Information
  - Witnesses • Allegations • Issues

XV. Meeting With Client
- Present Investigation Fact Findings
- Review Investigation To Date
- Identify Priorities
- Identify If Hypothesis Is Reasonable and Logical
- Identify To Do List

XVI. Court Preparation
- Identify Your Role
- Identify Witnesses
- Identify Evidence
- Identify Demonstrative Evidence
- Identify Your Testimony

XVII. Conclusion Of Case
- Pull Case And Store
- Provide Summary Conclusion of Case

Epilogue

It was ironic that **Don't Blame ME, Daddy** was first published in February of 1992 and that in August that same year celebrity actor Woody Allen was falsely accused of sexual child abuse out of a bitter custody battle with Mia Farrow, his estranged spouse.

But false allegations of child sexual abuse occur in many different arenas, besides the acrimonious divorce and custody context. Since the fruition of the 1974 Child Abuse Prevention and Treatment Act (aka, the Mondale Act), many accusations are leveled by professionals such as social workers, police officers and doctors, who are mandated by the Mondale Act to report suspected child abuse, regardless of the disposition well-founded or unfounded. Other accusations can be made in complete anonymity without accountability for same.

Many anonymous tipster accusations of child abuse turn out to be false. Laypeople are allowed to call a toll free hotline number to report suspected sexual abuse. Several of these claims are made in good faith by well-meaning, well-intentioned people. Such people don't understand the mechanics of our child "protection" system, and many wounded innocents are pursued and prosecuted.

Recent studies by the American Association for the Protection of Children indicate a 1700% increase in the number of child abuse reports since 1975. Moreover, in 1994, according to the National Center for Child Abuse and Neglect and the National Committee for the Prevention of Child Abuse, there were over 3 million reports of child abuse, of which 16% of the reports were attributed to sexual abuse. Of those approximate 480,000 reports of sexual abuse, published data indicates only 100,000 reports were confirmed cases, or about 21%.

In addition to SAID Syndrome (see chapter 8) type cases, and anonymous tipster type cases, there exists false accusations made out of the context of daycare and church settings. Such cases have hit the public spotlight hard in recent years.

After the McMartin preschool sex abuse scandal in California, which after its fruition in 1984 accounts for the longest and most expensive criminal trial in the history of this country, there's been the Margaret Kelly Michaels case from New Jersey, the Amirault case from Massachusetts, Little Rascals from North Carolina and Wenatchees witchunt from Washington. All of these cases depicted, via the news media, the accused as guilty. Yet, in all of the cases, those accused were either acquitted by a jury or their convictions were reversed by a higher court of law.

Charged to protect our youth from abuse, neglect and abandonment, the Departments of Social Services nationwide have exacerbated a problematic situation. This over-protective safety net that has been cast over America's children, has **swept** up many innocent families, also. The end result...while DSS is investigating and pursuing false complaints or erroneous information, there are **truly abused** children who are left at risk, simultaneously.

As I alluded to earlier, **ASHES to ASHES...Families to Dust** details the disintegration, death and future extinction of the American family, due to false allegations of child abuse. Many legislators are beginning to take notice of the familial destruction caused by unfounded accusations.

Rep. Goodling sponsored HR 3588, which if it had passed, would have in part repealed the Mondale Act. Congressmen Largent and Grassley sponsored the Parents Rights Act of 1995, which would allow corporal punishment not to be gleaned as physical abuse..another Pro-Family measure, which as of this writing has not yet become law. In Florida, I worked with state Senator James Hargrett (D-Tampa) for 3 years to adopt the "Spanking Bill" as law. Finally, in 1996 it has become law, allowing parents to administer corporal punishment in a Christian, disciplinary fashion without the fear of retaliation by the Florida Department of Health and Rehabilitative Services (HRS). (See letter to me by Sen. Hargrett).

Yet, we have much work to do before families can live "at ease," like they did so prior to the passing of the Mondale Act in 1974. Child savers and strident women's rights groups continue to push the **mindset**...we must protect women and children **at all costs** and if we must err we must do so on the side of women and children. Recently, Marian Wright Edelman, Executive Director of the Children's Defense Fund, coordinated "Stand Tall for Children's Day" in Washington D.C., an event that reinforced this **mindset.**

We must lobby our legislatures for a "Stand Tall for Families Day" and for a National Family Awareness Month (Month of the Family). With the divorce rate approaching 60%, with **NO-FAULT DIVORCE** laws the rule throughout the country, and with fatherlessness a top social concern in America still, the time is ripe to launch a national Pro-Family rights campaign with our legislatures, courts and media.

As I think back to my childhood days of the late 1960's-early 1970's, families **were not** immersed in such chaotic times. And, I pray that **ASHES to ASHES...Families to Dust** conveys an important message to all Americans: Families are in trouble in America. They are destined for extinction unless we can develop a system that is lined with checks and balances. Our laws must contain safeguards for protecting children **and protecting parents and families against frivolous and unfounded accusations of child abuse.**

Bibliography

Besharov, Douglas J.D. *Gaining Control over Child Abuse Reports*. Washington D.C.: Public Welfare/Spring, 1990.

Blush, Gordon & Ross, Karol. *The SAID Syndrome*: Sterling Heights, MI., 1986.

Clauss, Eliot. *Counterattack and Control: Keys to Successful Defense of False Child Abuse Accusations*. Northfield, MN.: IPT, 1989.

Daimmond, H. *Let's be Rational: An Attempt to Use a Logical Problem-Solving Approach to a Highly Emotionally Charged Situation in Order to Defend Accused Child Molesters*. Unpublished.

Dzieca & Schudson. *On Trial*. Boston: Beacon Press, 1989.

Eberle, Paul & Shirley. *The Politics of Child Abuse*. Secaucus, NJ: Lyle Stuart, Inc., 1986.

Gardner, Richard. *The Parental Alienation Syndrome*. Cresskill, NJ: Creative Therapeutics Publishing.

Giovannoni & Becerra. *Defining Child Abuse*. New York: The Free Press (Division of Macmillan), 1979.

Hechler, David. *The Battle and the Backlash*. Lexington, MA: Lexington Books, 1988.

Herzog, Paul. *Child Hearsay vs the Confrontation Clause: Can the Sixth Amendment Survive?* Northfield, MN: IPT, 1989.

Kiefer, Louis. *The Child as Witness in Allegations of Sexual Abuse Part III: Defense Strategies for the Falsely Accused Individual.* Northfield, MN: IPT, 1989.

"The Liberator." *Fighting False Abuse Charges* (taken from "The Liberator," Forest Lake, MN, June, 1990, quoting Thomas W. Pearlman, Esq., in *FACE*, April, 1990).

McIver, William II, Hollida Wakefield, Ralph Underwager. *Behavior of Abused and Non-Abused Children in Interviews with Anatomically-Correct Dolls.* Northfield, MN: IPT, 1989.

Petty, J. *Comprehensive Child Abuse/Neglect Evaluation Program.* Wilmington, NC: Human Growth and Training Associates, 1988.

Pope, Robert. *Manipulating the Child Sexual Abuse System.* Northfield, MN: IPT, 1989.

Pride, Mary. *The Child Abuse Industry.* Westchester, IL: Crossway Books, 1986.

Schultz, Leroy. *One Hundred Cases of Unfounded Child Sexual Abuse: A Survey and Recommendations.* Northfield, MN: IPT, 1989.

Schultz, Leroy. *The Child Protection Teams: Defenses for the Falsely Accused.* Northfield, MN: IPT, 1989.

Schultz, Leroy. *The Social Worker and the Sexually Abused Minor: Where are We Going?* Northfield, MN: IPT, 1985.

Spiegel, Lawrence. *A Question of Innocence.* Parsippany, N.J.: Unicorn Publishing House, 1986.

Underwager, Ralph and Wakefield, Hollida. *The Real World of Child Interrogations.* Springfield, IL: Charles C. Thomas, 1990.

Wakefield, Hollida and Underwager, Ralph. *Manipulating the Child Sexual Abuse System.* Northfield, MN: IPT, 1989.

Warren, John III, Ph.D. *Psychological Assessment of Defendants in Child Sex Abuse Cases.* Charlotte, N.C., 1990.

Yates, Alayne & Musty, Tim. "Preschool Children's Erroneous Allegations of Sexual Molestation."American Journal of Psychiatry, August, 1988.

Suggested Reading:

Ferguson, Dana. *Bad Moon Rising: A True Story.* Nashville, TN: Winston-Derek Publishers, Inc., 1989.

Underwager, Ralph & Wakefield, Hollida. *Accusations of Child Sexual Abuse.* Springfield, IL: Charles C. Thomas Publishers, 1988.

Underwager, Ralph & Wakefield, Hollida. *Issues in Child Abuse Accusations.* Springfield, IL: Charles C. Thomas Publishers, 1989.

Wexler, Richard. *Wounded Innocents: The Real Victims in the War Against Child Abuse.* Buffalo, NY: Prometheus Books, 1990, reprinted 1995.

Ceci, Stephen Ph.D. and Bruck, Maggie. *Jeopardy in the Courtroom.* American Psychological Association, 1995.

Ceci, Stephen Ph.D. and Bruck, Maggie. *The Suggestibility of the Child Witness: A Historical Review and Synthesis.* Psychological Bulletin, 1993, Vol 113 No. 3.

Scott, Brenda. Out of Control: *Who's Watching Our Child Protection Agencies?* Huntington House, 1994.

Kauser, Janson Esq. The Social Service Gestapo: *How The*

Government can Legally Abduct Your Child. Huntington House, 1995.

Guzman, Ingrid. Parent Police: *The United Nations Wants Your Children.* Huntington House. 1995.

Engel, Marjorie. *The Divorce Help Sourcebook.* Gale Research, Inc., 1994.

Pendergrast, Mark. *Victims of Memory: Sex Abuse Accusations and Shattered Lives.* Upper Access Publishers, 1995,1996.

Tong, Dean. *Don't Blame ME, Daddy: False Accusations of Child Sexual Abuse, A Hidden National Tragedy.* Hampton Roads Publishing Company, Inc., 1992.

THE FLORIDA SENATE

Tallahassee, Florida 32399-1100

SENATOR JAMES T. "JIM" HARGRETT, JR.
21st District

COMMITTEES:
Transportation,
  Vice Chairman
Agriculture
Commerce and Economic Opportunities
Rules and Calendar
Ways and Means,
  Sub. A (General Government)

June 11, 1996

Mr. Dean Tong
VOCAL
14304 North 22nd Street, Apt 153
Tampa, Florida 33613

Dear Mr. Tong:

It gives me great pleasure to inform you of the passage of the bill that will allow parents to corporally punish their children without the threat of being arrested by HRS or law enforcement officials. The legislation was incorporated into HB347 that the governor allowed to become law without his signature a few days ago. I have attached a statement that I issued on this momentous occasion.

I would like to express my sincere appreciation to you for your committed support toward this worthwhile piece of legislation. Our years of persistence have finally payed off. Starting now, Florida's families will be able to take back the responsibility for raising their children. They will be able to concentrate on teaching them how to become productive members of our society.

The state of Florida owes you a debt of gratitude. Please call me if you ever need my assistance.

Sincerely,

James T. "Jim" Hargrett, Jr.
Senator, 21st District

enclosure

REPLY TO:
❑ 2107 East Osborne Avenue, Post Office Box 11025, Tampa, Florida 33680 (813) 272-2990
❑ 330 Senate Office Building, Tallahassee, Florida 32399-1100 (904) 487-5059

JAMES A. SCOTT	MALCOLM E. BEARD	JOE BROWN	WAYNE W. TODD, JR.
President	President Pro Tempore	Secretary	Sergeant at Arms

Other Products by **Dean Tong**

Order Form

Don't Blame ME, Daddy	1 Book@ $10.00
	+$3.00 S&H $_____
ASHES to ASHES ... Families	1 Book@$15.95
to Dust	+$3.00 S&H $_____
Sexual Allegations in the 90's:	1 Video@$19.95
Tools You Can Use	+ $3.00 S&H $_____
Sexual Allegations in the 90's:	1 Audio@$9.95
Tools You Can Use:	+$3.00 S&H $_____

Total $_____

Price Reduction for Multiple Copies,
Call 1-800-987-7771

Name:_____

Title:_____

Organization:_____

Address:_____

City/State:_____Zip_____

Phone:_____Fax:_____

Visa No.:_____

Master Card No.:_____

Acct. No.:_____Exp. Date:_____

Signature:_____

Mr. Tong is available to speak to your company, organization, or firm on issues relating to families, divorce, custody, parental alienation, child abuse, false child sex charges, repressed memories, etc., on a negotiated fee basis. Please call for speakers availability and fees, 1-800-987-7771, or 1-813-885-6173

http://www.emrkt.com/books/dbmd.html

8017